THREE GENRES

The Writing of Fiction, Poetry, and Drama

PRENTICE-HALL INTERNATIONAL, INC., *London*
PRENTICE-HALL OF AUSTRALIA, PTY., LTD., *Sydney*
PRENTICE-HALL OF CANADA, LTD., *Toronto*
PRENTICE-HALL OF INDIA (PRIVATE) LTD., *New Delhi*
PRENTICE-HALL OF JAPAN, INC., *Tokyo*

THREE GENRES

The Writing of Fiction, Poetry, and Drama

Stephen Minot

Trinity College
Hartford, Connecticut

PRENTICE-HALL, INC., ENGLEWOOD CLIFFS, NEW JERSEY

Acknowledgments

I am indebted to Dick Tuttle for his invaluable illustrations and to William Ritman for his permission to reproduce his set design for Pinter's *The Collection*. Further, I am most grateful to George Nichols, Frederick Gwynn, and other members of the English Department at Trinity College who offered valuable comments and suggestions.

I am also indebted to the publishers of the following:

The poem "Trees" by Joyce Kilmer. Copyright 1913 and renewed 1941. Copyright renewed and assigned to Jerry Vogel Music Co., Inc., 112 West 44th St., New York 36, N.Y. Used by permission of copyright owner. "Portrait of the Artist as a Prematurely Old Man" by Ogden Nash. Reprinted by permission of the author. Copyright © 1934 by The Curtis Publishing Co. "Buffalo Bill" and "The Hours Rise Up," by E. E. Cummings. Copyright, 1923, 1951, by E. E. Cummings. Reprinted from his volume *Poems 1923-1954* by permission of Harcourt, Brace & World, Inc. From "The Hollow Men," "The Love Song of J. Alfred Prufrock," "Journey of the Magi" in *Collected Poems 1909-1962* by T. S. Eliot, copyright, 1936, by Harcourt, Brace & World, Inc.; © 1963, 1964, by T. S. Eliot. Reprinted by permission of the publishers and Faber & Faber, Ltd. From "A Refusal to Mourn" and "Fern Hill" from *The Collected Poems of Dylan Thomas*. Copyright 1953 by Dylan Thomas. Reprinted by permission of New Directions, J. M. Dent & Sons, Ltd., and the Trustees of the Dylan Thomas Estate. "A Solitute" and "To the Snake," from *The Jacob's Ladder* by Denise Levertov. © 1961 by Denise Levertov Goodman. Reprinted by permission of New Directions and the author. "First Confession," quoted with permission of the poet, X. J. Kennedy. "On the Poet's Leer" by David Ray, by permission of the author. From "Howl" by Allen Ginsberg, quoted by permission of the publisher, City Lights Books. From "The Lovemaker" and "The Wandering Jew," quoted by permission of The Cummington Press. From "The Ungrateful Garden" and "The Intruder" in *The Ungrateful Garden* by Carolyn Kizer, reprinted by permission of Indiana University Press. From "Another Song," quoted by permission of the poet, Donald Justice. "The Wild Swans at Coole," reprinted with permission of the publisher from *Collected Poems* by William Butler Yeats. Copyright 1919 by The Macmillan Company, Renewed 1946 by Bertha Georgie Yeats. From "Mowing," "Birches," and "Fire and Ice" from *Complete Poems of Robert Frost*. Copyright 1916, 1921, 1923, 1934 by Holt, Rinehart and Winston, Inc. Copyright renewed 1944, 1951, © 1962 by Robert Frost. Reprinted by permission of Holt, Rinehart and Winston, Inc. "To the Western World." Copyright © 1957 by Louis Simpson. Reprinted from *A Dream of Governors* by Louis Simpson by permission of Wesleyan University Press. From "Local Places" by Harold Moss, reprinted by permission of The New Yorker. From "Elegy Just in Case" by John Ciardi. Quoted with permission of the poet. From "The Division of Parts" and "The Farmer's Wife" from *To Bedlam and Part Way Back* by Anne Sexton. Reprinted by permission of the Houghton Mifflin Company. From "A Tribute to the Founder," quoted by permission of Kingsley Amis. "American Primitive" from *Poems 1947-1957* by William Jay Smith, Copyright 1953, by William Jay Smith, reprinted by permission of Atlantic-Little, Brown and Company, Publishers. "In a Station of the Metro" from *Personae* by Ezra Pound. Copyright 1926, 1954 by Ezra Pound. Reprinted by permission of New Directions, Publishers.

Library of Congress Catalog Card No.: 65-14938

Printed in the United States of America 92027-C

Current printing (last digit):

12 11 10 9 8 7 6 5 4

This work is dedicated to Virginia
who provided coffee, criticism, and enthusiasm
without fail from the first draft to the last.

PREFACE

This book ends with the statement that "creative work is a way of life, and the effort to publish is an important but not a central portion of that life." The sentence serves equally well as a preface, for it is the key to why I wrote the work, who should use it, and what I expect it to do.

Creative work covers a lot more than writing, of course. Many people find it in music, painting, acting, or even in a nonapplied science. What all these individuals share is a sense of satisfaction in sharpened awareness, in skills which are practiced for their own sake, and in productivity which is an end in itself. The creative life requires a kind of controlled instability in which the individual is constantly growing.

There are many authors, poets, and playwrights with these values. Yet until recently about the only texts which were available for the apprentice writer were the "How To . . ." books which solemnly promised hard cash sales in two to three weeks or, on the other hand, critical works and anthologies designed for the student of literature rather than for the writer.

A text was needed which would deal with all three genres strictly from a writer's point of view, treating each as a genuinely sophisticated art form. In working toward this goal I have used those concepts which my students have found valuable in the process of developing their own individual styles, and I have tried to avoid all those which are of interest mainly to the literary critic.

I have had three types of readers in mind. The first is the student in a college or university who is taking a course in creative writing. The second is the writer who is working on his own. Finally, there is the reader who, although not an active writer, constantly explores the intricacies of literature simply for the pleasure of it.

Students taking writing courses are often puzzled about why that type of course seems to require an annual defense in the pages of the *Atlantic, Harpers*, or the *Saturday Review*. So am I. It is an odd fact that those who have to be reassured about the value of these courses are perfectly prepared to accept the legitimacy of courses in painting, sculpture, or aspects of musical composition.

The question which concerns me is not whether these courses should exist but whether they can be made more effective. I think they can.

A good writing course has, among other characteristics, a rapid and provocative interchange of ideas. By *interchange* I mean that the students talk to their classmates and their instructor fully as much as he talks to them. More significant, students should not simply answer questions but be willing and able to initiate discussion. This is what distinguishes a seminar from a lecture course, and most writers who teach find that the seminar approach is an ideal method of conducting a creative course.

There are, however, certain basic concepts which the instructor must explain each year to each new class; this is why many seminars need occasional lectures.

The purpose of adding an analytical text to a creative writing seminar is *not* to bring the course closer to the traditional methods of teaching literature but to preserve the flexibility of the informal seminar. The text should *not* come between the instructor and his students; it should intensify that relationship by increasing the time devoted to discussion.

The primary problem of the writer who is working on his own is quite different. It is a matter of isolation. His friends tend to give criticism which is highly subjective, and the publishers to whom he submits are usually too busy to say much more than "yes" or "no." As a result, it is difficult for him to evaluate his own work. Eventually he may repeat the same style and even the same thematic concerns without being aware of it. No amount of determination will compensate for lack of growth or development.

A text like this one does not provide specific techniques and rules. Those methods are effective only when working with very rigid conventions such as greeting-card verse or pulp-magazine fiction. But if the independent writer applies each chapter of this work both to his own writing and to the literature he has read and respected, the process should awaken a wide variety of new reactions. What the independent writer needs most of all is refertilization. Writers' clubs are often stimulating, and some summer conferences can be helpful too, but only through a text can one re-evaluate one's basic literary values at leisure.

The third group I have in mind is made up of nonwriters for whom literature is more than a means of escape. Most of these have taken a few English courses in college but no longer have a way of sharpening their literary perceptions. Like the independent writers, these readers run the risk of going stale.

They will find that *Three Genres* differs from the purely critical text and the critical anthology which were assigned in literature courses. The primary concern here is not so much the final literary creation as the methods used to create it. This approach is in some respects like Homer's description of the design on a shield which he presented in temporal sequence, describing each step of the craftsman. This text describes literature in terms of process.

Turning now from *who* should use it to *what* I hope it can do, I move directly into a paradox. I expect this book to probe, nudge, jar, and possibly crack the reader's preconceptions about the nature of literature and the creative process; yet I also hope that the reader will end with a harmonious and internally consistent view of his own literary ideals.

This view should be individual. Each writer, like each piece of literature, ideally achieves a kind of internal logic. The first stage is forming it; the next—which comprises the rest of a writer's life—is developing its potential.

As I pointed out in the third chapter, the primary intention of this text is "to close the gap between that stage of conscious, laborious manipulation of craft and the more rewarding, though no less laborious, stage in which much of the creative process is directed by what might be described as 'a feel for the medium.'"

I am convinced that the greatest eventual service this text can perform for any one writer is to render itself obsolete.

S.M.

CONTENTS

PART ONE

The Writing of Fiction

1

THE RANGE OF FICTION

The value of basic *definitions;* the distinction between *descriptive writing* and *literary writing; fiction defined* as a form of literary writing; *simple fiction* distinguished from that which is *sophisticated;* ways in which each employs standard literary devices; *other devices* found only in sophisticated fiction; different *motives* of the writer.

The primary duty of the writer is to write. He has no need for critical distinctions which he will not be able to use.

There are, however, certain concepts which are extremely useful both during the creation and in the revisions of a literary work. The most basic of these has to do with the definition of *literary writing.* What is it? Almost as important is the method of evaluation. What is *good* and *bad?*

Suppose, for example, a writer has tried to recapture the day on which his grandfather died. A subject like this could be unified with a number of different thematic concerns and could be handled with a variety of tones from tragic through neutral to the ironic or even comic. But more basic than any of these choices is the question of why and how much the original experience should be altered. In short, at what point does the work become literature?

If the author is uncertain about this fundamental definition, he may spend valuable time and energy considering principles rather than writing. The danger is compounded in writing classes.

The most effective solution is to adopt Northrop Frye's distinction between *descriptive writing* and *literary writing* (see *Anatomy of Criticism,* Princeton University Press).

Descriptive writing is that in which "the final direction of meaning" is tied to the real world about us. This category includes such forms as the essay, thesis, editorial, article, or history text since each is fundamentally an attempt to describe or interpret some aspect of man's "real" environment. We judge them first on the basis of whether they are "true" or "false." Returning to the account of the dying grandfather, we would classify it as descriptive if it took the form of a medical report, news account, or autobiography in the strict sense, for each of these must be true to the facts no matter what the style.

Literary writing, on the other hand, is what Frye calls "an autonomous verbal structure" by which he means writing that creates its own universe. If, for example, our deathbed scene were handled as fiction, poetry, or drama, it is freed not only from the real-life experience but from the natural order of life as well. The author, of course, is still influenced by the memory of real events and may decide to use the facts faithfully. The point is that he is *free to create* any situation, group of characters, setting, or action he wishes. He can even create a whole new world in which ghosts come back (as in *Hamlet*) or men turn into giant cockroaches (as in Kafka's "Metamorphosis"). When we shift from descriptive to literary writing our main attention (both as writers and readers) shifts from the nature of the real world to the nature of a created world—from matters of reality to matters of art.

This division, of course, is not absolute. There are literary characteristics in essays and descriptive elements echoing the real world in most literature, and certain forms like the parable seem to lie between the two classifications. The general distinction is, none the less, enormously helpful for the writer. I will return to it repeatedly in this text.

Fiction, then, is the form of literary writing which tells a story in prose. As I pointed out above, there are nonliterary methods of narration also—the news account, for example—but they come under the heading of descriptive writing.

Fiction is popularly subdivided in many different ways, but most of these classifications are either vague or misleading. The terms *creative writing* and *imaginative writing* are often intended as antonyms for *commercial writing,* yet some of the most creative and imaginative novelists of this century have also been commercial in the sense of being financially successful. The publishing world distinguishes *pulp writing, slick writing,* and *quality writing* from each other, yet the true pulp market (so-called "confessions") is almost extinct, and there is no longer a sharp distinction between the fiction of the slicks, such as *McCalls, Redbook,* and the *Post,* on the one hand and the so-called qualities, such as the *Atlantic* and *Harper's,* on the other. Even those favorite terms *good* and *bad* have become so subjective that they are often no more than expressions of preference.

The most effective way to avoid the black gumbo of vague terminology in this case is to borrow from science. To the biologist, simple forms of life are *simple* and complex forms are *sophisticated.* Thus, the bird is not *better* than the jellyfish, but it is far more sophisticated in the sense that the potential of living matter has been developed much further.

Compare, for example, the Tarzan series of Edgar Rice Burroughs with the work of William Faulkner. They are similar in that they are both samples of literature—as defined above. They both tell stories in prose, they both use action and dialogue, they both contain characters which are quite unlike our neighbors next door, they both make use of animals, and they both contain initiation rites and other mythical patterns. The works of both authors were commercially successful and they each have followers who will swear that one is "good" compared with the "nonsense" written by the other.

But these two authors are utterly separate in the degree to which they have made use of the potential of fiction. As a character, Tarzan is *simple* and so are the stories in which he appears. As a character, Thomas Sutpen is *sophisticated* and so is the novel in which he appears. One must be careful here to distinguish this literary use of *sophisticated* from its popular use which describes personal characteristics. Benjamin in *The Sound and the Fury* is an idiot and as an individual is far from sophisticated in the conventional sense; but as an element in fiction he is enormously sophisticated, as is the work in which he appears.

Since this text is primarily concerned with writing which is sophisticated, we should examine the term carefully. There are three ways of viewing it: first, from the use sophisticated fiction makes of those standard devices found in all forms of fiction; second, from the literary devices which are not generally found in simple fiction; and finally from the kind of motives which stimulate a writer.

The Use of Standard Devices All fiction has *plot.* Sophisticated fiction has a plot which is not a simple refashioning of an old formula or convention but an apparently fresh sequence of events which draws the reader into the story as if he were living it himself. More will be said about plots in Chapter 4, but they deserve a brief introduction here.

There is no one "correct" method of constructing a fictional plot. Some, like Hemingway's in "The Short Happy Life of Francis Macomber," are elaborate and carefully constructed with a series of minor crises which build toward a major climax and a catastrophe. Others, like Updike's "The Crow in the Woods," are "open-ended" in the sense that they seem to begin at an apparently arbitrary point and close with poetic rather than dramatic significance—not with a bang but a metaphor. Such works are sometimes called "slice-of-life" stories since they often create the illusion of an average day in the lives of the characters rather than some outwardly dramatic turning point. This, of course, in no way suggests a lack of complexity in plotting.

Most fiction makes use of literary conventions in plotting. But a simple, unimaginative reproduction of plot formulas results in simple fiction. Such conventions include the varieties of Boy-meets-girl, Husband-is-tempted-and-then-returns-to-wife, Businessman-is-caught-in-the-web-of-Madison-Avenue-and-commits-suicide, and the like. The difference between a simple and sophisticated plot lies not so much in the convention itself as in the way it is developed. Tolstoy, after all, used the unfaithful-wife-faces-wrath-of-society-

and-her-conscience in *Anna Karenina,* but only the editors of *Classic Comics* could confuse this with a slick-fiction version of the same formula.

Some student-writers become so wary about literary conventions that they abandon plot altogether. These stories often become lost in a maze of speculation which, though seen through the thoughts of a character, converts the fiction into a disguised essay. Frequently this fault stems from a praiseworthy admiration for Joyce and a failure to note that the last fifty pages of *Ulysses* is not a short story but a scene in a carefully plotted novel.

All fiction has *characters.* Sophisticated fiction usually has characters of some complexity. The lowest order of simple characterization as seen in pulp and, often, in slick writing has only one quality. The hero may be "wise," "brave," or "fraught with integrity." I place these in quotation marks because they are stock types, as simple and stylized as the masks worn by Greek actors. One step above this—and still simple—is the level of "two-note characterization." The hero may be "tough but with heart of gold" or "kindly but addicted to drink." This level is no more complex in a literary sense than a tune on a two-noted flute, yet it is the basic formula for nine-tenths of so-called commercial fiction and television drama. Indeed, the primary distinction between the old Western films designed for Saturday matinées and the modern "adult Westerns" is a shift from one-note characterization to the two-noted, a shift which was as slight as it was profitable.

There are two general types of character complexity which we associate with sophisticated fiction. The first, sometimes referred to as "the onion approach," involves revealing successive layers of a personality through a succession of situations. This should not be confused with "character change" since it is only the reader's view, not the character himself, which changes. The other method of achieving complexity is through true character change. Hemingway's Macomber, for example, is dramatically transformed in the last third of that story.

There are, of course, exceptions. Stories like Alfau's "The Beggar" and Pirandello's "The Jar" adopt the manner of a folk tale with a minimum of characterization. These and other departures are analyzed in Chapter 5. The general pattern of fiction, however, demands complexity of character not as an end in itself but as a means of inducing the reader to accept the work as something more than an essay illustrated with dialogue and action.

Almost all fiction makes use of *action* and *dialogue*. Sophisticated fiction makes subtle use of both. For the craftsman, action is not merely a means of advancing plot but is at the same time a method of revealing character, establishing tone, creating ironies, developing themes—and occasionally all five of these intentions are combined in a simple gesture.

Dialogue on its simplest level may also be used as a kind of verbal glue to stick together units of action. But the writer who is willing to extend the limits of his craft can employ direct quotations of either speech or thoughts to develop the same five ingredients: plot, character, tone, irony, and thematic concerns. In general, no line of dialogue in sophisticated fiction serves only one function.

Literary Devices Peculiar to Sophisticated Fiction Returning to the analogy with biology, relatively simple organisms "see" in the sense of perceiving form. But only sophisticated forms of life are capable of extending this ability to the point where they can distinguish colors, judge distances, determine speed of moving objects, and, through computations of the mind, predict where an object will be at some point in the future. Sight on a human level is so far removed from that of, say, the ant and contains so many complex elements that we must consider it as a distinct, though related, characteristic.

In the same way, theme, tone, and overtone are in a vague and shadowy sense present in simple fiction, but when we consider how they are developed in sophisticated fiction it is fair to say that they are devices peculiar to this type of writing.

Sophisticated fiction does not usually limit itself to a specific theme. There is, rather, a collection of related thematic concerns.

More specifically, sophisticated fiction is rarely didactic. That is, it does not have as a primary purpose the teaching of any ethical, social, political, religious, or even philosophical point. This is not to say that fiction does not concern itself with these important matters. *Anna Karenina*, for example, clearly implies that those who do not have values which extend beyond themselves are doomed to a hell on earth; *Crime and Punishment* preaches that no man is beyond the scope of moral law; Faulkner's "That Evening Sun" is in part an attack on the sentimentalized view of "the good old South" and the "ditch" between the white man's world and the Negro's. But to insist that these concerns are the core or the "final meaning" of these works would place them together with *Uncle Tom's Cabin* or *Pilgrim's Progress*, fiction which we now read mainly for its historical significance.

Didactic elements, then, are significant but not primary—particularly in twentieth-century fiction. Further, when they do appear, they are almost always presented in an oblique fashion. Often it is not until we finish reading the work that we, acting as critics, begin to see this character as a subtle attack on some human characteristic or that situation as the author's view of some particular ideal. Returning to Hemingway's "The Short Happy Life of Francis Macomber" again, our initial interest was stimulated not because of some moral point but because of the dramatic sequence of events involving three highly credible characters. Only secondarily, and for most readers only after finishing the story, do we perceive Wilson's code of behavior as an aspect of the author's ideals and Macomber's "happy life" as those final minutes in which he discovered the validity of these ideals. If this search for and final discovery of an ethical code had been made the primary concern of the story and had been presented in a direct, blatant fashion, we would have a sample of descriptive writing—a kind of illustrated article in which the core is a proposition, not a literary concern.

To sum up, sophisticated fiction usually contains a multitude of themes or "areas of concern"; but the thesis, a specific proposition, is either absent or so carefully woven into the fabric of the work that it becomes only a part of the total pattern.

By way of contrast, simple fiction usually has a blatant thesis. The Western, now seen in film more than read on the page, is an excellent example. The action changes, but night after night the same moral messages are repeated: This-shootin'-and-killin'-must-stop, No-man-should-take-the-law-in-his-own-hands, and No-man-must-rat-on-his-friend. The fact that these endlessly repeated morality tales do not convert anyone suggests only that those addicted are less concerned with the message than the mental massage.

Our only concern here is that theses are repeated in ritualistic fashion, as simple a form of art as the instinctually repetitive ant is a simple form of life.

Tone is for many authors just as important as theme. In a simple sense, all stories have some sort of tone. An adventure story is exciting; a love story is sad or gay; science fiction is eerie. But sophisticated fiction employs tonal shifts the way music does. Salinger, for example, often begins short stories with sharp satire and ends with pathos. Malamud combines serious statement with comedy so that frequently we laugh at the moment of greatest insight. Faulkner often links the grotesque with the noble. Hemingway uses the stark, unadorned style of journalism for scenes which come close to sentimentality.

These are not arbitrary violations of that old rule demanding unity of tone. They are devices designed to pry the reader out of his complacency, to jar him, awake him, and move him, sometimes protesting, into the world established by that story.

Finally, there is the matter of overtone. I am using the term here in its broadest sense to include all forms of oblique suggestion. When a simple story has two girls, it often differentiates them simply by the color of their hair and they are recalled, if at all, not by name but as "the blond" and "the brunette." Sophisticated fiction usually suggests character through hundreds of small details: the way he or she talks, walks, makes decisions, lights a cigarette, pats a cat, drives a car, eats a meal, or acts with children. Most of what a reader knows about a character has come from indirect sources like these rather than from direct analysis.

In the same way, there are overtones or suggestions which expand the thematic concerns of a story. Usually these take the form of symbolic details. Conrad's speculations on the nature of man in *Heart of Darkness,* for example, are amplified indirectly in almost every passage describing the jungle. Contrast this method with that of simple fiction which bludgeons us with phrases like, "The African jungle is a place where the dark corners of a man's soul are revealed with savage intensity."

The oblique method is sophisticated not merely because it is more complex but because it transmits a far richer variety of suggestions while still maintaining that illusion of an as-if-real world.

In short, sophisticated fiction "does" more things with words, just as a bird "does" more with life than the simple jellyfish.

Motives of the Writer Contemporary criticism is not generally concerned with *why* the writer wrote the way he did, and this is one area in which writer and critic must peacefully part company. It is wise for a writer to examine his own motives honestly.

The term *commercial writing,* which I rejected as a literary term earlier in this chapter, has some value when applied to the way an author views himself. Generally speaking, a commercial writer is one who defines his work as a craft and his primary goal as monetary reward. His product is entertainment. With some exceptions, what sells is "good" and what does not is "bad." He studies the market carefully and invests his time and energies in those areas which seem to have potential profit.

The work of this frequently maligned profession tends to be conservative and conventional mainly because that is what the readers of large-circulation magazines pay for. Like the businessman, his work consists of supplying a demand.

The motive of the literary writer who is concerned with sophisticated fiction differs significantly. He also would like to be paid for his efforts, but this is not usually his primary concern. There are easier ways to make money. He is guided more by a variety of inner rewards. One of these is the pleasure of communication, which does not necessarily entail wide distribution. If the work is complex, it may reach only a small number of readers; but it often provides a genuine sense of satisfaction for the author when he knows that some readers have entered into the work fully. In addition, most writers have a need merely to express. This has nothing to do with the reader. Like singing to oneself, the act itself gives pleasure. Finally, and for some this is the most important, there is a very private reward in achieving what one personally considers excellence. Sometimes this takes the form of competition with those authors living or dead whom one respects.

Every writer has his own personal drives, and one can see what variety there is from reading *Writers at Work* (edited by Malcolm Cowley) which contains some of the best interviews conducted by the staff of the *Paris Review.* What I am concerned with here, however, is not the variety but that which is shared: a common respect for literature as something of value in itself. Without this, and without fairly broad reading to support it, no text can help an individual to create literature.

The range of fiction, then, is as wide as the human imagination. It includes both the somewhat stylized conventions of simple fiction as well as the intricate and subtle conventions of sophisticated work which are the subject of this text.

2

THE SOURCES OF FAILURE

Fiction as rooted in *experience* and in literary *conventions;* sterile conventions seen as *formula writing;* an analysis of seven stale and unproductive formulas: the *Television Rehash,* the *Adolescent Tragedy,* the *Preadolescent Tragi-Comedy,* the *Poe Gimmick,* the *O. Henry Twist, Mock Faulkner,* and the *Gray Flannel Tragedy.*

In almost nine out of ten cases the failure of a story to achieve significance, credibility, or even interest is due not to the revisions but the origin, the source from which the story developed. These stories are doomed at conception. It is for this reason that I have included what will be a largely negative chapter so early in this section.

Fiction stands on two legs, convention and personal experience. By convention I mean the patterns of storytelling such as specific points of view, methods of revealing characters, types of conflict and tension, symbolic or suggestive use of setting, and the like. These conventions (discussed in Chapters 4-11) are found not only in sophisticated fiction but in all other forms as well: slicks, pulps, television drama, and even the comics.

By personal experience I mean everything the individual remembers of his own life: the actions, the talk, the thoughts, the scenes, and the settings which remain either clearly or only vaguely in one's memory. Put another way, experience includes that great reservoir of stimuli from all the five senses: objects seen, sounds heard, odors smelled, textures felt, and material tasted. But we must add to this list a sixth "sense" of thought and emotion.

Fiction which depends almost wholly on experience without regard for convention tends to become unintelligible. An extreme example of this is so-called automatic writing in which the practitioner types steadily and without conscious direction for five hours and saves the last hour for publication. It is interesting as dreams are interesting, but it is not to be confused with stream-of-consciousness writing, the carefully controlled literary device developed by Joyce. Because automatic writing is produced without artistic concern it is literarily simple and, for most, boring.

Excessive concern for convention, on the other hand, can lead to the sterile formulas seen in slick and pulp fiction, "soap operas" on radio and now television, adventure stories, and that most highly stylized form of storytelling, the comic strip. Every story, of course, uses convention; it is only when those conventions become blatant, rigid, and without elaboration that we call them formulas. We use the term primarily with reference to patterns of plot, but the highly conventionalized expressions of love which Shakespeare satirized so ruthlessly in "My Mistress's Eyes are Nothing Like the Sun" were another kind of formula and were found in nonsophisticated poetry of the time.

Starting with a formula or a fragment of a formula is the primary cause of failure in the writing of fiction. Since this sort of failure originates with the first draft, hours of work are wasted. It is, therefore, essential that the writer be able to spot these literary ruts early so that he may strike out on his own—the subject of the next chapter.

The following, then, are seven deadly sins of fiction which, because of their sterility, corrupt any attempt at sophisticated writing.

The Television Rehash usually comes in two forms, the abbreviated Western and the war story. It is extraordinary how many well-read, articulate students revert to these standard plots, somewhat disguised but still complete with their stylized, almost ritualized representations of such virtues as manliness and courage as well as their antonyms, weakness and cowardice. The result is almost always failure.

The frequency and the strength of this temptation is due, I believe, to the fact that there are many intelligent individuals who have, by the time they reach twenty, absorbed more television drama than they have literary works. If, for example, you have watched five television dramas a week for four years, you have absorbed 1,040 separate (but similar) plots, at least 3,120 attempts at characterization, more than 4,160 separate dramatic scenes, and the equivalent of 20,800 pages of dialogue. It is true that not much of this material was studied carefully, but the repetition of plot types, stock characters, and highly formal patterns of diction and syntax are presented in a day-to-day sequence which outdoes the most scientific presentation of programmed learning yet devised by educators.

The danger is not due to the subject matter. Good novels have, after all, used nineteenth-century western United States as a setting, and several great novels have made use of war. The reason these shows prove to be so disastrous as source material is that they have almost nothing to do with the complexity of genuine human experience or even genuine human beings. The script writer himself is not writing from experience. He has as *his* source nothing but a set of stylized conventions involving situations, characters, and the use of language. The reason Marlon Brando's dialogue and actions and even his gestures in *On the Waterfront* are all so similar to his dialogue, actions, and even his gestures in *The Wild Ones* is *not* due to a similarity between boys living on the East Coast and those living in California. It *is* due to the fact that both films are based on the same convention. This may not be "bad," but it certainly is simple.

Most writers consider themselves beyond or "above" such influence. Many are. But one should always be on guard. When a plot begins to have a familiar sound to it, examine carefully just what the source might have been. More important still, when a character begins to slide into an easy pattern, when he begins to become predictable, it is time to examine just where his genesis was. And when dialogue begins to be infiltrated with phrases which you cannot associate with someone known, hunt down the true source ruthlessly.

The Adolescent Tragedy. This, of course, can be combined with the Television Rehash in what then becomes a compounded failure. But more often, the story is initially based either on the experiences of the author or one close to him. It takes various forms: the breakup of an adolescent relationship; the innocent male and the sophisticated female—or the reverse; the case of the insensitive parents (alcoholic, materialistic, mean, or all three); first introduction to prejudice or other forms of injustice.

Insofar as these stories use genuine and fresh detail from personal experience, they can succeed. But there are three dangerous pitfalls: lack of perspective, unconscious borrowing from slick and conventionalized fiction, and sentimentality.

The author's lack of perspective or a sense of proportion stems from the fact that in many cases the experience is too fresh. The author is still *in* the story rather than *above* it; he cannot control it. Thus, what appears to be a true tragedy to the author-protagonist appears to the reader as pallid comedy.

Sherwood Anderson was acutely aware of this when he wrote "I'm a Fool." The literal story involves a boy who is ready to commit suicide over his mildly fraudulent behavior with a girl. This portion of the story is exactly the sort of adolescent tragedy I am warning against. But in this case the author, with a fine sense of perspective, adds just enough satiric tone so that the theme becomes not the boy's "tragic" loss of the girl but his melodramatic view of himself. Thus, while the title quotes the boy's own evaluation of himself, it also becomes the author's ironic suggestion that the boy is more of a fool than he thinks. (This, incidentally, is a simple version of the highly complex irony found in Eliot's "Prufrock," where our judgment of the narrator is more severe than his own condemnation of himself.)

This is not to say that no adolescent faces tragedy. Many do. And these cases should not be adulterated by a patronizing author. But when they are that serious, they are unique and are far more complex than the simple loss of a girl friend or a pet dog. Faulkner's "Barn Burning," for example, is on one level a story of a boy's loss of respect for his father—an adolescent tragedy. But it is compounded by a larger concern, a conflict in the boy's mind between the code of his family and that of society generally. This conflict is echoed in the dialogue and actions of the other characters. The implications here are far wider than the horizons of the adolescent world.

Slick fiction may be a loose term which does some injustice to those magazines which, in addition to their formula stories, occasionally print sophisticated material, but the conventions which the term suggests are quite specific and there is no injustice whatever in attacking them. The adolescent boy, for example, must be tall, thin, awkward, have an adenoidal condition, be perpetually in love with a variety of young girls and old cars. Those who don't read women's magazines pick up the formula in crude form from the so-called comics or even from Booth Tarkington's lesser works; but no matter what form this extended cliché takes, it is as far removed from the adolescents of Faulkner, Hemingway, Steinbeck, Updike, Salinger, and Cheever as Disney's Mickey is from real mice.

Few serious writers accept the slick pattern in its entirety, and rarely is the borrowing conscious. What usually happens is that the writer who is short of clearly remembered material quite unintentionally borrows from that refuse heap of hackneyed detail because it seems easier. It may be only a Dagwood-like father or a Model T Ford with "Lulu Belle" written on the side, but it often requires checking the origin before one realizes that the former is an overworked caricature and the latter is the invention of script writers who haven't looked at a high school parking lot for twenty years.

Sentimentality comes directly from the slick magazine field. Here the lonely, misunderstood little boy, the plain little girl with glasses, the neglected old woman, and the kindly grandfather facing the bewildering complexities of a world too busy to hear his pithy mutterings are all paraded before the reader for the sole purpose of short-circuiting the emotions and eliciting tears. When this is done blatantly in the commercial field, it is a cynical act on the part of the writer. There's money in those tears. But when it is imitated by the serious, young writer, the motive is only lethargy and the result inexcusable.

The hardest version of sentimentality for a critic to attack is that which is based on the plight of a racial minority. But no matter how admirable the theme of a story may be, it is cheapened by the fundamental dishonesty of sentimentality. The source of these stories is not life but the trappings of experience rigged to produce a single emotion.

Sentimentality, like propaganda and pornography, can best be judged not on the motive of the writer (since all three can be produced unintentionally) but on the basis of whether the story or passage is so designed as to produce only one reaction or one emotion to the exclusion of others. Sophisticated fiction, on the other hand, produces a complex set of reactions and expands rather than restricts the vision of the reader.

Adolescence, then, is a rich source for fiction. But it must not be distorted by a lack of proportion or adulterated by threadbare conventions. The story must be true to the complexities and intricacies —whether comic, tragic, or only insightful—which make that age worthy of a writer's effort.

The Preadolescent Tragi-Comedy. For some reason, female writers are more attracted to this dangerous formula than males, but this may only be due to a masculine reluctance to identify himself as writer with the preadolescent, a phenomenon which has more to do with psychology than literary judgment. In any case, the story turns an age which can be truly comic or terrifying or intricate in its perceptions into something which can only be described as "cute."

Once again we must distinguish between what is a rewarding source for fiction, the preadolescent period, and what this particular type of failure is based on, a convention. If the author of a "sweet little story about a girl of five in love with a man of thirteen" honestly looked for the source of the story, the search would end in the pages of women's magazines, not in his or her own life. The mechanics of the situation may be real; it is the author's tone which adds that extra cup of sugar and fulfills the recipe for "cute fiction."

The formula for the preadolescent boy is no less absurd than the one for the adolescent. He has freckles, is preferably a redhead, keeps frogs and snakes in his pocket, proves his virility by fighting, and uses bad grammar to express occasional nuggets of great wisdom. Recently he has been made to represent various ethnic minorities without any visible improvement either of the formula or of the dignity and traditions of the group so graced. He is a stylized Tom Sawyer mummified by writers who are more familiar with Lassie than Mark Twain. He serves no purpose but financial gain for the popular writer and so should be returned to the commercial world from whence he sprang.

Once again, honest analysis of the origin of one's fiction is the best means of separating the sterility of literary formulas from the potency of experience and observation.

The Poe Gimmick. One does not have to abandon one's respect or even admiration for Poe's inventiveness in order to scorn the well-worn and essentially boring imitations of his work. There are three reasons why warmed-over Poe is generally unsuccessful. The first is an historical consideration: Poe was working in a period when the short story as an independent genre was just being born. His tricks were fresh and truly surprised readers who were, in this area, naive. Since then, our expectations have increased. We are no longer content with pure melodrama such as we find in "The Pit and the Pendulum" or "Ms. Found in a Bottle." We now expect fiction to contain more elaborate characterization, more complexity of theme, and greater variety of tone. Even that last bastion of melodrama, the horror film, could make no more use of Poe's material in the film called *The Raven* than to treat it as fodder for the lowest sort of satire.

Another reason for the collapse of the Poe market as a source for good fiction is that most of his gimmicks were one-shot affairs. That is, once the trick has been used, we can no longer be truly surprised by it. And when almost the entire impact of the story is based on the melodramatic elements, the contemporary writer cannot borrow without being obviously imitative.

The third and most significant danger stems from the fact that in so many cases the author who appears to imitate Poe is not really familiar with more than one or two of his works. He is imitating the imitators of Poe as seen in film, simple horror stories, and even (though he rarely admits it) *Classic Comics.* Once again we return to this problem of originality: When fiction is based on an imitation of an imitation, it is so far removed from human experience and the subtleties of human reaction to experience that it no longer suggests an insight into anything.

The O. Henry Twist. This is, I hope, almost self-explanatory. Everything which I have pointed out about imitating Poe's technique of melodrama applies here to O. Henry's sentimentality. In most cases, the imitative trick ending is added to a story which is extraordinarily dull up to that point. There is a half-century of difference between the kind of sustained irony with which authors like Roth and Cheever vitalize their fiction and the one-shot ironic twist with which O. Henry so often ended his stories. In most cases, the imitators miss entirely the kind of charm with which O. Henry built the body of his story. What he achieved was not fiction in the contemporary sense but an entertaining, well-told, after-dinner anecdote. This tradition has continued, but has been taken over by the columnists and is almost wholly out of the fictional tradition.

Mock Faulkner. No writer can help being influence by his favorite modern author, but the attempt to imitate him (either consciously or unconsciously) often results in unintended satire. Hemingway and Salinger are frequently borrowed from, but Faulkner is truly contagious. My favorite example is an early attempt at fiction by a college sophomore who managed to pack into a single story one seduction, one rape, one case of incest, and a suicide—all in 2,000 words. Grim as the subject matter and the author's intention were, the end result was a hilarious burlesque.

The origin of that story was not, of course, Faulkner's work but a corrupted memory of selected passages. There was no awareness of the intricate structure of a Faulknerian novel in which violence, which does often appear, becomes woven into the fabric of the entire work. In *Sanctuary,* for example, the scene which is so frequently branded as objectionable is in fact so obliquely presented that many readers are not aware of just what happened until later in the novel—or even until they have turned to the critics for help.

In addition, the imitative story showed no awareness of the relationship between the length of a story and the degree of violence which it can contain without spilling over into the area of melodrama. If one thinks of violence as electrical voltage, it is easy to see that what is successfully sent through a heavy-gauge woven cable will burn out if sent through a single strand of light wire.

By way of specific example, it is worth noting Faulkner's "Dry September" and J. F. Powers' "The Eye." Both stories involve a brutal lynching. Both stories mute the degree of violence by refusing to describe directly the actual lynching scene. Neither author can be accused of literary cowardice. Inclusion of the lynch scenes in these two stories would have overloaded the circuit and the result would have been melodrama; exclusion, in these cases, allows for the maximum possible impact.

The Gray Flannel Tragedy is the last of these seven deadly sins. It is by far the most prevalent, springing up perennially in almost every writing class like tenacious dandelions in the best of lawns. And like the dandelion, it is one of the few species which is not subject to cross-fertilization and thus is deprived of any genetic variation whatever.

The theme of these stories ("Man-does-not-live-by-Success-alone") may have once been vaguely influenced by Dreiser's *American Tragedy,* and it certainly is linked with the more recent "businessman novels" such as *The Man in The Gray Flannel Suit* and *Sincerely, Willys Wade.* But I find it highly significant that in almost no case has the author of these repetitious imitations read these works. Nor, I might add, is the characterization based on their own parents.

Yet in spite of this, the pattern is incredibly similar. I have included a full description of the formula in the section on drama as an example of "false realism"; it is sufficient here to point out that in the imitative versions the protagonist is always a businessman, always drives for social success, always has a neglected wife and neglected children, and always commits suicide. The only variation is the choice of execution: window-jumping is first choice, but revolvers-to-temples are a close second.

Since the authors in question have not read the same fiction, and since the phenomenon they exhibit is too recent to be classified as a Jungian archetype, we must turn to other possible sources. One such source, I suspect, is the "adult drama" of television. How else could these authors all describe the same mahogany desk with the identical set of three telephones? More speculative, however, is the hypothesis that the formula represents a kind of latter-day folk myth passed on by word of mouth, a kind of shorthand used in bull sessions starting off with "Now, take the hard-driving businessman with three phones on his desk. . . ."

In either case, the formula is as far removed from Dreiser's vision as it is from the student-author's own experience. The true origin, as in the other six cases of unsuccessful fiction, is neither literary nor personal; and the result is painfully monotonous.

All this, of course, is highly negative. The entire chapter is a repetition of "Thou Shalt Not." One of the primary functions of this text, however, is to reduce the agonizing period of basic trial and error in the creative process so that the writer can as quickly as possible move on to problems which are more intricate and increasingly individual.

There is no greater waste of time for a writer than hours spent writing and revising a piece which is so rooted in stale conventions that it can never succeed. If he is in a writing class, he must go through the entire process before the pointlessness of his efforts is exposed. Those writing on their own must wait for the mute and infuriatingly uninformative series of rejection slips. But those who have learned to reject plots, character, and scenes which were borrowed, even unintentionally from subliterary sources are ready from the start to examine the true source of fiction: the life experiences of the author himself.

3

THE SOURCES OF IMAGINATIVE FICTION

Selection of experiences which have fictional potential, including: *shifts in attitude* toward members of the family or those outside it; shifts in *self-evaluation;* and *memory fragments* drawn from settings, characters, or incidents; *metamorphosing experience* for purposes of *clarification, complexity,* or a more objective *perspective.*

The last chapter involved clearing away the rubble—that unproductive junk pile of old formulas. This chapter will deal with the source material which has real potential in the construction of fiction.

It is easy enough to point out that most fiction springs from the experience of the writer and then, consciously or unconsciously, is refashioned by the imaginative use of literary conventions like those that will be analyzed in the next seven chapters. But every individual has an enormous backlog of experiences recorded both in the top drawer of easily accessible material and in that vast file of the subconscious. It is not easy, particularly at first, to know where to start looking. Nor is the transforming of material a "natural" or "instinctive" process. As with any art, one usually begins with a conscious awareness of each step. When the techniques of looking for and then shaping material have become internalized, the creative process becomes a highly individualized effort and the writer no longer needs a text. The intent of this chapter—and of the entire text—is to close the gap between that stage of conscious, laborious manipulation of craft and the more rewarding, though no less laborious, stage in which much of the creative process is directed by what might be described as "a feel for the medium."

There are usually two phases in the genesis of a story. The first is selecting the experience or some aspect of an experience, and the second is the matter of reshaping this material which, because it is often so basic a transformation, I shall call metamorphosis.

Selection of Experience One of the first areas of personal experience which should be examined carefully is the event or sequence of events which changed one's attitude toward another person. The quietest, most uneventful life is packed with such moments. In fact, I have never been able to see any clear difference in the quality of work done by those whose lives have been spiced with travel and adventure as opposed to those who have "done nothing." The really significant distinction is between those who have been observing everything that has happened to them and those who either do not observe or are unable to recall.

Examine the relationship between a child and his parents. Ideally, it consists of sustained love, but actually it is constantly in flux. In very general terms, it is apt to be a progression from idealization through disillusionment to a new acceptance usually based on a fairly realistic evaluation. But this is a vast oversimplification, and stories which are based on a simple thematic statement of "The day I discovered my father was no saint" are apt to turn out thin and unconvincing. The writer has to probe deeper in order to discover and dramatize those unique shifts in his own attitude. Often it is some *specific* characteristic of, say, the father that is altered in some slight but significant way which lends itself to good fiction.

In addition to child-parent relationships, there are a variety of other intrafamily attitudes which also shift significantly: brother and sister, a boy and his younger brother, two brothers and their father, two sisters and a maiden aunt, daughter and mother, three brothers or three sisters, or any combination of these and an uncle. All of these relationships keep shifting in real life, and the shifts are remembered because something was done (action) or said (dialogue) or thought in such a way as to dramatize the change. In some cases the writer can draw on such relationships directly, but more frequently he has to metamorphose experience into something related but different—a process which I will explain shortly.

Next, turn from family relationships to those outside the family. The girl-boy relationship is a field which is heavily mined with stereotypes. One false step (like "But darling, we're married in the eyes of heaven," or "Her eyes were like limpid pools") and the story has exploded in your face. In most cases you can find a safe path by asking these two essential questions: What *really* happened? What was there about the action, the thoughts, the dialogue which was truly unique? There are times, however, when what really happened (action and dialogue particularly) would on paper appear so close to a cliché that the author must either turn the piece into a satire or alter the facts to make the fiction credible. When the author gives as an excuse, "But it really happened that way," he is exposing a basic misunderstanding about the nature of fiction. Experience can be an important ingredient in fiction, but it is not a model for the final product.

Some of the best relationships to examine are those which involve an age difference. It is often difficult (though not impossible) for a young writer to enter the lives of characters who are far older. One way to bridge the gap is to make use of those real-life situations which were the first means of gaining insight into the lives of those much older. This includes significant child-adult relationships outside the home.

Most fiction is based on situations which involve two or more people. It is in this area that one should look first.

Yet there are valuable experiences which occur when one is alone. These too are worth examining. They may consist of a struggle against nature, such as when on a solitary camping trip or when sailing; or the "antagonist" may take the form of a mechanical object, such as a plane when one is flying solo or a car when one is driving in a blizzard.

The big danger in these stories is the tendency to slip into the standardized conventions of the adventure story. If one doesn't build convincing characterization and some complexity of theme, the story may end up close to those thrillers we used to read under the titles of "Yukon Patrol" and "What I Learned on Lake Stormy."

A less obvious danger is the difficulty of exposing a character in depth without the aid of dialogue and interaction. There are various tricks, of course. The protagonist can talk to himself, study his own face in the mirror, read letters, and recall past scenes. But these devices can become contrived. It is for these reasons that while solitary experiences often initiate a story plan, the final work usually contains more than one character.

Another method of stimulating one's memory involves working with a setting, a character, or an incident which *for some reason* has remained vivid. Here the author begins not with an analytical understanding of just what the significance is; he begins with the assumption that for this particular detail to have remained fresh and clear there must have been some special meaning in it for him.

Such a memory may be highly fragmentary. Settings like a particular drug store, a specific field or grove where the author used to play, a view from a car window, or a living room seen only once often stand out with extraordinary—and usually significant—sharpness. Characters (not to be confused with "characters" who are "unforgettable" because of their quaint similarity to clichés held dear by the *Reader's Digest*) may remain in the mind only from an overheard conversation or a quick glimpse: a subway attendant, a store clerk, a hitchhiker, or an auto mechanic. And incidents do not even have to be directly connected with the observer. They may involve an argument overheard in a supermarket; the smashing of a window; an automobile accident; or the playful flirtation of a girl and three boys on a beach, a park, or the Staten Island Ferry.

One of the first things to do with such a memory-fragment is to recall every possible detail: the visual minutiae, the sounds, and the intricacies of one's own feeling. From these one may discover why that particular experience remained in one's memory while so many others drifted beyond recall. The final story may or may not include the author himself, and it will doubtless be far removed from the facts of the experience, but it has the advantage of being rooted in an initial fragment of the author's experience.

In all these searches for the raw material of fiction it is essential to remember that the experience need not be highly sensational or even very dramatic. It is true that the moment of decision for *Lord Jim* involved a choice of whether to stay with a doomed ship or leap into a waiting lifeboat, and that Francis Macomber's turning point came quite significantly while hunting in the African bush country; but it is not true to hold that this is the only or necessarily the best form for fiction to take. The moment of awakening which Joyce called the epiphany in his own short stories is often so subtle that the careless reader can miss it altogether. The short-story writer who feels compelled to cast his fiction on the high sea or the African bush country merely to achieve dramatic impact shows not only that he has missed the true nature of drama but that he has no idea of what is the true origin of fiction. And incidentally, he has not read Joyce's *Dubliners* or Updike's *Pigeon Feathers* or Salinger's *Nine Stories.*

Metamorphosis of Experience Experience, then, is the usual origin of fiction. But only occasionally is the final product unaltered fragments of autobiography. Fiction develops—consciously or unconsciously—through a process of literary metamorphosis. Such shifts in the basic conception of a story idea usually stem from two diametrically opposed needs: to clarify or sharpen the patterns which made the experience memorable in the first place and, conversely, to break patterns and relationships which seem too simple, too obvious or contrived. There is a third justification for metamorphosis which is often ignored: when the experience is still so close to the author that he cannot manipulate it objectively.

Sharpening and clarifying is basic to fiction. It is an oversimplification to say that all literature is the transformation of disordered experience into communicable patterns of events, thematic significance, and character revelation. But like many oversimplifications, it is a part of the truth. Take thematic unity, for example. Suppose the experience consisted of a hot August day on which plans for a family picnic in the country were ruined when the car boiled over in the heart of the city's slums. The thematic elements which have kept the experience itself vivid in the writer's mind may consist of such varied details as the boy's first awareness of his father as a man hopeless in a crisis, a surprising insight into the instability of his parents' relationship, a recognition of a special bond between father and daughter, the beginnings of social consciousness in the face of an economically repressed community, an introduction to racial distinctions, and an ironic contrast between the narrator's sense of high adventure and his parents' sense of disaster.

A good story can echo all of these themes. But the writer will probably want to focus on just one or two. Here is the first stage of the metamorphosis. But with any one of the elements, there will be contradictory details. The primary impression, for example, may have been based on the father's inability to take control of the situation. Yet it is quite possible that in certain areas he was calm and competent. In such a situation the author may have to make extensive modifications to clarify his theme.

More radical, the final story may end with no children involved—this would swing the attention directly to the parents. Or the entire family might be dropped in order to build from some minor sequence of events observed while waiting for the car to be repaired. Occasionally all one retains is the flavor of the setting and a few individual details, such as a man's conversation with his girl leaning out of a fifth floor window or an impatient cab driver waiting for his car to be repaired at the garage.

In making such revisions, a writer often feels two "pulls"—one is his concern for the fiction as artistic creation and the other is his sense of loyalty to the experience itself. These represent the two fundamental types of writing as outlined in Chapter 1: the literary and the descriptive.

If he responds to only the former, his story is apt to turn out contrived and artificial. But if he gives in totally to the second, he has little control over his work. This may by pure chance turn into fiction, but more frequently it becomes a journal entry—a kind of literary doodling.

The first and primary reason for metamorphosing experience, then, is to sharpen the focus and to clarify the literary concerns such as theme, characterization, motivation, tone, and the like.

The second function of literary metamorphosis is the reverse in that occasionally the patterns of experience are too neat, too contrived for fiction. When the theme of a story is blatant, we are acutely aware of an author at work and no longer enter into the story as if it were an extension of experience. It becomes only a trick. And there is nothing to be gained by telling the reader that "it really happened that way." If, for example, the father in the story outlined above really was consistently irascible or without exception dependent on his wife's suggestions, he would become a "flat" character, a cliché of fiction. Variation and further insight would be needed not to clarify characterization but to make it more convincing. Or if the story ended up so obviously in the category of "The day I discovered father was not perfect," the author might be well advised to add other thematic elements so that we no longer have the feeling that it has become an extended anecdote.

A fine example of this principle is seen in the rather complex plot development of Hemingway's "The Short Happy Life of Francis Macomber." This is described further in Chapter 4, but it is worth noting here that what is essentially a simple contrast between two days, the first involving an act of cowardice and the second an act of courage, is made far more subtle by breaking the time sequence with a series of flashbacks. The natural chronology of the story would seem contrived and obvious; the rearranged sequence of the plot actually used keeps the reader from perceiving the structure of the story while preserving its advantages.

The third and final justification for these basic transformations is the experience which has not yet been emotionally digested. In most cases it takes a year or more for an author to look on a personal experience with some objectivity and perspective. True, some experiences turn into fiction without much change. But this is far rarer than most people realize. And when one is still very much involved in an experience, one has little control over it. If the writer resists the suggestions of his critics with the statement, "But, it didn't happen that way," he can be sure he is still too close to the origin of the story.

In these cases, it is sometimes helpful to break the mold set by the experience itself. This is usually done through an initial metamorphosis of the story. Childhood experiences are sometimes converted in this way by dropping the child and seeing the story through the eyes of an adult; the original setting can be shifted to some completely different place; ages can be changed; even the sex of a character can be shifted (as in the extraordinary source of Proust's Albertine), and, most basic of all, what originally came to mind as a minor or secondary theme can be developed as the primary theme of a story. Through this technique, the author can often re-establish control over a story which might otherwise have been only a journal entry.

All the steps outlined in this chapter can occur quite unconsciously. In such cases, the author is unable to explain where his plot or his characters came from or why he made the initial changes which, from a critic's point of view, seem so basic. And some authors depend more on such unconscious processes than others.

But whenever one finds it difficult to start a story, and whenever the first draft seems to fall short of one's own standard, it is extremely important to follow these steps. First, make sure that the story itself is not rooted in some well-used situation which is far removed not only from your own experience but the experience of the writers who have profited by it. Second, examine all the memorable experiences of your own life, particularly those which seem to shift either your own views or the attitudes of others. Next, consider a number of radical transformations or metamorphoses which might, on the one hand, sharpen both themes and characterization and, on the other hand, keep the story from becoming contrived or artificial.

A good story is rarely unaltered personal experience and never is pure invention. The blend of these two elements varies not only with the author but with individual works by the same author. When one considers the extraordinary variety of experience stored in the mind of an individual and the endless number of "inventive" devices available to anyone who is well read, the matter of linking the two becomes as complex as is the arrangement of chromosomes which make each organism unique. This is the true meaning of *creative* writing.

4

THE PLOT

Freeing the story from the experience; *story* and *plot* defined and contrasted; variations in *chronology* illustrated; the *formal* and *open-ended* plot defined; a *case history* of a specific story showing development of a plot through successive drafts.

A plot can be borrowed directly from life. But a writer cannot see the potential variations of that plot until he has freed himself from the tyranny of experience.

The easiest way to achieve this freedom is to recall the distinction between descriptive and literary writing. As I pointed out in the first chapter, descriptive or assertive writing is *wedded* to the real world because in order for it to be "good" it must by definition also be "true." The worst criticism we can make of an essay is that it is untrue. Literature, on the other hand, requires only a flirtation with experience. It is then free to go where it will—or where the artist wills it to go.

This freedom is granted through a system of *assumptions.* The reader assumes that, say, a newspaper account will be more or less bound to the facts, whereas a fiction will be a lie worth reading for other reasons. Yet oddly enough, the same piece of writing can be read either way. It all depends on what clues are given. Take, for example, the following passage.

> Max Haffinrapper unlocked the door of his bookstore and stepped from the cool, fresh air of a spring morning to the familiar atmos-

> phere of molding leather, glue, and commercial disinfectant. He breathed deeply—a sigh of satisfaction like a man come home again. And then, through the twilight of dust-laden air, he saw a figure sitting on his desk. He couldn't be sure, but it appeared to be the ghost of Dante.

First, let's assume that this is an Associated Press report read in the morning paper—the type of human interest account which is used as a filler when there are not enough genuine crises to fill the first page. The very existence of "A.P." at the head classifies the story as descriptive, and we assume that it must represent the facts of the real world. Quite unconsciously we make the following predictions: (1) This mysterious figure will turn out to be a flesh-and-blood thief, a book-lover, or an agent from the Department of Internal Revenue and *not* the ghost of Dante; or (2) this Max Haffinrapper will end up at Bellevue for "observation." Because we do not accept the existence of ghosts in the real world, our first effort is to "make sense" of the story by revising either the nature of the "alleged ghost" or the sanity of the observer. All this from the key letters "A.P." which we translate as "descriptive writing."

But now let us shift the same account to the pages of, say, the *Kenyon Review* or the *New Yorker*. Our first question becomes, "Is this *really* the ghost of Dante?" In asking the question, we do not take a stand on the existence or nonexistence of ghosts, nor do we assume that the author has taken such a stand. The order of the real world is quite outside the world of this particular piece of fiction. What we are asking, then, concerns the kind of logic which will be used in this particular story, the kind of rules which will apply to this story alone.

The author is free to fill that entire bookstore with ghosts without making any comment about the real world, just as Thurber may have (we can't be sure) placed a real unicorn in the garden, and Updike a real centaur in a high school. In a sense, the logic of literary writing is the logic of dreams: It is "real" while we are in the midst of the narration, yet no matter how symbolic, it is not a literal representation of the real world.

But before the writer can use this freedom effectively, he must understand the distinction between *story* in the strict sense and *plot*.

The clearest explanation of these two terms appears in E. M.

Forster's *Aspects of the Novel.* He defines *story* as "a narrative of events arranged in their time-sequence" (p. 130). *Plot,* on the other hand, is "a narrative of events, the emphasis falling on causality." Plot, then, may use the natural chronology of the story and merely emphasize motivation, or it may abandon that time-sequence altogether in the interest of developing the intricacies of causality. Conrad's *Lord Jim* and Faulkner's "A Rose for Emily" are good examples of fiction in which the plot is presented in an entirely different order than that of the *story.*

Forster's choice of terms is unfortunate since the word *story* must also be used to designate any short piece of fiction. For the sake of clarity, I shall italicize the word when using it in his special sense.

Story is significantly linked with descriptive writing. A reporter may write his *story* several times, each version being more detailed than the last; but he maintains the chronological order and pays little attention to causality.

"Bookstore owner sees 'ghost,'" he may begin. This is the whole story in headline form. Then he will start again with:

> When Max Haffinrapper, 63, opened his small bookstore on 58 West 4th Street Manhattan at 6:35 this morning he saw a figure which he believed to be the "ghost" of Dante. He threw a book at the apparition, smashing a large, plate glass mirror behind his desk. Haffinrapper was committed to Bellevue Hospital for observation.

This is pure *story.* It moves chronologically with dogged determination. It does not tell us much about causality. We are left wondering if Mr. Haffinrapper threw the book because he was frightened of ghosts or had a hatred for Dante or was generally irascible or was crafty in the art of publicity. The story also contains some unnecessary information such as the exact time and place.

The first change which a plot makes is to add information about causality. Insanity, implied in the newspaper report, has perhaps the least potential. But even if the author selected such a course, he would probably concern himself with the question of "why Dante?" Why not Shakespeare or cousin Irving Haffinrapper on his father's side? And why that particular day? All this is causality or, more specifically, motivation. And the author cannot go very far with these questions before he begins to wrestle with theme.

The second change plot might make in the basic and reportorial *story* is a shift in the chronological order. The meeting with Dante (or "Dante" if you insist) might serve as an opener, but the piece could just as easily begin ten years later with Mr. Haffinrapper as an accomplished medium or an executive in an unscrupulous public relations office—depending on the imagination of the author.

There is no answer to the question of where the *story* in a strict sense actually began. We can argue that it had its origin with the purchase of the store with Haffinrapper's army bonus in 1918 or with his first reading of *The Divine Comedy* at the age of twelve or with his listening to Gothic tales at his mother's knee from the age of three. Nor does it stop there. If we apply John Galsworthy's tenacity to this story we may end with a *Haffinrapper Saga* in which our Max is but a chapter.

An entirely new set of possibilities appears when we develop Dante as a true ghost. Now we deal with *his* motivation: why did he select Haffinrapper? Is he a free agent like Hamlet's father or merely a part of a bureaucratic system like the dead in Sartre's *Les Jeux Sont Fait?* The reporter is professionally committed to the facts of real life; the author, however, is artistically committed to exploring the potential of the world he has created.

Once the writer feels free to manipulate his material and truly understands the difference between *story* and plot, he is ready for the technical problem of revising *chronology.*

Let us assume, for the sake of simplicity, that a particular *story* is made up of seven scenes running chronologically from Monday through some sort of resolution on the following Sunday. The author can, of course, use this same chronology for his plot. But he should consider at least some of the infinite number of alternatives.

One arrangement would be to use a *single flashback.* The story might begin with the events of Wednesday and Thursday, move back to Monday and Tuesday, and then finish with the climactic weekend. This would be particularly valuable if the *story* had a slow start. Quite often one adds a flashback like this only after several drafts have been written.

This is a true flashback and should not be confused with simple references to the past either by the author or through dialogue. Since the flashback requires a whole new scene complete with setting and some indication of the date, it should not be used to present incidental material which could have been handled either through dialogue ("'The poor girl had her fiftieth birthday last week, you know'") or through direct author's statement ("It had been only a week since her traumatic fiftieth birthday").

The usual method of slipping into a flashback is to use the past perfect tense for two or three sentences and then to return to the simple past, as follows: "The preceding Monday, Max had been most pessimistic. He had, in fact, told his Uncle Irving at lunch that the scheme would never work. They spent the entire meal arguing about it." The scene is now launched and will continue in the simple past tense.

Eventually one must come out of the flashback. One approach is the direct statement: "By Friday, however, the entire situation had changed." Another method is simply to plunge the reader back into the scene which he left at an earlier point. This can, of course, be confusing if the flashback has been a long one or if the scene to which the reader is returned is similar to the one in the flashback. If, for example, the plot moves from a Monday lunch with Uncle Irving to a Friday dinner with the same man, the reader may be needlessly baffled. If, on the other hand, the author had left the protagonist swimming in rough seas off Newport, Rhode Island, he could jolt his reader out of that meal-time flashback simply by starting a new paragraph with, "A wave caught him smack in the face."

A second arrangement of this hypothetical seven-scene *story* would be to concentrate on the last scene, Sunday, and to include earlier material with *multiple flashbacks.*

One reason for using this arrangement would be to add a special emphasis to that scene. It could also gather together material which otherwise seemed scattered and poorly unified. The great danger, however, is that the story may become unnecessarily cluttered. Complexity of plot does not *in itself* lead to sophistication; it must be used in such a way that the story "does" more or, if you prefer, "says" more.

A third arrangement of plot would be to begin with the climactic events of Sunday noon just as in the arrangement described above, but to replace the scattered flashbacks with a chronological treatment from Monday through the entire week. The final scene in such a story would probably push through to Sunday night for a resolution. This is sometimes called a *frame story* since the bulk of the narration is enclosed by two portions of the same scene. (Some critics, however, restrict this term to the story told by a character in a larger work, such as the separate narrations within Chaucer's *The Canterbury Tales.*)

When the opening and closing scene is highly dramatic, using it as a frame tends to distribute the tension throughout the length of a story. An extreme form of this can be seen periodically in television melodramas which begin with the hero firing a revolver or slapping an hysterical woman. Like every literary device, this one can be commercialized. A milder form of the frame story is that in which a narrator begins by talking to a visible audience and ends in the same scene. Conrad was particularly fond of this method as a means of developing the character of the speaker obliquely. In some cases, however, it only clutters a story.

Variations in chronology like these are found more frequently in *formal plots* than in those which are *open-ended.*

The term *formal plot* simply designates those in which form is emphasized. They are characterized by one or more rises in dramatic action, some measure of suspense, a climax, and usually a resolution. It is close to drama in this respect. It may take the form of a series of scenes each with its own rising action, as in Conrad's "Youth," or just two, as in Hemingway's "The Short Happy Life of Francis Macomber," or, especially with shorter stories, only one. The case of Hemingway's story is interesting because although the *story* in the strict sense is a perfectly symmetrical presentation of two days, one in which the hero acts the coward and the other in which the hero acts with determination and enthusiasm, the author has refashioned the *plot* by means of flashbacks primarily to disguise the form. It is still a formal plot in the sense defined above, but what might have become obtrusive plot formation has been made a subtle construction.

The *open-ended plot,* on the other hand, appears to start arbitrarily and closes not with a climax and resolution but simply with a period. There is no clear resolution and usually little which could be called dramatic.

But even this is illusion. The open-ended story would be dull if we as readers did not make some sort of discovery about motive or character or the patterns of action. The open-ended plot often contains an epiphany—a moment of understanding; or our perception of significance may come subtly and gradually as with the long, apparently wandering stories which have become associated with the *New Yorker*.

Ideally, then, the writer begins with an experience, frees himself from it by separating the *story* from whatever plots seem to suit it, considers various chronologies, and finally sets his work down on paper. But no creative process is that neat. In point of fact, the writer usually muddles his way through draft after draft.

The following case history of a published short story is fairly representative. Notice that in spite of apparently arbitrary vacillations, the general direction of the revisions is from descriptive (biographical) to literary and from simplicity of *story* to complexity of plot.

The author had spent much of his childhood sailing small boats in open sea. He came to think of the sea as somewhat anthropomorphic—a wrathful version of the Old Testament Jehovah. And on one occasion, after a half-hour struggle in which he almost lost his life, he expressed his jubilation by the ungrateful gesture of spitting into the sea he had outwitted.

So far we have pure *story* with descriptive or assertive overtones. The experience went down on paper without much mutation under the title of "To Wrestle With Gods." Result: It was thin in implication and bloated with melodrama.

The second draft increased the complexity by adding a father (through flashbacks) who became a source of the rebellion. The original theme of childish (and rather ungrateful) man against the sea, the gods, God, fate, and the like was retained. The mortal father merely added causation. Result: more complexity, but dangerously close to the convention (formula) of rebellious adolescent proving self against his father.

The third draft shifted the emphasis from the father by adding a twin brother. Since the original protagonist was rather like Jacob in his willingness to wrestle with Jehovah, the brother was called Red, a reference to Jacob's twin brother Esau who was born "hairy and red." And the father, less subtly, became Isaac. We now have a competition for the father's approval (blessing) through behavior in a small boat at sea. Result: enough complexity to bury the original assertive and biographical roots; but there was something rather trite (too obviously a literary convention) about adolescent competition for father's approval.

The fourth draft (after several years) shifted the age of the boys so that in the metamorphosed version they were in their thirties, veterans, and returning home for a family reunion. A whole new level was added through the fact that Red, now called Harry (a play on hairy), is an enthusiastic navy veteran like his father and Jay is a pacifist who slid into military service through the draft. This also added a new irony in that the pacifist twin fights harder to win the father's blessing than does the apparently militant twin, Harry. The title was then shifted from the thesis-ridden "To Wrestle With Gods" to one with overtones of combat and independence: "Windy 4th."

The story in its final version may be found in *The Virginia Quarterly Review*, Winter 1964.

The point of this case history—and of the entire chapter—is that whereas *stories* in the strict sense are found in almost every portion of a writer's life, *plots* are by definition the invention of authors. They are literary constructions. In fact, it is the artistic manipulation of plot which establishes one of the fundamental differences between life and fiction.

5

THE VIEWER

The means of perception as the essential vehicle for all fiction; *person,* first vs. third; *experimentation* in viewpoint; *selecting* a point of view by conscious decision; *the spectrum of viewpoint* offering limitless choices; *dangers* inherent in such choices.

The Means of Perception This term simply refers to the agent through whose eyes a piece of fiction appears to be presented. For example: "He looked at his grandfather, wondering if the old man had understood." Here the means of perception is clearly the boy. We know his thoughts and hopes. We don't know the grandfather's reaction and will not until he speaks or makes some gesture to the boy. Our view of the scene, then, is not the author's but the boy's.

The means of perception may be used synonymously with *point of view* and *viewpoint,* but both these older terms have become confused with *mood* and *tone.* When a critic writes, "The story is told from the point of view of an embittered and sarcastic old man," he not only is saying that the means of perception is the old man, he is suggesting that the mood of the story is bitter and the tone is, at least in part, ironical.

Most fiction—particularly the short story—limits the means of perception to a single character, regardless of whether the first or third person is being used. This means that as readers we enter the mind of only one character, we do not know factual material that he doesn't know, and we are not addressed directly by the author. In the example given, for instance, we would be surprised to have the next sentence read, "Actually Grandfather did agree, but he knew that he could never tell the boy." We would be even more surprised to read, "Little did either of them realize that on the very next day Grandfather would take a trip to the hospital." Here we not only moved out of the boy's world, we moved out of the story altogether. We have the sense of the author talking to us which, although possible, is a sharp break in the convention, similar to that when the playwright jumps to the stage and describes the next act.

The primary advantage to limiting the means of perception to a single character is that the reader is more readily drawn into the story. This is partly due to his sense of identification with that character—a feeling which should not be confused with sympathy, respect, or even approval. More important, it is due to that aspect of fiction which is illusion as opposed to factual or assertive writing.

Here, for example, is a sample of factual writing in the form of a police report:

> The driver and sole occupant of the car, Miss Templeton, remained at the scene of the accident until a large crowd had assembled. Then she left the scene and was observed to run south, down Franklin Street toward Main. No explanation was given for her departure.

In a sense there is a means of perception here: It appears to be a combination of those questioned and the policeman himself. We can sympathize with the woman in the way we do from reading newspaper reports. But we remain detached. We do not become either the policeman (who has quite properly kept his feelings out of it) or the woman.

A case worker or a psychologist could add further analytical details. He might, for example, help us to analyze her sense of guilt and her need to escape from the disapproving stares of the crowd. But she would still be a case history, a subject for analysis. We, the readers, would remain detached.

A fiction writer, on the other hand, might describe part of the episode like this: "She had waited there as long as she could stand it. Then she ran. A path opened for her but she saw only a haze of stern faces on each side and heard only their unassailable silence."

This leaves out many facts. We don't know the woman's name, the name of the street, or which way she ran. But it gives us material we did not have before. We know something about the agony of waiting as the crowd grows; we can feel some of the suddenness of that flight. We share her view of the crowd and feel, as she does, some of the hostility which is suggested in "their unassailable silence." The means of perception has shifted from the outside—policeman, reporter, or case worker—to the character herself. And as we share her view, her feelings, we enter the story with some measure of emotional involvement.

In addition to drawing the reader into the story, there are two other advantages to limiting the means of perception to a single character. First, it serves as a natural device for withholding information. The scene between the boy and his grandfather at the beginning of this chapter, for example, maintains a tension by limiting the means of perception. We wonder as the boy wonders just what the grandfather will think. In fact, almost every example of suspense in fiction is based on the limitation of the means of perception.

The final advantage is that it gives the author the opportunity to provide the reader with incorrect or biased material. It is quite possible, for example, for the reader to share with a character a delusion or a misinterpretation of the true facts. The grandfather might be thought of as a kindly man for the length of a story and then be exposed as actually selfish. Restricting the means of perception to a single character is a simple and natural way to establish such misinterpretations.

The writer of fiction, then, is not simply reporting a sequence of events in the clearest possible fashion. He tries to create an illusion of reality convincing enough to draw the reader into the scene and into the mind of at least one character. Authors like Hemingway, Faulkner, and Conrad have created some startling departures from the single means of perception, and these experiments in viewpoint will be discussed later in this chapter. The fact remains that even for these experimenters the single means of perception presented in first or third person remains the primary vehicle for fiction.

Person A child's first piece of original fiction is usually a mixture of autobiography and fantasy. Without thinking of technique he selects the first person.

"And I went down behind Mr. Syke's house where the woods are and I saw a little pond and right next that pond lying down was a blue lion and I *ran*."

Everything is here: a setting, a sequence of action, a climax with man pitted against beast (at the age of five, stories are apt to be epic and archetypal), an emotional response, and a resolution. But if you ask him why he used "I" instead of "he," the child can only shrug and say "it happened to me, that's why." This answer has a certain charm at the age of five, but it loses its luster when it is repeated at the age of twenty. And so does the story. When one adopts the techniques of a five-year-old, one must settle for the same limited audience.

Actually it is dangerous to select the first person just because the story is based on personal experience or third person because the incident originally happened to someone else. The decision should be made not on the basis of where the story came from but what the story as a literary work is to become.

One use of the first person, for example, is not to reveal the most personal feelings of the author but to satirize the speaker. When Swift decided to write *Gulliver's Travels* from the point of view of Gulliver speaking in the first person, it was not to reveal Swift's own views directly through his protagonist. Some of the finest satire in that book comes from the author's subtle ridicule of conventional middle-class views as seen in Gulliver's reactions.

Exactly the same technique was used by Sherwood Anderson in the short story "I'm a Fool." Again, we have the first person used by the protagonist. A fine irony is drawn from the fact that this poor boy is a far greater fool than he ever suspects, not because of what he has done but because of the melodramatic way in which he tells it. Here again, the author has not selected the first person to reveal his inner convictions or secret life but to gain a new dimension by allowing the reader to learn more about the character than the character himself knows. In this way the satire is sharpened with irony.

Another use of the first person occurs in stories of reminiscence. Having a mature character look back and report on his earlier experience actually provides a kind of double viewpoint. One of the best and most complex examples of this is in Conrad's long story "Youth." Here the protagonist as an old man tells a story about himself as a youth. The age and attitudes of the teller are made clear both at the beginning and at the end as well as in intervals during the story. The listeners are old and there are old men in the story itself. Thus, attitudes of youth and age are compared and contrasted throughout the work. All the advantages of the single means of perception are preserved, yet a double vision is presented vividly.

In addition, the first person is the best form with which to create the illusion of a storyteller speaking out loud. Almost every author has tried his hand at this form, but it has limited uses. It adds to the irony of Anderson's "I'm a Fool" and to the regional flavor of Faulkner's "Spotted Horses" and to the character revelation in many of Conrad's works. It should be noted, however, that it is a difficult form which depends as much on a good ear for dialogue as music depends on a good ear for tone. There is a tendency among amateurs to stress the dialectic variations excessively (see Chapter 9) and to use the informality of daily speech to excuse a kind of thematic haze which has settled on the work.

The fourth and final advantage of the first person occurs when it is used to place the means of perception outside the protagonist. In Fitzgerald's *The Great Gatsby*, for example, the protagonist, Gatsby, cannot be given the means of perception because so much of the novel depends on the mystery of his past. And it would be awkward giving it to his love, Daisy, because she has never been able to understand Gatsby's values. So the "I" of the story is a secondary character who is related to each of the other two in his value and background. He never views impartially, but he does provide the reader with equal insights into two different worlds.

The popular argument that the first person lends to a story "immediacy" or "realism" or "credibility" which cannot be achieved in the third person is absurd. These abstractions (which are often offered as a muddle of synonyms, a kind of verbal stew) are, if they mean anything whatever, goals for every author. And if these goals were in any way easier to reach through the first person, surely that would have become, in a hundred years of short-story writing, the favored form. But the fact is that less than half of the stories being written in this century are in the first person. Clearly we cannot argue which form is better for fiction, only which is better for this story or that novel.

The advantages of the third person are not as easy to categorize. There are, of course, some very simple considerations: It is the form to use if the story is to have more than one means of perception. It is clearly the form to use if the protagonist dies at the end of the work. And it has a certain advantage if the protagonist is the sort most readers would have difficulty identifying with. But these are not enough to explain the popularity of the third person.

The most persuasive defense for the third person is its flexibility. Whereas the first person sets the author squarely within the mind of a single character, the third person can fluctuate between a kind of neutral style and that which is truly an echo of first-person narration. In the following passage, for example, the means of perception remains with the boy, but there is a shift away from the neutral view toward the boy's own speech.

> He had been kept after school again. It was a simple matter of writing "Good boys do not cheat" fifty times and then cleaning up the classroom, but it took the length of the afternoon. Now he was in a hurry to get home because the shadows were long and it would be dark and scary soon. The short cut was through crazy old Mr. Syke's back lot—"Old Mr. Syke is higher than a kite" they used to chant, though no one had ever seen him actually drunk. He slipped through the hedge, down across the corner of the lawn, and under the trees. The air was still. He walked fast and held his breath. A few more feet and he would be past the pond where. . . . But there it was again, the enormous blue lion. It lay calmly by the edge of the pond, its paw dangling in the water. "Run" he thought, and he was running.

This is no longer a story written by a child. We have some factual material at the very beginning which, though known by the character (and therefore in harmony with the means of perception), is told in neutral terms. Then the passage begins to echo the phrasing of what might be the boy's own telling. The first hint of this is the word "scary" which is borrowed from his own vocabulary. And we are then prepared to accept Mr. Syke as "crazy." All this leads us to a quick and natural acceptance of the blue lion.

Here the third person borrows some of the objectivity of the clinical report and some of the subjectivity of first-person narration. It avoids the cold detachment of a psychologist's statement which would humorlessly place "crazy old Mr. Syke" and "blue lion" in quotation marks to indicate that these are not the "truth." And it avoids a slavish adherence to a child's vocabulary which, particularly in longer pieces, becomes difficult to maintain.

This kind of flexibility is more widely used than the casual reader realizes. In stories like Hemingway's "The Short Happy Life of Francis Macomber" and Faulkner's "Barn Burning" it is often impossible to distinguish thoughts from "objective" comment. In fact, it is this very flexibility in the third person which lends these stories a sense of "immediacy," "realism," and "credibility."

Experimentation in Viewpoint The most common variation of the single point of view is perception distributed among two or three characters. One of the most famous examples of this is Hemingway's "The Short Happy Life of Francis Macomber." The bulk of this story is told alternately from the point of view of the husband and Wilson, the guide. But a few brief insights are given into the private mental world of Mrs. Macomber, and two solid blocks of thought and feelings are given to the wounded lion.

But this should not be thought of as the "omniscient point of view." The author is quite careful not to skip rapidly from one mind to the other. Long sections of the story are given to first one and then another character. And the wife, an essential character, is seen largely through the eyes of others. Even at the very end where her intention becomes the crucial point of the story, Hemingway refuses to enter her mind.

Student authors often try to write from a truly omniscient point of view. This tendency comes from the fact that in school they wrote many more expository papers than stories. But experienced authors in this century have generally avoided this form. If Hemingway had used a truly omniscient view in his story, there would be much jumping from mind to mind. Worse, he would lose the chance to withhold periodically the reactions of his characters.

Faulkner has experimented a good deal with point of view. One of the most interesting is in the novel *As I Lay Dying*. Here he uses the first person exclusively, but he shifts the means of perception from chapter to chapter. In a sense he shifts the fictional world, leading us to view one situation in several different ways. This, of course, lends itself better to a long work. Each chapter becomes a short story in itself with its own individual style.

Another interesting experiment is in the story "That Evening Sun." The story opens with a first-person narration in which an unnamed narrator longs for the charm of the old South. In the body of the story, however, the "I" turns to "we," and it is only with some searching that one discovers which of the children included in that pronoun is actually the original speaker. This is not just a trick. The story itself is a refutation of the sentimentalized introduction, and shifting from first person singular to first person plural dramatizes this separation. The original speaker, the "apologist" for the old ways is not fully present in the story which exposes his sentimentality. But it is worth noting that, while the "I" is almost wholly abandoned in the body of the story, no information is given which was not seen by the original speaker. In this way our sense of being there is preserved.

The same technique is used by Conrad in *The Nigger of the "Narcissus."* The "we" refers generally to the crew. We are not aware of an "I" until the crew disbands at the end of the cruise. But a close examination of the text reveals that, just as in Faulkner's story, there is a single viewer.

Maintaining a means of perception is partly a matter of avoiding author's intrusion. Authors must know almost everything about their characters but only occasionally are they willing to enter the story directly.

There are, of course, a few recent examples of author's intrusion being used as a conscious literary device. John Cheever's rambling novel, *The Wapshot Chronicle* is probably the best illustration. It is, however, a risky model for writers of short stories.

Selection of a Point of View Point of view is too often selected unconsciously. As has been pointed out, there is a tendency to base the choice of person on the origin of the story rather than the desired outcome. The same is true for the decision of which character is to serve as the means of perception.

All fiction has a "natural starting point" in the writer's mind. A story may begin as an abstract idea such as suspicion and be translated into characters such as: "a young husband's financial insecurity reflected in his attitudes toward his young wife." Here the natural starting point might be third person with the husband as the means of perception. Or, preferably, a story may begin with personal experience—say, a misunderstanding between a girl and her boy friend. Here the natural starting point might be first person from the girl's point of view. In many cases this natural starting point, this first conception of the story, may be the best for the final version. But the author should be aware of the many choices available. Only if he resists the temptation to be slavishly loyal to the original conception can he be sure that the final version is the best possible presentation.

In the following passage there are three characters. Clearly the husband, Max, is the means of perception.

> When Max came home his wife was sprawled in their only comfortable chair, sipping a Coke, and watching "The Light of Her Life" on Channel 3. The boy was at the table with arithmetic book and papers before him, but his eyes were on the television show too. Keep calm, he told himself. Play it cool.
>
> "Where were you?" he asked, hanging up his coat as if it were a casual question.
>
> "When?"
>
> "This afternoon. I called and there was no answer." He wasn't going to tell her he called seven times. A wife, he figured, should never feel she was worth seven calls.
>
> "I was here," she said. She hadn't once taken her eyes off the shimmering screen. "Phone must be busted."
>
> She looked up at him and smiled.

The story has begun. We have a setting, three characters, and a tension bound to the mystery as to where she was. But most of all we have a clear means of perception which is going to shape the course of the entire story. No matter what we may think of a man who won't let his wife know that she is worth seven telephone calls, we have identified with him. We are in his mind, see what he sees, and wonder about the very things he is wondering about.

The whole direction, tone, and possibly the theme as well shifts when we change the means of perception.

> When Celia heard him open the door she tensed. But there was no need for that, she told herself, no need to feel guilty. After a morning of cleaning house, washing clothes, waxing floors—which most husbands offer to do themselves—and making meals for the boy

—after all that a woman deserved escape. And why shouldn't she spend the afternoon at a double feature? Yet she knew she would not tell him. Bad enough to be caught watching a show like this on television—impossible to admit spending the afternoon watching *Red River Rodeo* and *Sioux City Belle.*

While this paragraph is a simple rewriting of the first version, it suggests a totally new story. Whether it will be better or worse than the story suggested by the first opening is up to the author to decide. My point here is that the author should make this decision knowingly.

But there are other approaches possible. In both of these versions the boy has been all but neglected. A third story is suggested by giving him the means of perception.

For an hour he had fingered the arithmetic book, staring sightlessly at the page headed with "Problems in long division." But ahead of him, beyond the book, just past his mother's left shoulder, was the television set which had drawn him into a doctor's private world. Jim Noble was arguing with his wife who was saying "So what's wrong with split fees, Jim? We've got bills to pay like everyone else." The words made no sense, but the way they talked to each other made his stomach feel like it was filled with marbles. And then he saw his father standing in the doorway looking as if he had just lost his job or something.

Here the problem of marital division is taken from the boy's point of view. Presumably the satiric scene from the medical soap opera and possibly even the reference to "problems in long division" foreshadow an aspect of the theme. The parents are significant only insofar as they affect the boy. It is a third story.

Next, there is the matter of person. Each of these three versions could be told in the first person. This decision, as I have pointed out, has to be made in terms of what the story is to become. It would be quite possible, for example, to present the story from the husband's point of view in the first person, allowing him to defend himself as a fair and reasonable man while showing the reader just how immature he actually is. The same could be done from Celia's point of view. Or the boy could present his parents in what he feels is a kindly light while actually showing how selfish they are. "Every afternoon," he might report quite sincerely, "when I come home from school she's gone to a movie so she won't bother me with housecleaning and stuff when I should be doing my homework.

That's why I'm first in my class." In this single statement presented from the boy's point of view in his own words, we the readers make a judgment about Celia which is contrary to the boy's. If this differential between the boy's interpretation of his mother and our evaluation of her continues, we have a story in which the first person has created a sustained irony.

But whose story is it? That is, which character is the protagonist? In the last instance we might assume that it would be the boy's story since he is telling it. But if the mother emerges as the most fully drawn, the most completely analyzed, the story could easily become hers. The boy, then, would be simply the naive reporter, the innocent narrator who thinks he is describing a kindly and considerate mother while in fact he reveals a portrait of adult immaturity. Or the mother, given the means of perception, might present a story which primarily concerns either the boy or her husband.

Thus we have three factors to consider: the means of perception (who presents the story), the person (first or third), and the focus (who is the protagonist). Seen schematically the number of choices looks like this:

A story primarily about	CELIA	MAX	THE BOY
Seen through the eyes of			
CELIA	1, 2	3, 4	5, 6
MAX	7, 8	9, 10	11, 12
THE BOY	13, 14	15, 16	17, 18

Here the odd numbers represent first person presentations and the even, third person. The total of eighteen versions represent not only eighteen first paragraphs but that number of different stories as well. No writer can take the time to sample all of these choices before moving into the body of a story. But one should never be blind to the alternatives.

Spectrum of Viewpoint The preceding diagram suggests that all fiction can be categorized as being either first person or third person. This is fair if we revise the statement to read "most fiction."

But even then it is really an oversimplification. The number of choices open to a writer of fiction is almost limitless because, instead of having certain specific types of viewpoint, one has a kind of verbal spectrum. Just as it is easier for the artist to speak of "blue" and "green" as clearly definable entities, it is easy for the writer to speak of "first person" and "third person." But the writer at home with fiction can sense more subtle distinctions.

These gradations run from the most inward, limited, and personal to the most external and impersonal.

1. *Stream of consciousness* is the most subjective form of writing. In a sense it is the purest form of the first person. But because it is limited to a seemingly random flow of thoughts, it eliminates such valuable devices as action, dialogue, and setting. For this reason it is rarely used as the sole medium for a story. For further treatment of this device, see Chapter 9.

2. *First person as-if-told* allows us to move outside the mind of the narrator insofar as he describes the actions and dialogue of others. But the echoes of everyday speech ("Well now," "Like I said before," "Ain't nothin' to worry about," and so on) present limitations in diction.

3. *First person in neutral style* avoids the restriction of common speech, though it too has limitations, as noted above.

4. *Third person* is the most flexible approach to fiction, though normally it is limited to a single means of perception.

5. *First person plural* ("we") is a very rare and difficult form to be tried, if at all, only by those who have been writing for some time. It is included here simply as a significant step in the progression from the most subjective to the objective forms.

6. *Objective reporting* is the final stage. This, of course, is out of the realm of fiction. Fiction may resemble it, as Hemingway's sometimes does, but resemblance is far from identity.

Dangers The primary failure in handling point of view is the summary conclusion. There is an apparently overwhelming need on the part of some beginners to add a final paragraph which sums up the theme of the story. At worst it comes out as a moral: "He learned once and for all that . . ." or, "After that, Tom was careful about what he said when the old man was around; and never again did he bring up the touchy business of World War I."

Although good authors occasionally speak for themselves in their fiction, they rarely attempt to summarize an entire story. This reluctance is due in some cases to a conviction that a story ought to explain itself through action and dialogue. More often, it is due to the fact that most sophisticated fiction cannot be summarized in a paragraph. To try would merely reduce complexity to unjustified simplicity. Because of this, an urge to summarize frequently serves as a danger signal indicating either that the story is in fact a simple one or that it did not show what the author hoped it would.

The second most common failure is the summary introduction. "It was a beautiful August day on Lake Placid," an inept writer begins, "and there was little to suggest that before sunset Tom would learn much about the vicissitudes of weather and perhaps a bit about himself as well." The story is now dead. Here again the means of perception is the all-seeing author rather than Tom. Worse, it gives promise of boredom through literary simplicity.

Another common weakness is shifts in the means of perception. As has been pointed out, the most common form for short fiction is the single viewer. This is particularly true of works which are less than 4,000 words long. And in those rare cases where two or more characters *are* used, the shifts are usually kept at a minimum.

Finally, there is the fascination of the bizarre point of view: the adventure story which assures us that the hero will live because it is written in the first person, until we discover at the end that it is a note written in a bottle; the first person poor-little-boy story which turns out, in the last sentence, to be about a happy-little-dog; the father-son story which turns out in the last sentence to concern two creatures from outer space. Such a warning should not be necessary; but it is. The fact that certain authors such as Poe and Kafka have used plots which are clever, even tricky, does not justify a story whose single purpose is to entertain the reader by surprising him. Such singularity of intent reduces the story to the most unsophisticated level.

As pointed out in the last two chapters, the source of a story and the formation of plot are of fundamental importance. Selecting a means of perception is equally important. In fact, of the three concerns, this last is the most frequently neglected. Many students who feel free to metamorphose experience and experiment with plot continue to leave the viewpoint unchanged and unquestioned in draft after draft.

The writer of fiction is not in full control of his craft until he can imagine and truly *feel* just what changes he could create in a particular story by altering the means of perception.

6

CHARACTERIZATION

Characterization defined as an *illusion* made credible through *internal logic* and developed by *complexity;* two basic *methods* of characterization analyzed: *direct analysis* and *oblique suggestion* through such techniques as *dialogue, thoughts, physical details,* and *character change.*

The first step in developing the art of characterization is understanding that it, like all aspects of fiction, is an illusion. That is, when we as readers say that a fictional character is "convincing," "vivid," or "realistic," it is not because he resembles the person next door but because we have the illusion of having met and come to know someone new.

By way of specific example, it is not necessary to have even traveled in the South to feel that one has "met" Faulkner's Snopses, nor do we have to have lived in Dublin in order to accept Joyce's Stephen Daedalus. And we certainly don't have to have known six-foot cockroaches to feel a genuine sense of compassion for Kafka's Gregory.

It is true, of course, that most fictional characters, like most plots, have their origin in the author's own experience. They are then metamorphosed in a variety of ways, both consciously and unconsciously. But the fact that we as readers can accept both Anna Karenina and Huck Finn as "realistic" should be enough to indicate that our judgment is not based on any direct relationship between our friends and those we meet in fiction.

This illusion, which we call "credibility," in characterization is the product of two fundamental elements: internal logic and complexity. The first, logic, applies to all levels of characterization from Dick Diver to Dick Tracy. The second, complexity, differentiates sophisticated characterization from the simple.

Internal Logic The word "internal" means within the boundaries of the story, for we are not primarily concerned here with any relationship between the fictional character and an individual in the real world. When a writer defends his fictional creation with the words, "But she really was just like that," he has denied the art of fiction just as thoroughly as if he had defended his plot with the words, "But it really happened like that." In short, he has confused the source of characterization with the final creation.

The word "logic" used here is not a tight, syllogistic form which we associate with argument but is an interrelationship between a character's actions, dialogue, thoughts, and even physical details like dress and possessions from which a reader draws inductively certain conclusions both consciously and unconsciously. It is on the basis of these relationships that the reader comes to the opinion that a certain character is plausible.

On the simplest level, plausibility is pushed to the point of predictability. We know, for example, that Dick Tracy will never under any circumstances take a bribe or physically assault an innocent man. For many readers this set of rigid conventions destroys the illusion of credibility; yet for others it is so effective that they send letters and presents to the fictional character in care of their local paper, utterly confusing art and life.

On the level of sophisticated fiction, plausibility is often based on that which was unexpected but which in retrospect can be explained. In Frank Rooney's "Cyclists' Raid," for example, we come to know Joel Bleeker as a peaceful man who detests the military aspect of the motorcycle troop. We are shocked and startled when toward the end of the story he rejects everything he has stood for by beating an innocent man to the ground. Yet the act is "credible" because the author has so carefully developed his smoldering rage, his sense of utter frustration, and his despair at the moment of his daughter's death. It is worth noting how carefully the author has compounded this despair by inserting earlier in the story information about Bleeker's wife who years before had died as violently as did the daughter. His own violent action is startling and unpredictable, but from what we have come to know of his background and personality it is understandable.

The principle of internal logic applies not only to the outcome of a character but to each stage of his development as well. One of the finest examples of this is Nelson Algren's "A Bottle of Milk for Mother." The story opens with a character named Lefty Bicek who is being questioned by the police. They have charged him only with having trailed a drunk, but then they begin to accuse him bluntly and apparently without evidence of being a "jackroller." The attitude of the policemen and the reporter in the room is such that we immediately sympathize with Lefty. We brace ourselves for a story of police brutality. But as Lefty begins to defend himself, we are startled to learn that he really did intend to rob the old drunk. The shift could not have been predicted, but it is consistent with what we have already learned about Lefty. The next surprise comes when his story shifts again: He really did "strong-arm" the old man. By this time we have more material to work with, so again the shift in our evaluation of Lefty appears to be "logical." As the story develops, our opinion of Lefty is knocked down step by step; and when we hear him confess that he did have a gun, that he did fire it, and when we learn that he has murdered a father of five children, we see Lefty as a pathetic, brutal, insensitive thug. And our opinion of the police has become much more complex—a mixture of basic respect and some scorn. At the very end we see Lefty in his darkened cell. He appears to be praying—another reversal which we are ready to accept as possible. But he is only looking for his cap—more credible. Then, cap found, still on his knees, he ends by softly telling himself "I knew I'd never get to be twenty-one anyhow."

The story demands one reappraisal after another; yet each one has been prepared for so that it appears natural or logical. This logic does not depend on our knowing the Polish district of Chicago during the depression. It does depend on our ability to put the pieces together in such a way that one element leads to or prepares the way for the next.

Complexity As I pointed out before, all fictional characters contain some measure of internal logic. Only in the case of sophisticated fiction, however, do we have complexity of characterization.

There is, of course, no sharp division between characters who are presented with complexity and those with simplicity. But when we look at the extremes, it is clear that they are divided not just by degree but generically as well. The character who is presented on a purely simple level usually reflects a generality, a convention which we can label as "a typical. . . ." A character who is presented on a complex or sophisticated level, on the other hand, is the raw material from which those generalities were formed.

By way of specific example, take the type found so frequently in the murder-mystery detective which we can call "the Irishman." He is, by convention, outgoing, flirtatious, aggressive, only moderately educated, anti-intellectual, opposed to the responsibilities of marriage, as true to his friends as Robin Hood, fond of drink but opposed to drunkenness, and invariably successful.

Such characters are tailor-made to fit the convention, and the author learns the technique by reading as many other samples as he can find and drawing from them a pattern. The process is essentially the same as the one whereby the concept of "the typical Italian" or "the typical salesman" are created: a statistical average taken from samples.

By way of contrast, take the highly individualized Irishmen which we meet in the works of James Joyce, Frank O'Connor, and others. These are not statistical averages; they represent the endlessly varied samples from which generalities are usually drawn.

This distinction is an important one because so many young writers who try to create individualized and complex characters manage to slide back into a rigid convention. There are good reasons for this weakness. First, most of our education has been spent drawing generalities from specific cases. In history courses we are trained to identify "the typical attitude of the eighteenth century" or "the typical British worker of the nineteenth century" and the like. In psychology we learn patterns of "the typical neurotic," and in sociology we master terms like "upper-middle-class attitudes." Second, much of our nonacademic learning leads us unwittingly to identify such concepts as "the typical German" or "the typical Catholic." And finally, even our literary training tends to stress patterns such as "the rogue," "the tragic hero," "the non-hero," and "the foil."

It is for these reasons that some student-writers found a character not on individualized characteristics but upon statistical patterns. None go so far as to have an American parent with 3.5 children, but the results are no less absurd when a writer consciously tries to create "the typical teenager."

This point is made clear when one thinks of the fully drawn and complex figures one has come to know through literature. Raskolnikov in *Crime and Punishment* is not a typical Russian or a typical adolescent or a typical anything. He is a character who happens to be Russian, happens to be young, and is also filled with a great egotism which is blended with an inwardness, a solipsism, a childishness, an insecurity, and an instability of emotion all interrelated through a system of internal logic so that we as readers take him seriously as an as-if-real character.

It is true, of course, that his name may come up as an example when we are discussing Russians or adolescents or neurotics or converts to the church or egotists or heroes. But he will be only one of many examples. Like every individual, he serves as the material from which we draw conclusions. He is not the conclusion itself.

Before going on to specific methods of characterization, I should point out that the principles of complexity and internal logic described here apply equally well to the construction of plot. More significantly, one cannot discuss these basic techniques of character development without making reference to plot. From this it should be clear that although an analytical text can separate plot and character as separate entities the writer of fiction cannot. When one moves from theory to practice, one no longer thinks of "character" as a separate problem. One works with a specific character in a particular situation, and the two are more or less perfectly blended in somewhat the same way that color and form are in painting.

Methods of Characterization Shifting now from goals to methods, there are two basic approaches in the development of character. The first is the direct introduction of character analysis and background; the second is the oblique suggestion of character through action, dialogue, and other elements in the story itself. Most stories make use of both methods in differing proportions, but for the sake of clarity I shall treat them separately.

The direct approach often seems easier. The writer wants to include aspects of personality and biographical background and so leaps at the task with forthright determination. The result might be something like this:

> At fifty-two John Carrington was a failure. His marriage had ended in divorce, his shoe store had been leveled for the new Interstate 95, what the state had paid him was now "loaned" to a collection of cousins and friends who thought him a fool for his generosity, and his battle against obesity had collapsed utterly when the rusting scales hit 200.
>
> Yet for all this, Carrington was happy for the first time in his life. Somehow it was easier to deal stoically with failure than it had been to face the harassment of his wife, his business, his friends, and calories. Besides, as custodian of the town hall he could give somber and sage advice to whoever would listen—from the young things seeking marriage licenses to the Mayor himself.

These two paragraphs provide a fund of information which the author may draw on later. We have from the very start a block of biographical notes, a general appraisal, an apparent contradiction to this appraisal, and at least one significant physical detail about his appearance.

The direct approach, then, is fairly easy to write, is honest, is easy for the reader to follow, has some literary precedent, and appears to free the writer for the really serious matter of developing plot.

But each of these "advantages" should be qualified: It is not really an easy task when one realizes that characterization is almost always a continuing process which runs through the entire piece. What one reveals in the opening block of analysis—or any such paragraph—is not the whole story. One must decide just what the reader should be given and what should be withheld. Quite often such a block of direct analysis is ironic, intentionally leading the reader astray by giving false or superficial characteristics and leaving to the story itself the task of exposing the truth. This is particularly effective when the analysis comes from the apparently authentic voice of the character himself. In Peter Taylor's "A Spinster's Tale," for example, the opening bit of narration is analytical: "My brother would often get drunk when I was a little girl, but that put a different sort of fear into me from what Mr. Speed did. With Brother it was a spiritual thing." This much is stated. But as the story develops, we as readers learn what the protagonist does not: that her fear of her brother's drunkenness was not at all a spiritual thing. In fact the entire story is based on the irony that the protagonist is revealing much more in her story than she herself realizes.

We can see from this that although direct analysis of character is frequently used, it is not necessarily easy for the author nor is it any more "honest" than an oblique introduction of the same material. In fact, it may be evasive, ironic, or both. No matter how carefully the author describes his characters at the beginning, he is never "free" to concentrate on plot development alone since plot and character are forever interlocked. In the case of "A Spinster's Tale," for example, there are two sets of character development. First, there is the chronological biography of a girl who grows into a determined spinster; and second, there is the analysis by symbolic action which reveals to us bit by bit just how wrong she is in her analysis of herself and what the true situation is. Put these two methods of character development together and you have the plot.

The second general method of developing character is oblique, devious, fragmented, and runs through the length of a story. It makes use of action, dialogue, thoughts, physical details, and shifts in the reader's evaluation as manipulated by all of these.

Action is perhaps the most frequently used device. On a simple level, when a man kicks a dog we make a judgment about his character; when he kicks a dog and then cries, we make another. On a less blatant level, when a character habitually drives fast (as do the Buchanans in *The Great Gatsby*), we make an unconscious appraisal even if this action is not stressed. Such a character is quite different from one who never exceeds thirty-five. It would take a great deal of explanation and would probably stretch our credulity, for example, to visualize Tom Buchanan as a slow driver.

The range of significant action is enormous, running from Raskolnikov's butchering an old woman to the husband in Katherine Mansfield's "A Man With No Temperament" unconsciously turning his wedding ring. In a sophisticated story, almost every bit of action contributes to the reader's perception of character.

In selecting significant action, don't forget that an extremely minor detail can make a major contribution to a story if it is repeated or reinforced by details which are similar. If, for example, a wife of a chain-smoking husband empties an ashtray during a conversation, the reader learns nothing. The action serves no purpose. But if she does this three times during a single scene, the reader will consciously or even unconsciously make a judgment about her. One can achieve the same result if she interrupts the conversation at various points by picking a piece of lint off his jacket, straightening the pillows beside her on the couch, putting away the magazine he has dropped next to his chair, rubbing her finger over the coffee table to test for dust, *and* emptying that ashtray.

In addition, there are those little details which do not have to be repeated because they are somewhat startling in themselves. The reader reacts in very specific ways when a character picks his nose, probes his ear with his finger, cleans his nails with a mother-of-pearl penknife, gnaws at a fingernail, cracks his knuckles, picks at a pimple, or yawns so widely that tears come to his eyes.

Mature readers respond readily to such cues. It is not usually necessary to label them with explanatory phrases like, "Always meticulous, she . . ." and "Disgustingly, he. . . ." Remember that drawing conclusions from the actions we see is exactly the technique which we use in daily life to analyze those about us. We say that a person is mature because we have seen him remain calm in a moment of crisis; or that he is a hypocrite because, while lauding the Boy Scouts, he won't let them use his woods for camping; or that she is still a child at forty because she collects dolls and reads bed-time stories to them. These are the specific examples of action from which we draw inductive conclusions. Judging character and attitude in fiction, as in life, moves from the specific to the general and abstract.

In addition, there are actions in fiction that are external to the character which they comment upon. When Mrs. Macomber sleeps with the guide, Wilson, the action reveals not only something about them but about the character of Macomber himself and the true nature of his marriage. Or when Mr. Speed in "A Spinster's Tale" "spat on the snow, and with his cane he aimed at the brown spot that his tobacco made there," we learn, not about Speed (who is never developed as a complex character), but about Betsy, the spinster. We as readers know that he is harmless, but her descriptions of his actions become not only repulsive but sexual as well. Or when Conrad in "Youth" describes the fire on the *Judea* as one which cannot be smothered, the action of the fire itself is compared with the nature of youth and in turn is an insight into the character of the young Marlow. This, of course, is a highly elaborate use of action and requires the author's exposition, scattered through the story, to make the equivalents. But once we make the link, it is as difficult to separate the character of the young Marlow from the leaping flames as it is to think of the old Marlow without recalling the action of the old ship slipping beneath the sea—"more pitiless than time itself."

Dialogue deserves an entire chapter to itself, but it is worth noting here that what characters say and think (two versions of the same thing) is a basic device in the revelation of character. The most common weakness in the works of novice writers is dialogue which describes character directly.

"The trouble with you," we read either as dialogue stated to our protagonist or to himself in reflection, "is that at fifty-two you are a failure. Your marriage has ended in divorce, your shoe store has been leveled for the new Interstate 95. . . ."

Passages like this read like a script from "This is Your Life." This is damning enough, but notice that what has really happened is a blatant exposure of the author's intention. We no longer have the illusion of being there; we have slid back to descriptive writing now poorly disguised as either the dialogue or the thoughts of a character. The character himself becomes reduced to a puppet mouthing a thesis. Thus, the analysis, which was intended to make the character more "convincing," defeats its own purpose.

In general, then, dialogue does not *state* what a character is really like, it *shows* it. "When I saw them bulldozers level the old store," our character might say, "I felt like getting right out there in front of them—let 'em heave me up on that pile of boards and brick like another piece of junk. But by the time they got through and smoothed it all out so you couldn't recognize the old block at all, things didn't seem quite so bad. And on my way home that night . . . well, I caught myself whistling. Hell, I haven't whistled since I was a kid."

Here the character is describing his feeling to another person, but he is not fully aware of just how much he has revealed his life as rubble or how the new lack of responsibility has reduced him, ironically, not to despair but to the freedom of childhood.

This brings us to a second method of employing dialogue as a vehicle for character revelation: the unconsciously ironic statement or thought. We have already seen how the spinster in "A Spinster's Tale" reports completely invalid interpretations of her true feelings. Since the story is told in an as-if-narrated form, all the action also can be seen as a form of dialogue. This is a fairly common method of character revelation. Sherwood Anderson's "I'm a Fool" and the introductory paragraphs of Faulkner's "That Evening Sun" are also fine examples. But it can equally well be employed in third-person stories. Character revelation in Algren's "A Bottle of Milk for Mother" is handled largely through the protagonist's own dialogue and is developed through a series of lies—some intended to fool the police officers and others to fool himself.

The next method of character revelation, through physical details, appears on three levels. The first makes use of those objects which the character quite consciously selects to reflect his personality, his goals, his values, and his attitudes. In *The Great Gatsby*, for example, we learn a great deal about the protagonist from his house and his clothes; and Gatsby himself is perfectly aware of how suggestive these objects are.

On the next level, there are those physical details which unconsciously reveal aspects of character. Owning a Cadillac is a rather obvious and overused device, but the subtle distinction between a Mercedes and an Austin Healey or between a black Ford sedan and a blue Ford convertible is worth noting. Our society is overloaded with such distinctions: a tie with yellow dots one-quarter of an inch in diameter is one type, and a tie with yellow dots two inches across is quite another; a house with an iron stable-boy with a ring in his hand on the lawn is one sort of home, and one with pink plaster flamingos is another; and neither would be likely to talk to a man with old truck tires and a rusting fender on his lawn. Following the principle of internal logic, we might expect the stable-boy home to have an S. & H. Green Stamp print of Degas in the livingroom; the flamingo home might have a set of plastic "conversation piece" Spanish dancers on top of the television set; and the tire collector might have a gray engraving of a man scything a field with the inscription, "The Reaper," and a dairy company calendar with a picture of a little-leaguer at bat beneath a smiling, shadowy face of Babe Ruth with the inscription, "In His Shadow."

If emphasized, each of these physical details can become satiric; if merely touched on in passing, they can become background which the reader will use, knowingly or unknowingly, to evaluate the characters.

On a more subtle level, physical objects which have nothing whatever to do with the character's choice are often used. Setting, for example, can go beyond just establishing mood and can actually add to characterization. A particularly good example of this is seen in "The Nightingales Sing" by Elizabeth Parsons. The opening scene is a country road on a foggy evening which is described in some detail. When the girl's companion says "I hope this is the right road. . . . I've only been here once before," we accept the statement as merely filling in a minor bit of background. But by the time we are half-way through the story, the old farm house they visit clearly becomes an aspect of the adult world—full of mystery and the chance for unhappiness—which the girl sees for the first time and then leaves for a while. Her stage of adolescence—looking forward to a new and more sophisticated world with both anticipation and some trepidation—is matched by her early feeling about the setting itself. In a sense, that opening scene became a subtle symbol for adulthood; but what concerns us here is the fact that a complex set of physical objects were used to develop important aspects of her character.

Like any literary convention, this can be pushed to the level of the hackneyed. When we read of funerals accompanied by rain, weddings by sun, and rage by thunder we mutter darkly about the *pathetic fallacy*, the artificial use of nature to echo human emotions. And when we see the happy couple in a family-type film walking hand in hand toward the rising sun, or a whole colony doing this as in the final scene of *San Francisco*, we laugh. The convention is used without skill or subtlety. Yet the storm scene in Shakespeare's *King Lear* is still effective and "The Nightingales Sing" makes beautiful use of nature. Once again, the difference between hackneyed and sophisticated use of a literary convention is a matter of subtlety and originality.

The final method of showing character obliquely is revelation through change. Character change may refer only to a simple shift in the character's attitude, such as that seen at the end of "The Nightingales Sing." Or it may involve a shift in our evaluation of a character, such as I described in "A Bottle of Milk for Mother." Only in longer short stories and in novels do we have a basic shift in personality, such as occurs in "The Short Happy Life" and *Crime and Punishment.*

There is a wide range to choose from here, but it is well worth noting that in nine cases out of ten a story which is described by readers as "flat," "dull," or "dead" is one which has not made use of such change. Further, one of the most noticeable differences between simple and sophisticated fiction is both the degree and the subtlety of character change.

Returning to our original point, characterization is an illusion. But to be sophisticated it must contain both internal logic and complexity. The methods used may include solid chunks of analysis, but one cannot do without the oblique revelation of character through action, dialogue, thoughts, physical details, and significant changes.

7

CONFLICT AS CATALYST

The *need* for conflict; conflict as an *end in itself* seen only in the simple adventure story; the concept of the *catalyst* in fiction; four basic types of conflict: man against *nature*, against *society*, against *man*, and against some aspect of own *self;* the technique of *developing* conflict and *compounding* it in successive drafts.

Though every writer knows that conflict is an integral part of fiction, many stories are damaged by too much, too little, or the wrong sort of conflict. The first step in avoiding this sort of failure is to re-examine just *why* conflict is such an important part of fiction. Then we can go on to analyze specific types of conflict.

The usual explanation takes this form: Fiction is necessarily dramatic; the essence of drama is conflict; therefore, the essence of fiction is a conflict. This is valid, of course. It is a neat syllogism. And it is helpful insofar as it correctly describes one link between drama and fiction. But *is* fiction necessarily dramatic?

A much simpler and more helpful explanation can be based on an analysis of what actually happens when fiction is written. As I have already pointed out, a story is any prose piece describing events which are essentially hypothetical or self-contained as opposed to writing which attempts to explain or describe aspects of the real world. And we have seen how simple, unimaginative, or overused events often result in simple fiction, such as so-called commercial fiction, slick writing, or comics. In exactly the same way, events which proceed monotonously without complication will result in fiction which is simple and monotonous.

Thus, there is no rule against writing fiction with no conflict. But such works will have no complication and little elaboration except for what one can draw from the language itself. This is one reason why authors like Updike who frequently provide so little action turn naturally to highly poetic prose, relying on metaphor, on symbol, and even on rhythms for impact and subtlety. In most fiction, however, it is conflict and not the techniques of poetry which provide both the power and the intricacies of plot, character, and theme.

By way of specific example, take a story about a doctor who goes on a house call, examines a young girl, discovers she is sick, leaves a prescription, and goes home. This is certainly a story. It is also a very simple story. As soon as we think of complications and elaborations, we think of conflict.

But conflict for its own sake produces fiction which is only somewhat more sophisticated. Tarzan faces conflict (man against beast and occasionally man against man—*never* man against wife). Every detective story and murder mystery is loaded with conflict and complications as ends in themselves. Every western is based on conflict of a highly dramatic, though stylized, form. If we spice our dreary doctor story with a patient who is suspicious of doctors (because, say, she was once jilted by one), we have a doctor-against-woman plot and might squeeze a television script out of that. It would be more sophisticated than our first version, but it is still a far cry from what William Carlos Williams did with the situation in "The Use of Force."

Sophisticated fiction like this employs conflict not as an end in itself but as a means to an end. Or, to borrow T. S. Eliot's term, it is the *catalyst,* the element which causes or speeds up some change. Williams first uses a conflict between the doctor and the sick girl who is unwilling to be examined as a means of exposing a more subtle conflict: that part of the doctor which is calm and professional pitted against that which is impatient and sexually charged. As the scene begins to take on overtones of a rape, the implications about the nature of men and women become enormously complex. The catalyst here has not only caused and sped up a change in the nature of a character, it has elevated the entire story from the level of a slick script to highly sophisticated fiction.

Turning now to specific types of conflict, we could list a baffling array of combinations. But for simplicity's sake, I shall reduce them to four which are frequently used in contemporary fiction: man against nature in its broadest sense, man against society, man against man, and man against some aspect of himself.

I begin with man against nature because in some respects it is the clearest convention; but it is certainly not the most frequently used. On the simplest level, it is the adventure story: Tarzan against the jungle, the Rover Boys against the vicissitudes of the North Atlantic, and, on a slightly more complex level, Buck in London's *Call of the Wild* against the brutal environment of the Klondike.

I am using "nature" in its broad sense here, including all things natural, from weather and the environment generally to beasts and even insects. Such conflicts are shown in those preliterary cave drawings at Lascaux in which wild animals are artistically killed with arrows.

Contemporary use of the man-against-nature conflict can become highly complex. Conrad, for example, used it frequently. As I mentioned earlier, Marlow in "Youth" pits his youthful energies against the sea. This much is pure adventure. But when the sea is repeatedly associated with time, we see in Marlow that part of us all which battles time and, specifically, our own mortality. This is echoed by the old ship, the *Judea* (from the Old Testament, complete with a steward named Abraham), which is eventually consumed by water (time), allowing the young Marlow to set forth in one of the three small boats heading for the "mysterious East" and eventually guided by a beacon on the jetty (just as the three wise men headed for the star in the east), which an old cynic who had arrived earlier claims never existed. This entire system of symbolic relationships between aspects of youth (the young Marlow, the yearning for the mysterious East, and the fire itself) and age (Captain Beard, the old ship *Judea,* the steward) and the overwhelming force of time (the sea) is superimposed on a story which was originally taken as a somewhat sentimental adventure story told by an old man about his youthful conflict with the sea.

Setting aside our own individual value judgment of whether this is "good" or "bad" fiction, this is clearly and objectively a highly sophisticated use of a convention.

It is not necessary, however, to be so elaborately symbolic to achieve a high level of sophistication. In *Typhoon*, for example, Captain McWhirr faces nature with a kind of naive assumption of human superiority; his primary and most dramatic discovery is that the full impact of nature in the form of a typhoon is incredibly more powerful than man or even what man can imagine. This much is adventure with only minor secondary implications. What makes the story complex, however, are the changes in McWhirr's own personality. The proud-man-made-humble is a well-used convention, but what makes *Typhoon* almost as sophisticated a work as *Oedipus Rex* and *King Lear* is the intricate, step-by-step conversion of an entire personality from kingly self-confidence to deep humility in the face of nature. Sophistication here depends not so much on symbolic relationships, as in "Youth," but on the scope of the implications—that all humans tend to have an unjustified sense of superiority over nature—and the penetration into the intricacies of one particular man.

Less symbolic yet still highly sophisticated is Lawrence Hall's "The Ledge" (O. Henry Award, 1961—in *Best Stories of 1961*). Here a man is caught on a ledge with two boys in December. Their rowboat has drifted off, and the ledge will be covered at high tide. There is almost no chance for survival. The only choice for the protagonist is how to face his last hours. He does so with such dignity and inner strength that the story achieves an impact greater, in my opinion, than Conrad's *Typhoon*. This is extraordinary in view of the fact that the work is fairly short, that there is no real character change (except in the sense of our increased understanding of him), and that the ending is almost predictable—though one maintains hope until the end. Sophistication in this case is achieved, I think, through massive understatement—without which the story would become either sentimental or melodramatic—and highly individualized detail of action and reaction. What is lost in scope through the lack of symbolic suggestion and character change is made up for in minute examination of the situation itself.

Different as these three treatments of the man-against-nature conflict are, all share that quality which separates simple works of fiction from sophisticated: In each case the conflict is introduced, not as an end in itself, but as a catalyst which initiates and develops a wide variety of implications.

The second general type of conflict is man against society. It is similar to man against nature in that the individual is dealing with something larger than himself and generally omnipotent. Like all forms of conflict, it is not the exclusive property of any one historical period. Although we do not have Lascaux cave drawings depicting the individual facing a tribal judgment, we do have many scenes in the *Iliad* and the *Odyssey* in which the relationship between the individuals and the "court" of gods is a clear echo of conflicts between the individual and society.

Contemporary fiction frequently develops this conflict by means of a courtroom trial. In fact, this device has recently become almost a fad not only in novels but in stage and screen dramas. The temptation to use the trial stems from the fact that it is naturally dramatic, leading step by step toward a climax and a resolution. There is a great danger, however, in using any convention which is currently undergoing heavy exploitation: One tends to be drawn into the ruts of simple fiction. Another difficulty is a kind of literary claustrophobia which comes from being held so closely to a single, interior setting.

In a more general way, man's conflict with society has taken the fictional form of a struggle to enter a social group or class. The problem is rarely just a matter of making money; it involves a great number of trials imposed by a closed society on those who would join it. We can see this pattern in such works as Dreiser's *An American Tragedy* and Fitzgerald's "Winter Dreams" and *The Great Gatsby.*

The convention is so thoroughly overworked that it is difficult to achieve freshness or originality. Yet it is just as possible to metamorphose a convention as it is experience, and a good example of this is seen in Saul Bellow's "Mr. Green."

The conflict in this case is between an individual working for the Welfare Department and the highly suspicious society of Chicago's Negro district. There is irony in the fact that the protagonist's job is not to harm but simply to deliver a relief check which is probably very much needed by a certain Mr. Green. The primary conflict arises partly from the clan-like loyalty in the society which keeps its members from giving an outsider any information whatever.

Since his effort is to enter a closed society, we have the same pattern as seen in works like *An American Tragedy*. However, what Bellow has done is to invert the order, making the seeker distinctly better off than those in the group he hopes to enter. The wall he meets is not one of wealth but poverty.

On the second level, the conflict reflects racial barriers. This does not take the form of hatred or even antagonism as in Faulkner's "Dry September" or J. F. Powers' "The Eye"; the white protagonist is treated with general good will and even warmth by the Negroes he meets. But for all this, they will not give any information concerning the man Green and where he might live. In this story the primary taboo held by the majority against the minority of one is "Thou shalt not inform."

Equally emphasized is a third level of conflict: government against citizens. The protagonist finds that no matter how clearly he insists that he only wants to deliver a check, he is taken as a representative of the government and as such he is mistrusted as a detective or police officer might be. Bellow adds a completely different aspect of the same conflict by inserting a scene in which a white woman—the exact opposite of the elusive Mr. Green—lays siege to the welfare office in order to receive further financial assistance. The external differences have been reversed, but the conflict between the individual and the state is essentially the same.

Finally, and most subtle of these four areas of conflict, is the fundamental problem of communication between individuals. This, of course, is not a conflict between man and society, but it adds rich overtones to the other three. The end of the story is left ambiguous: We do not know whether the check will ever reach Mr. Green. There is an echo here of the most basic human dilemma: We never are absolutely sure whether we have made contact with another person no matter what words we may use.

There are two points worth noting about this story. First, the technique of metamorphosing a convention is remarkably similar to what one does with experience. The transformation here is fundamental, yet much of the original pattern remains. Second, what may come to the writer as a simple and obvious conflict often can be deepened so that layer after layer emerges. Occasionally such conflicts appear in the first draft; much more frequently they are developed slowly in the way described at the end of Chapter 4.

It is not always necessary to be so ruthless in revising a convention. Sherwood Anderson's "The Egg" achieves originality in quite a different way.

Like Bellow, Anderson here rejects the overused young-executive type. His protagonist is a man who until the age of thirty-four was a "cheerful, kindly man" who worked as a farmhand. But after marrying a school teacher, he and his wife "became ambitious. The American passion for getting up in the world took possession of them."

This is, of course, a blatant use of the convention. But the author then slides off into what appears to be an independent essay on the nature of hens and eggs. This quite literally lays the foundation for a complex set of symbols which are used both directly and satirically. The protagonist's successive failures as chicken farmer and then as restaurant keeper are both hilarious and pathetic; but in the course of this story it is easy to forget that we are dealing here with a man's hopeless struggle to achieve "success." In the final restaurant scene when he tries to play the "public entertainer" and "jolly innkeeper" he is rejected as an absurd freak, not only by the solitary customer, but by us, society at large. His failure to battle his way to "success" in this scene is thematically close to the one in *The Great Gatsby* when Gatsby tries to impress his friends with his luxurious wardrobe.

But not all conflicts between man and society involve class mobility. Conrad's "Amy Foster," for example, deals with the plight of a foreigner trying to live in a small and highly provincial English town. He struggles not for supremacy but mere acceptance—and loses dramatically. In "Do You Like It Here?" a slim story by John O'Hara, society is represented by a boarding school, and again the goal is only acceptance. A more complex treatment of the same boarding-school plot is seen in Fitzgerald's "The Freshest Boy," and once again the same plot with minor revisions appeared in the play,

Tea and Sympathy. In each of these cases the individual is a student, both literally and metaphorically, and society is portrayed as the school itself.

Contemporary fiction tends to be pessimistic about the conflict between the individual and society. In all the examples given above, only one—"The Freshest Boy"—ends in a clear victory for the individual. This is not, I suspect, due to the gloomy nature of writers; it has its roots in our view of society. Writers of fiction, like poets, often see it as immovable and vaguely threatening to the individual—and the impact of the depression and two global wars has intensified this general feeling. More fundamental than these social concerns is the literary fact that what was once seen as man pitted against unalterable fate, as in *Oedipus Rex, Electra,* and again in *Macbeth,* now seems to take the form of man against society. What appears to be pessimism may be more of a literary tradition. And it is well worth noting that often the failure of the individual on one level is accompanied by a type of behavior which is ennobling and a positive affirmation of man's behavior. The protagonist in "Mr. Green," for example, never smashes the wall of social separation, but there is something quietly heroic in his attempt. This is similar to the struggle of the protagonist in Hall's "The Ledges," where the battle against nature is lost but the method of fighting—with dignity and self-restraint—is a victory of grave importance.

With the third general type of conflict—man against man—we shift from situations in which the individual is outclassed in a struggle against something far larger than himself to ones in which the odds are fairly even. This direct relationship between two individuals may take the form of a deadly struggle, as in Maugham's "The Outstation" or Sinclair Lewis' highly melodramatic "Virga Vay and Allan Cedar." It may end only in boiling frustration, as in Powers' "The Valiant Woman" or the husband-wife relationship in Salinger's "Uncle Wiggily in Connecticut." Or it may be treated as comedy on various levels, such as in Stephen Crane's "The Bride Comes to Yellow Sky," Thurber's "The Catbird Seat," and Frank O'Connor's "My Oedipus Complex." This final example, by the way, is well worth careful study in that it is a comic treatment of the same conflict which is developed with such power and dramatic intensity in *Oedipus Rex* and in at least an aspect of *Hamlet*.

Only rarely does the conflict between individuals take the form of a physical struggle. Once again, there is no rule against this particular way of dramatizing the conflict; its infrequency stems from the attempt to achieve subtlety and freshness. The stock barroom fight in the western is "bad" only insofar as it is monotonous and fails to suggest anything beyond the satisfaction of watching a very simple ritual. The observer may safely predict that the villain will use one of the standard "unfair" weapons such as a knife, a broken bottle, a chair, or an accomplice; further, the hero will at some point be flat on his back and save himself only by raising both feet against the onrushing antagonist; also, someone will be thrown against either a table or the bar in such a way as to smash it; and, finally, the hero will win. Now there is much to be said for this type of ritual: It has a kind of crude grace rather like an unimaginative ballet troupe, it allows the viewer to fantasize himself as heroic without placing any demands—either physical or psychological—upon him, and it "kills time." But popular as these rewards are, they are somewhat removed from those which we associate with sophisticated literature.

In many cases, the "fight" is won by maneuvering others into finishing off the antagonist. Maugham developed this with some seriousness in "The Outstation" and Thurber did the same, with hilarious results, in "The Catbird Seat." Since the struggle is only a catalyst, it is often brought to a draw without losing the dramatic impact of the story, as in the final scene of "The Valiant Woman." Another variation is the use of irony. In "Virga Vay and Allan Cedar," for example, the protagonists could have "won" had their suicide pact succeeded; their final defeat comes not through their deaths but by the success of their antagonists to keep them alive. This is a very simple and blatant version of Macomber's ironic victory in death over his wife—only one of a series of conflicts which are woven into that story.

The fourth and final type of conflict is the most complex of all. It is man against himself. More specifically, it is one aspect of an individual played against another. The three other types of conflict almost always involve in some way this fourth type as well. Conrad's "Youth," for example, serves neatly as a sample of the conflict between man and nature. But it is also a metaphorical conflict between the youthful and romantic Marlow and the old, nostalgic, yet slightly cynical Marlow who narrates the story.

An even clearer example is seen in "Mr. Green," which I have described as a conflict between the individual and society on purely social as well as racial and governmental levels. The story is also a study of an internal conflict: that part of the protagonist which is the driving force behind the search for the elusive Mr. Green as opposed to that part which would just as soon go home to his own warm room and comfortable bed. This particular aspect of the story reaches the level of an internal "fight" in the final scene and the result is a draw.

Almost every sophisticated story can be broken down analytically into more than one type of conflict. They echo each other. More than that, they amplify each other. The greater the length, of course, the more opportunity there is to compound these interrelated conflicts. In fact, one of the distinctions between a short story and a novel is the degree to which the work has multiplied the number of conflicts. It is for this reason that Conrad's "Youth" is closer to what we think of as a novel than Kerouac's *On The Road,* an effective but relatively simple treatment of the same theme.

But writing requires more than the ability to analyze the fiction of others. To make use of this analytical material in the actual process of writing and revising one's own work, it is often helpful to follow these steps.

1. Analyze just what the conflict has become in the first draft of your story. To do this, you must isolate not only the type of conflict but the true outcome.

2. If the story seems thin or conventional, invent fresh and varied ways of dramatizing the conflict which already exists. This may involve additions as minor as subtle shifts in action, dialogue, thoughts, or even setting. Or it may entail entirely new scenes, additional characters, or a basic shift in plot.

3. Next, consider other types of conflict which might amplify or echo the one already there. If, for example, the conflict in the first draft is essentially one of husband and wife, are there ways in which either of them could represent the views or the values of society, making the other partner in some respects opposed to this larger group? More significant, can either character be developed in a way as to reveal an inner conflict which echoes the overt dispute either directly or indirectly? Few individuals in real life are "single-

minded" about anything; in the same way, most positions taken by characters in fiction represent only a part of their true feelings.

For a specific example of this type of development, turn back to the end of Chapter 4. The case history of a story given there concerns plot development through the course of several drafts, but it also can be seen as the gradual compounding of conflicts starting with man against nature, building into man against society, and emerging as a set of internal conflicts which amplify rather than negate the other layers.

Conflict as an abstract concept rarely serves as the origin of a story. But it almost always is present, at least on a simple level, in any situation which has the feel of potential fiction. The analysis in this chapter then is not intended to help in the task of finding material as much as in the laborious effort of revising what has gone into a first draft. Conflict as a catalyst is one of the fundamental means of converting the embryo of a story into a complex and original piece of sophisticated fiction.

8

TENSION

Tension defined as an abstract form of conflict; *value* of the concept; types: *curiosity* as withheld information vs. the desire to know, *suspense* as hopes vs. fears, *irony* as assumptions vs. outcome, *paradox* as logic vs. truth, *satire* as normal view vs. exaggerated view, and *shock* as the incredible made credible; means of implementation.

The preceding chapter on conflict was limited to dynamic relationships between characters and those forces which opposed them. In analyzing them, we were able to draw on experience since that sort of conflict is common in daily life.

Tension as used here is also a type of conflict, but it is a much more abstract and purely literary concept since it deals with the relationships between aspects of the story itself. Specifically, tension can take the form of *curiosity*, which is essentially withheld information opposed to the reader's desire to discover it; *suspense*, which is hope played against fear; *irony*, the literal statement contrasted with intended meaning; *paradox*, our sense of logic baffled by the facts; *satire*, the true view distorted by the author's exaggerated view; and *shock*, the incredible made credible.

It is natural enough to think of these literary elements as isolated and separate from each other. There are fundamental differences among them. But from a writer's point of view there are two distinct advantages to considering them under the single heading of tension. The first comes when diagnosing a story which appears to be generally "flat" or "uninteresting." The feeling is easy to detect, but the writer must be more specific if he is to do anything about it. Such a sensation—common enough—may be due to a lack of conflict or poor development of a conflict such as was described in the last chapter. But it is just as likely that the story lacks tension. For a careful and effective diagnosis, one should consider all six types of tension.

The other advantage of considering these literary elements as a group comes when actually making revisions. Friends, classmates, and critics may offer such suggestions as "it needs some kind of twist," or "fuzz it up—you know, like Faulkner," but it is up to the author to translate these vague and easy offerings into specific plans for revision. "Some kind of twist" may best be treated as a moment of shock or it may be sustained throughout the story as irony with or without the addition of satire. "Fuzz it up" (a particularly abhorrent bit of advice) usually implies the need for curiosity, suspense, or paradox—three related yet distinct approaches.

In brief, the theory of tension in fiction provides a means of analyzing just why a story seems to "sag" or "lacks voltage," and further, opens up not just one but a number of different alternatives for effective revision.

Curiosity, like the other forms of tension, is dependent on two elements; withholding information creates no dynamic result unless the author also has created a desire to find out what is missing. For example, a story might begin with: "Ellinton Bates stood there calmly surveying his guests who were much too absorbed in their conversations and their drinks to notice him." There is nothing wrong with this opening, but it is quite different from: "Dripping wet, Ellinton Bates stood there . . ." or "Bleeding profusely from the head, Ellinton Bates. . . ." The first opening is factual and may have withheld some of the same information which the other two did; the other two also withhold information, but enough is given so that the reader is determined to find out what happened just before the opening scene.

What is a fairly simple device in openings can become highly complex when used in the body of a story. In *The Sound and the*

Fury, for example, Faulkner's "complexity" is primarily a matter of exploiting the tension of curiosity to an almost agonizing degree. Because we receive the first section of the novel through the eyes of an idiot, much of the factual material—what actually happens and the time-sequence—is withheld. But equally important is the material which we *are* given—sensual details of sight and touch, fragments of dialogue, unexplained movement. We recognize enough of the story to make more sense of it than the protagonist, but we never cease struggling to fill in the gaps.

Like all conventions, this particular device can be used in a blunt and obvious way which makes the reader too consciously aware of a literary formula. This is most frequently true of openings. It is well worth examining the first paragraphs of a series of short stories from any anthology. Few will have anything as bizarre as the example I gave above. And almost never is a prophecy used, such as "Later that day he would learn the meaning of love." Although this of course does not constitute a "rule" of fiction, it does serve as a reminder that the reader's curiosity is usually achieved by subtle means.

Another misuse comes under one of the headings used in Chapter 2: "Mock-Faulkner." In these cases, pointless obscurity is employed like a smoke screen to hide what is usually a stillborn story. Curiosity is rarely achieved in these cases because the reader is apt to lose the desire to learn more.

The degree and type of curiosity appropriate for any particular story is usually decided more or less unconsciously in the first draft. It is with the revisions that one is well advised to analyze just what one has revealed at which points. If the story seems flat and dull, increasing the areas of curiosity may prove to be a helpful antidote. If, on the other hand, the story has become weighed down with unnecessary complexity, it may be wise to "open it up" for the reader somewhat.

Suspense is often thought of as merely an intensified form of curiosity. But there is another significant difference: Whereas all the examples of curiosity we examined had to do with what has already happened or what was happening at that moment, suspense is strictly limited to what might happen. In other words, suspense involves possible outcome and is essentially the tension created between what we hope for and what we are afraid may happen.

The term has become somewhat pejorative from its frequent association with melodrama. "A suspenseful drama" has become a newspaper critic's polite way of describing films like *I Was a Teenage Werewolf* or summer-stock productions of *Dial M for Murder*—a technique of placating the advertisers without actually lying.

But all this indicates is that suspense, like all literary conventions, can be used so blatantly as to reduce the subtlety of the work as a whole. A standard murder mystery employs suspense as the central literary ingredient, and many intelligent people enjoy these works in the same way one enjoys a "suspenseful" baseball game. Guessing the outcome is part of the fun, but the fear that one might be wrong is equally important. If the reader knows with assurance who committed the crime, the detective story has failed.

Crime and Punishment also employs suspense, but it is not a murder mystery in the usual sense. There are two basic ways in which the convention of the simple mystery has been refashioned. First, we know from the start who is guilty, and the suspense is shifted from "who done it?" to the question of whether the murderer will perceive his act as a moral crime. In this way the central concern shifts from external and mechanical manipulations of plot to internal—psychological and moral—development. Second, this suspense is only one thread in a highly complex pattern of fictional material, such as social and moral concerns, contrasts and similarities between characters, character development and disintegration, and the like. Suspense is important in this novel, but like yeast in bread its effect depends upon the skillful balance of other ingredients.

Sophisticated fiction, then, usually avoids two dangerous extremes. On the one hand there is the story made simple and unimaginative by excessive dependence upon suspense. It turns out to be a game, a kind of light entertainment for those either momentarily or chronically lazy. On the other hand, there is the story which even if clever or intricate fails to draw the reader through to the end. Such work is sluggish, without strength of its own. As author, one can sit back and blame a Philistinian public for not struggling harder, but it would be more constructive to consider the forms of suspense which could be used to intrigue sophisticated readers.

Subtlety and careful integration with the other aspects of the work are the keys to the successful use of suspense.

Irony in its conventional sense can take three forms. First there is the statement, either by a character or by the author himself, in which the literal meaning is the opposite of the intended meaning. This is *verbal irony* in that it always takes the form of words, but it might also be called conscious irony because it is usually used knowingly by a character or directly by the author. Frequently this verbal irony is merely an extension of understatement. If during a hurricane, for example, a character says "Quite a blow," we take the comment not as inaccurate but as a commonplace use of understatement. But if he says, while watching his house and property destroyed by the pounding surf, "Great day for sailing!" the understatement has been pushed to the point where it is exactly the opposite of the intended meaning and we have verbal irony. If he is bitter, as well he might be, we may also say he is sarcastic.

Verbal irony can be used in brief flashes or it can be a sustained tone throughout an entire work. As an example of the former, we have Nelson Algren's description of Lefty's knife in "A Bottle of Milk for Mother": "His own double-edged double-jointed spring-blade cuts-all genuine Filipino twisty-handled all-American gut-ripper." On the first level, this is a description of praise; all but the last hyphenated modifier are taken from advertisements in (ironically) comic magazines. But the very excess of praise and the final modifier are enough to assure us that the author's view of the weapon is exactly the opposite.

Another example of the same type of irony can be found in Joseph Heller's *Catch-22,* a novel which is permeated with both irony and paradox. "He was a militant idealist who crusaded against racial bigotry by growing faint in its presence." Note how "militant" is not only nullified but reversed by the final phrase. Or: "He knew everything about literature except how to enjoy it." Or: "The case against Clevinger was open and shut. The only thing missing was something to charge him with."

When verbal irony is sustained throughout an entire work, it is usually a vehicle for satire. That is, the author continually reverses his actual feeling in order to make the ridiculed more ridiculous. In nonfiction, Swift's "A Modest Proposal" is perhaps the best-known example. His proposal to solve the overpopulation problem in starving Ireland by eating small children is presented with such restraint, such logic, such modesty that every year a small number of literate freshmen read it straight, turning Swift from an ironic humanitarian into a sadistic cannibal.

In fiction, Anderson's "I'm a Fool" is a good example. Less subtle is Sinclair Lewis' "I'm a Stranger Here Myself" and *Babbitt*, in which the author takes no stand against his characters but allows them to damn themselves.

Dramatic irony is not limited to plays; the term refers to the fact that the final reversal turns on action. The classic example is in Sophocles' *Oedipus Rex*. When the messenger comes on stage saying "Good news!" those in the audience who know the story wince with the realization that the news will actually be catastrophic. For the others, the impact of the irony will be delayed until later in the play, as it will be for the characters themselves. Note that the reversal here turns on outcome. If, by way of contrast, the messenger had already given information known by him and the others to be disastrous and then added with bitter sarcasm, "Now *there's* a piece of good news," we would have verbal irony.

Dramatic irony could be called unconscious irony insofar as the characters are not aware of its presence. The playwright, of course, knows what he is doing, but the presentation is far more oblique than the direct statements quoted from the fiction of Algren and Heller.

Because contemporary writers rarely work with known plots, the hidden information must be made known to the reader in the course of the novel or story itself. This is achieved in Peter Taylor's "A Spinster's Tale" by the title itself. Because we know that this girl will grow into a spinster, much of her self-analysis which is naive on one level becomes highly charged and significant on another. Exactly the same technique is used in Frank O'Connor's "My Oedipus Complex" which, though with a much lighter tone, allows the "innocent" actions of a boy to take on significance which he does not realize.

The third type of irony is sometimes called *cosmic* or the *irony of fate*, though it may take the form of a very minor event. In general terms, it is any outcome which turns out the opposite of normal expectations. It is, however, more complicated than a simple reversal. It is not enough to have a normally brave man turn cowardly. The characteristic must be firmly identified with the agent, and the reversal must be a clear denial. For a man who has spent a lifetime being a fireman to die from smoking in bed, for example, is ironic enough for a news item—though it would make rather clumsy fiction. Good fictional examples from works already discussed can be seen in the conversion of the doctor in Williams' "The Use of Force" into a kind of metaphorical rapist, or the conversion of the mildest of all mild clerks in Thurber's "The Catbird Seat" into a man who masterminds the utter defeat of a fearfully dominant antagonist. Or, beyond the level of characterization, there is irony in Conrad's "Youth" where the scene in which the crew works desperately to save the sinking ship by pumping the water out is followed directly by one in which they try to extinguish the fire in the hold by pumping the water back in.

Verbal, dramatic, and cosmic irony are in some respects quite different from each other, and each form can be developed in an infinite number of ways; but they all establish a tension by playing expectations or assumptions against actual outcome. In verbal irony the assumption is that authors and characters mean what they say, but the reality denies this. In dramatic irony the assumption is that characters cannot know what they have not yet learned, but the fact is that they sometimes stumble very close to the truth either by direct statement or a reversal. In cosmic irony the assumption is that there is order in the universe, and we are jolted when this "logic of life" is reversed.

The analysis of irony can become an entertaining game for the critic in all of us, but one cannot use it successfully until one has read enough fiction to know the "feel" of it. Few literary devices are more elusive. In this respect, it comes close to wit, which can be analyzed to death in lectures and texts but which comes to the writer, if at all, primarily by reading *it* rather than *about it.*

Elusive as it is, irony is none the less important. It serves as a means of salvaging the story or novel which is too close to the author by providing a significant distance between fiction and experience. It can be made to provide the needed tartness in a story which has touched on the sentimental. And it can easily be used to add a kind of comic relief to a story which has begun to approach melodrama. In general—and including all three of these cases—the use of irony is the best antidote for the story which in any way has begun to "take itself too seriously," a particularly common ailment. This odd descriptive phrase in no way suggests that a story should not be serious; it does suggest that the tone of high seriousness is not always appropriate. When one has weighed down a simple story with deadly seriousness, the result may be absurd; the solution in some cases is to increase the magnitude of the story itself; but just as frequently the introduction of irony will be a wiser course.

Paradox is closely related to irony, but it differs in that the tension is created by upsetting only one type of assumption: logic. In brief, we assume that logic will result in the truth, but the paradox arrives at a conclusion which refutes logic. Some of the best examples are found in Joseph Heller's *Catch-22*. "The Texan," he writes, "turned out to be good-natured, generous, and likable. In three days no one could stand him." This is a perfectly balanced paradox. First we are given the material for a logical conclusion; then we are tripped by a reversal which is illogical but immediately acceptable as "true." The same "one-two punch" is seen repeated in his description of a modern farmer: "He advocated thrift and hard work and disapproved of loose women who turned him down. His speciality was alfalfa, and he made a good thing out of not growing any."

Sometimes paradox can be extended as plot. In the same novel, Yossarian, a bombardier, is called before his superiors for missing the target and requiring a second bombing run. The colonel is furious, shouting, "How am I going to cover up something like this in the report?" Yossarian says "Why don't you give me a medal?" After much argument, what began as a possible court-martial hearing ends with a citation for heroism, "For going around twice." This entire scene is the development of an absurd paradox just as any of the examples given in the paragraph above could have been developed.

Satire creates tension by playing an exaggerated view of characters, places, or institutions against the "true" or "reasonable" view. The distortion may be slight and the resulting "light satire" mildly chiding, as in the works of J. P. Marquand; they may be heavy but essentially comic, as with Peter DeVries' novels; or they may be bitter and corrosive, as with much of Sinclair Lewis and sections of Heller's *Catch-22*. But in spite of the variety, all satire has some measure of exaggeration devised to ridicule the subject.

Irony and paradox are natural ingredients in satire as many of the examples given above show. But these three forms of tension should not be thought of as inseparable. Certainly the dramatic irony of *Oedipus Rex* is not accompanied by satire, nor is the cosmic irony in Williams' "The Use of Force." It is difficult to find samples of good satire free from irony, but Mary McCarthy's savagely comic "Cruel and Barbarous Treatment" comes close.

There are two dangers in the use of satire which often damage early attempts. The first is a lack of focus. That is, the author has not decided just what the butt of his satire is and the resulting story is often diffuse and scattered. It is well worth examining the first draft of any satiric work with a cold, unsmiling critic's stare (which is particularly difficult when intoxicated with one's own hilarious wit). After one isolates the target of the satire—usually a type of person, a place, or an institution or some combination—one can peel off that which has been added at the time only because it seemed clever. This process often results in far sharper, more accurate ridicule.

The other danger is one of simple excess. I use this phrase quite consciously for satire which has become excessive is almost always simple. Rather than giving lengthy examples here I recommend first reading one entire issue of *Mad*, an excellent primer of blunt satire, and then reading a complex and sophisticated sample of satire such as McCarthy's "Cruel and Barbarous Treatment" or Heller's *Catch-22*.

Satire is often avoided on the unfounded assumption that a story must be either wholly satiric or strictly literal. This is unfortunate. Frequently a story can be intensified or enlivened by turning the satiric ridicule on a secondary character, an aspect of the society, or some institution involved in the plot. If the level of satire is kept light, there is not apt to be any damaging break in the tone of an otherwise nonsatiric story.

Shock is the last method of creating tension in fiction and is one of the most frequently misused. I have described it as the incredible made credible, and in most cases of failure the author simply has not made it credible. Occasionally such authors rely on a kind of blackmail which, were it stated directly, would come out as, "If you don't like it, you're square." But a reader's yawn in the face of unconvincing violence is neither square nor beat, it is roundly damning.

The general dangers of conventionalized violence are discussed more fully in Chapter 2; I am concerned here with the specific techniques of shock. There are two basic types: a sudden turn of events in the story itself, such as the death in Graham Greene's "The Basement Room" or Fitzgerald's *The Great Gatsby*, and the startling discovery on the part of the *reader*, such as the one in Faulkner's "A Rose for Emily." Both types depend upon convincing the reader that the jolt came as a natural and necessary development of what preceded. If it is artificially constructed or poorly prepared for, the reader will not be touched.

One brilliant and chillingly successful example of the first type appears in *Catch-22*. An idyllic day at the beach is shattered when a flyer named McWatt buzzes a soldier standing on a raft. Some "arbitrary gust of wind or minor miscalculation of McWatt's senses dropped the speeding plane down just low enough for a propeller to slice him half away." The following description of the body and the general panic on the beach converts this moment of shock into a nightmare.

At first glance, this may appear to be a *deus ex machina*—an agent brought into the plot arbitrarily the way Greek playwrights lowered their gods by ropes. But when one recovers from the shock, it is worth examining how carefully this scene has been prepared for. Two hundred pages earlier Heller began to give us a clear picture of McWatt and his method of flying. From countless different scenes we came to know him as one who took chances calmly, buzzing tents, buildings, and people as if the risk taken in regular bombing raids were not enough for him. The moment of shock is brutally effective, not just because the body of a man has been sprayed over a group of swimmers, but because while on the one hand we are jolted with something utterly unpredicted, on the other there is a part of us muttering "It was bound to happen."

Here, of course, we have returned to the principle of making events unexpected but natural, the core of internal logic as described in Chapter 6. The only difference is that the voltage of the unexpected has been increased.

One should never underestimate the value of the second type of shock, however. "A Rose for Emily" is a classic example of shock derived from the reader's discovery of an event which occurred years before. And Williams' "The Use of Force" employs the same technique insofar as it is not the physical violence as much as our sudden perception the actions' sexual significance that jolts us. There are the same overtones and the same sense of surprised discovery in D. H. Lawrence's "The Prussian Officer" and Faulkner's "Dry September."

These, then, are six methods of creating tension in fiction. It is not a complete list, but it provides a wide range of diagnostic vocabulary with which to analyze ailing fiction, and it should serve to stimulate inventiveness which is so acutely needed when rewriting.

The varieties of tension are like the types of conflict discussed in the previous chapter in that they are such a basic part of fiction that they are often taken for granted. Frequently they appear in the first draft without conscious planning. There is no danger in this except for those who confuse first drafts with finished work. A close critical analysis of both conflict and the forms of tension in a first draft is an essential step toward effective revision and rewriting.

9

DIALOGUE

Dialogue defined in its widest sense as any phrase or passage which appears to quote a character's words; three types of *external dialogue:* formal pronouncement, monologue, and conversation; the *multiple duties of conversation* such as suggesting theme, character, mood, and moving the plot; *internal dialogue,* directed thoughts, and stream of consciousness; *blending dialogue* into the fabric of the story.

In its strictest sense, dialogue refers to those passages in fiction which are spoken out loud to another character. Used in this way it is distinguished from *monologue,* lines which a character speaks to himself, and *interior monologue,* his thoughts. But the recent development of drama as a literature to be read on the page and the still newer emergence of cinema as an art form have required a more general term which would distinguish a character's own words (either as thoughts or speech) from action and description.

The term is not damaged when we expand it to fit our needs. *Dialogue,* then, has come to mean any phrase or passage which appears to quote a character's words directly.

This covers a wide range, but there are basically five forms. The first three of these are external in nature: formal pronouncements, conversations, and monologues. The other two are internal: directed thoughts (which include both interior monologues and inner debate) and stream of consciousness.

The Three Types of External Dialogue The formal pronouncement and the monologue are the most dangerous and for some the most tempting forms of dialogue. Their roots are in Greek drama, in which one finds an almost stylized presentation of material through fairly formal speeches. The tradition is preserved in Elizabethan drama where characters frequently present their ideas and feelings in speeches of some length delivered either to listeners or to themselves while alone on the stage.

In the twentieth century, however, the technique has become the stamp of second-rate film scenarios and unsuccessful fiction. "But look here, Ma'am," the fair-haired deputy sheriff says to the idealistic school teacher from back East, "the only law out here is my shootin' iron and if I don't go out there and face them. . . ." And when he is through with his formal statement he stands while she delivers the "But-Clem-when-is-this-shootin'-an'-killin'-goin'-to-stop?" speech. And as Walter Kerr has pointed out in his delightful book, *How Not to Write a Play,* this formula can be revised to fit the two-fisted man on the waterfront, the hard-as-nails detective, and the soldier. What Kerr fails to point out is that this particular stylization is not just a reworking of Ibsen; it is a corruption of Sophocles. Every hardened lawman is an oversimplified cartoon of Creon in the play *Antigone*, and every schoolma'am arguing for human dignity is a primer copy of Antigone herself.

One reason so many student writers allow their characters to stand still while formally pronouncing their convictions is that they remember the ancient tradition of formal address from the best of the classical and Elizabethan dramas. This is then reinforced by television's echo of the same tradition.

There are two good reasons why formal pronouncement does not often lend itself to sophisticated modern fiction. First, the Greek audience did not demand or even expect the sort of realism we are used to in fiction. Anyone who has watched a Greek tragedy presented in its original language in an open theater complete with robes and masks is impressed at how stylized the performance is. There is almost no action. The gestures are closer to ballet than modern drama. The strength of the play comes from the fact that eloquent speakers are presenting significant and moving verse. Without knowing the language well one can find the play overwhelmingly dull. But the modern reader of fiction is used to a balance of action, description, and dialogue by means of which he can enter the situation and identify with the characters. To allow a character to pontificate suggests to the modern reader that the author himself is lecturing. This is as true of works which are basically fantasies, like Kafka's *The Trial,* as it is of more conventional forms of modern realism.

A second reason that formal address usually fails in fiction is that it was devised to solve problems in drama which simply do not exist for the short-story writer. The monologues of Shakespearean heroes, for example, were a dramatic convention devised to present the inner thoughts of articulate men. The novelist does not have to have his protagonist pace up and down voicing his thoughts simply because the writer is free to penetrate the character's mind both directly by quoting thoughts and indirectly by presenting memories, dreams, and fragmented reactions.

For these reasons external or spoken dialogue in contemporary fiction is usually limited to conversations. Characters do not announce themselves, except in highly unsophisticated works, as representing democracy, truth, virtue, evil, corruption, or the Spirit of West Berlin. They do not explain the author's intent or even his convictions. In a sense, they do not *tell* much about themselves or the story in which they appear; they *show* the reader hints about both by what appears to come up in conversation quite by chance.

Take, for example, the following sample of blatantly self-analytical dialogue:

> The trouble with us is that we're all spiritually dead. We look to the past, we *live* in the past. We spend our time longing for what is gone, feeding on our own memories. It isn't just us here tonight, it's all of Ireland that's joined the dead.

Whether this be presented as a monologue—the hero staring into the mirror and searching his soul—or a dramatic speech by a rebel to an assembled group, it is poor fiction. It states a thesis as directly as an essay might. It converts the speaker into a wooden puppet of the author, and the reader cannot accept the illusion of reality.

Yet Joyce uses essentially this same theme in his story, "The Dead." And he presents it largely through dialogue. The reader, however, is not bludgeoned by a formal lecture either from the author or a character. He discovers the theme just the way one might in real life: by detecting a grim pattern in the conversation which the cheerful speakers themselves have not. The bulk of the story superficially suggests that the group is lively in every sense of the word. The scene is a large party with much laughter and gaiety. The conversation appears to be random. But gradually the reader notices a recurring concern for the past: the opera singers who have died and gone, the monks who sleep in coffins, and many more. The irony is twisted again at the end when one discovers, again through dialogue, that the one character who is truly alive, living as a vivid memory, is physically dead.

The Multiple Duties of Conversation In examining the three types of external dialogue, we can see that informal conversation is the most useful and the most commonly used in contemporary fiction. And clearly its primary function is not to state the theme of the story but to suggest it indirectly. The author tries to create the illusion that the conversation is developing naturally and in a random fashion as it does in real life, while in fact he is subtly inserting significant material from which the reader will draw conclusions as if they were his own unique discovery. "This may look like a gay and lively party," the reader of Joyce's "The Dead" says to himself "but something is going on here that they don't understand." Much of the delight in the act of reading comes from this fascination the reader has in knowing more about what is *really* happening than do the characters.

But almost every line of successful dialogue performs more than one duty. In addition to developing the theme, it reveals character, establishes the tone, and moves the plot. Often it is possible for an apparently simple piece of conversation to do all four.

Characterization was analyzed more fully in Chapter 6, but it is worth noting here how great a part dialogue plays. On the simplest and most obvious level this is a matter of diction. Take, for example, the range of greetings an old classmate might make: (1) "Excuse me, but aren't you Michael Thompson?" (2) "Say, you must be Mike Thompson!" (3) "Hello Mike, good to see you again." (4) "Mike, baby! Long time no see!" Even taken out of context, these phrases give the reader a cluster of presuppositions.

Developing characterization through conversation poses three related problems: the use of dialect, profanity, and obscenity. The important principle which applies to all three of these is that words of this nature stand out on the page far more vividly than they do in actual speech. A tape recording may prove conclusively that a certain individual is incapable of pronouncing the "th" sound and always says "dis" and "dat" for "this" and "that." But writing this down with blind loyalty to phonetic spelling so emphasizes the dialectal peculiarity that one feels the character is almost unable to speak. A good example of this is Poe's early experiment in Southern Negro dialect. In this story, "The Gold Bug," the phonetic spelling becomes so far removed from normal written usage that the reader often must puzzle over what is being said. The result is that the character appears to be almost inarticulate. Writers of fiction have since discovered that the illusion of dialect is best created not by literal phonetic spelling but by suggestion. One "dat" for every three or four "thats" will create the sound in the reader's inner ear. The The same applies for "you all," "youse guys," and "b' faith 'n by Gorry."

The impact of profanity and obscenity varies with the age. For Chaucer, taking the name of the Lord was an outrage, whereas words which referred to bodily functions were acceptable. It is an odd fact that we now accept profanity in print but hold strong taboos against obscenity. The rule for the writer is the same as the one applied to dialect: restraint. One four-letter obscenity in a chapter has more shock to it than twenty in a casual spoken conversation in the barracks. There is nothing absolute in this ratio, of course, and ultimately the author has to depend on his ear for the effect he wants. The principle, however, is clear enough: The art of convincing dialogue is not achieved by stenotypists; it depends on a writer's skill in creating the *illusion* of reality.

Characterization is shown not only through a character's choice of words but through the length and structure of the sentences he uses. Quite unconsciously a reader makes certain assumptions about a character who says, "When I hear that oily voice of his, or see him smile his way through some specious and smug argument, or catch sight of that handkerchief he always has folded just so in his breast pocket, I know that he is the one man on this earth I hate." We make other assumptions when the statement is cut to, "Him? He's the only man I really hate." The difference here is not in diction (as it would be if the second used "guy" for "man"), it is simply the complexity of articulation.

In addition to developing the theme and revealing character, dialogue can establish the tone. This is easiest to see in the extremes of Henry James on the one hand and Hemingway on the other. James' complex, involuted dialogue must be read slowly and keeps the reader constantly on guard for subtle paradoxes, ironies, and ingenious insights. Hemingway's dialogue is often the reverse, and the stark quality of his short-lined, short-worded, scantily modified sentences creates a different climate. These are the extremes. Most authors find some area of compromise. But no writer should be so fixed that he cannot adjust his dialogue to fit both character and situation. The diction and sentence structure which is appropriate on the deck of a sinking ship is not necessarily appropriate for the same character on an August evening in the apple orchard.

The final duty of conversation is to move the plot. When one wants to move a couple from a lower Manhattan apartment to the Staten Island ferry it is natural enough to use a kind of stage direction like this: "It was too hot to talk, too hot to think. They had to get out of the apartment, so they took the Battery Express and in fifteen minutes were on the ferry, watching the slick, oily waters of New York Harbor slide by." But the advantage of moving them there by dialogue is that one can perform more than one literary task with the passage.

> "Let's get out of here," he said. "I'm dying."
>
> "Relax," she said. "It's no cooler out there. You'll just get steamed up finding out. Take it easy, lover-boy. Save your strength."
>
> "I'm roasting in a damn oven and you tell me to take it easy. What d'you think I am, a Sunday chicken? Not me, no sir. I'm gettin' out of here."

"Relax."

"Come on, we'll take the ferry. For a dime we can stay cool for an hour. Big summer cruise for a dime."

"O.K. You win. Should I take my furs?"

The plot has moved. They are on their way. But in addition to getting them out of that apartment the author has also developed his restlessness, her placidity, their relationship, the tone of the story, the mood of the scene; and possibly a bit of the theme has been exposed as well. In short, dialogue has served several purposes at the same time.

Internal Dialogue One of the most significant progressions made by fiction in the past hundred years is the continuing penetration into the mind. This is partly a cultural phenomenon and can be linked historically not only to Freudian and Jungian psychology but to a much broader concern for the inner workings of the individual. Or it can be viewed as a resurgence. College students today are far more interested in Oedipus and Hamlet than they are in David Copperfield or Becky Sharp. What concerns us here, however, is the genuinely new set of literary tools now available to the writer of fiction.

There are two types of internal dialogue: directed thoughts and stream of consciousness. These should not be confused, nor should either of them be identified with the flashback (see Chapter 4).

In point of fact, the mind makes a very careless distinction between speech and the most articulate level of thought. When facing a decision we sometimes say out loud to ourselves, "Now, let's see, shall I write Harry or is it worth a phone call?" But if there is someone else in the room, the tendency is to "say" the same thing silently. On this level the words are the same. It is natural enough to reproduce this in fiction in the form of dialogue without quotation marks.

The reader accepts this in the form of complete sentences because on this level we actually think in sentences. This same inner debate might, for example, go on with, "No, the real problem is just how much I'm going to tell him." The structure of inner debate can be just as logical and formal as spoken debate. And the reader accepts the illusion of two voices (seen in "let's—let *us*—and such rebuttals as "No, the real problem . . .") simply because that is the way we think much of the time.

Shifting from spoken to silent dialogue is easy. The modern reader is so used to it that a simple "he thought" or failure to use quotation marks is sufficient. In Hemingway's "The Short Happy Life of Francis Macomber," for example, thought fragments are inserted frequently without the slightest risk of confusion. In this passage it is Wilson, the hunter, who is the means of perception:

> "You mean will I tell it at the Mathaiga Club?" Wilson looked at him now coldly. He had not expected this. So he's a bloody four-letter man as well as a bloody coward, he thought. I rather liked him too until today. But how is one to know about an American?

The first sentence is spoken dialogue as indicated by the punctuation marks. But readers find no difficulty in identifying the fourth sentence as internal dialogue even before arriving at the phrase "he thought" because, although it is phrased as dialogue, it contains no quotation marks.

It is worth noting the variety of techniques in these six sentences. From spoken dialogue we move to description ("looked at him now coldly") to analysis of his reactions ("had not expected this") to internal dialogue for the final three sentences. Hemingway could have used spoken dialogue throughout merely by changes in punctuation and certain words: " 'I didn't expect that of you. So you're a bloody four-letter man as well as. . . .' " Or he could have returned the entire passage to Wilson's mind: "Now he's wondering if I'll tell it at the Club. I hadn't expected this."

The fact that Hemingway *did* not choose these alternatives in no way indicates that he *could* not have used them; but this variety of choices is a clear explanation of why the act of writing is far more exhausting than reading.

Stream of consciousness is a newer technique. Unlike directed thoughts, it consists of an apparently random succession of reactions and impressions bound not by a logical system but by psychological associations. The flow from one thought to the next is directed in somewhat the same way that a word-association test is conducted, except that instead of a set list of words one works with the character's own constantly developing list. Take, for example, this brief sample of Molly Bloom's thoughts in Joyce's *Ulysses.*

> . . . after the Lord Mayor looking at me with his dirty eyes Val Dillon that big heathen I first noticed him at dessert when I was cracking the nuts with my teeth I wished I could have picked every morsel of that chicken out of my fingers it was so tasty and browned and as tender as anything only for I didn't want to eat everything on my plate those forks and fish-slicers were hallmarked silver too. . . .

At first glance this appears to be a somewhat arbitrary listing of reactions. But there is a natural sequence of associations which directs her from the Lord Mayor to Val Dillon to the taste of nuts to fingers to chicken to the silver.

Because a careless reading suggests that this effect can be achieved simply by writing fast and without plan, there was a fad for doing exactly that during the twenties. Much of this so-called "automatic writing" was published, but none of it has since been republished. Joyce's *Ulysses,* on the other hand, has.

Clearly there is a vast difference between automatic writing and Joyce's stream of consciousness. The former is sometimes entertaining, often interesting, and doubtless therapeutic; but the writer is simply going through a kind a nondirective psychoanalysis. The author, on the other hand, is primarily concerned with developing, exposing, and communicating to the reader the inner consciousness of a fictional character.

Briefly, this is the difference between pure, idiosyncratic therapy and literature.

Blending Dialogue Dialogue, like every other phase of writing, is best discussed by treating it as a separate and isolated technique. The successful writer must, however, blend it into the total fabric of the story. This is not easy.

There are many ways in which dialogue can spoil what might otherwise be a good story, but here are five causes which appear most frequently.

There is a tendency among apprentice writers to present dialogue in *solid blocks.* That is, instead of a natural give and take of informal conversation with its periodic interruptions, the author allows *A* to speak for one complete paragraph, and then gives *B* the stage for a paragraph. I suspect that this is a result of good training in expository writing, but it makes for bad fiction. The best cure is first to listen consciously to a non-intellectual, non-philosophical conversation. Note the brevity of each successive utterance, the fragmentation, and the repetition. Then turn to authors who rely heavily on dialogue (Hemingway, for example) and study how the illusion of these characteristics is created without risking the boredom which a tape recorder would inflict.

A second problem is the *failure to use the full scale* of dialogue. Although certain authors like Salinger sustain pages of dialogue without ever moving "up" the scale to indirect quotation or "down" to thoughts, this is a very risky technique. Large blocks of dialogue can often be summed up with a cautious use of indirect quotation like, "For two hours they discussed Mary Jane without ever mentioning to each other the central fact that he was hopelessly in love with her." And on the other end of the scale, dipping indirectly into the mind might also serve well in that same scene: "He let her ramble on, fascinated by the fact that she looked more like Mary Jane than anyone else he knew." Or directly quoting the mind: "Doesn't she know? Is she really that stupid?"

Dialogue also fails when its *function becomes too obvious*. Take, for example, those lines of stock dialogue which are used to present capsule views of character: "Let me drive you home in my new Cadillac"; "Don't get me wrong, some of my best friends are Jews"; "Look, son, you've got to understand that football builds character"; and "Darling, Mother knows best; that girl's just plain common." These are nothing but stylized and conventional cues to indicate such stock characters as the affluent businessman, the mincing bigot, the hypermasculine father, and the perennial monster-mother (see *The Silver Cord* by Sidney Howard). Even if these were in other respects genuine and carefully drawn characters, such lines of dialogue would tend to simplify them. They are close to the captions in silent films like "Unhold me, you cad!!"

The same is true of dialogue which is intended to highlight the themes at the very start. These usually are inverted with a vain hope of throwing the reader off the track, but too often the line becomes a dead giveaway which kills the story even before it is born. For example:

"Perfect day for a sail, Jim; not a cloud in the sky." (Prediction: A storm will come up and drown the speaker.)

"The trouble with college boys is that they're all stuffy and self-centered." (Choice: A Princeton graduate will face a mob and save the protagonist or a Yale student will risk his life to save a mongrel pup from the bottom of a mine shaft.)

"Girls are not for me." (Will fall in love.)

"Patriotism is passé." (Will fight in Korea.)

"The church. . . ." (Will join.)

And so on. The fact is that any pontifical statement in the first paragraph of a short story puts the reader on guard and leads him to suspect a formula story. The rambling and apparently directionless quality of so many good short stories (sometimes called "New Yorker Style") is in part a rebellion against this kind of formula, but it is not necessary to break the pattern of the story (see Chapter 4 on plotting) if one can avoid these giveaway lines of dialogue.

Although no rule solves any literary problem, it is helpful to recall here what I pointed out earlier in this chapter: That most lines of dialogue serve more than one purpose, such as hinting at character *and* some aspect of the theme, or suggesting mood *and* moving the plot. This is the best way to keep the reader from becoming preoccupied with the author's technique.

A fourth problem is the line of dialogue which fails simply because it is *not true to character.* The author must constantly ask himself, "Would he have said it that way?" Whenever one detects a stock line of dialogue such as those given above, one must honestly consider whether the character himself is stock. This is treated fully in Chapter 6; it should suffice here to point out that the "typical businessman" or the "typical doctor" cannot be given lines of dialogue which sound real because *he* is not real; he doesn't exist. But as soon as we have an executive in the Trans-Canadian Paint Company who would really rather be back in the army as a pilot and whose only son is doing poor work in the seventh grade, *then* we can start thinking about what kind of dialogue is natural and true to character.

The final way dialogue can fail to blend into a story is by *echoing a tape recording.* This rare but highly damaging failure is due to a fundamental misunderstanding about the artistic process. It has already been pointed out that the illusion of dialect is not achieved by exact phonetic imitation. In exactly the same way, the illusion of character is not achieved by taking dictation. Listening to how people actually speak is about 40 per cent of the training required. Studying the actual transcripts of presidential press conferences as given in the *New York Times* is a worthwhile adjunct to this. Analyzing dialect, intonation, and sentence structure is essential. But 60 per cent of one's training should consist of studying dialogue in contemporary works. If this 40–60 division seems artificial and removed from life, remember that the nonobjective painter has reduced his observance of nature to something like a 5–95 per cent division and the musician, who rarely tries to imitate the sounds of nature, has always maintained a 2–98 per cent division. Literature is still more closely concerned with actual experience than are any of the other arts, but this should not encourage the writer to confuse his art with mere mechanical recording.

Fiction is, first of all, an art; fictional dialogue is, therefore, first of all an artistic illusion.

10

SETTING

Examples of setting; *geographic* setting (nation, city, a specific house); *temporal* setting (year, season, time of day); *social* setting; methods of *revision:* heightening, muting, metamorphosing.

In its strict sense, setting refers to the geographic area in which a plot takes place, including both the country itself and such distinctions as urban, suburban, rural, at sea, and the like. Equally important, however, are temporal setting—the year, season, and time of day—and the social setting. In the following examples, the action and dialogue are constants, but aspects of setting are significantly different.

> It had snowed all Sunday, ruining his day of rest with the howling, rattling demands of his Eazy-All Sno-Blower. And that night the storm must have kept at it because by morning the walks were drifted over as if no one had touched them. He called the bank and told them he couldn't make it and went back to blasting the snow into his neighbor's yard. Normally he wouldn't have bothered—he hated the Eazy-All almost as much as snow itself—but the letter was bound to come that Monday and the postman wouldn't come to the door unless it was cleared and sanded. All this, then, for the sake of the letter. And when the postman finally did come, he still had to hand it over the last drift.

He had only to read the first line. Mildred must have seen the postman coming and was now standing in the open door in her bathrobe, shivering.

"Well?" she asked.

"Nothing," he said. Then he crumpled the sheet and threw it into the spinning blades of the machine which sent the shreds flashing into the street like snowflakes.

He didn't know until well into July why no one in his right mind spends summer months in Madrid. And since the leather exporters with whom he was supposed to be doing business were, apparently, all in their right minds, there was really nothing to do but drink warm wine and wait for the letter. In fact, for three days he hadn't even bothered to pick up his mail at American Express. But on Monday he made a special effort, moving through the deserted streets like a slug crawling over a hot rock. It was there, and for a moment he thought the hike might have been worth it. He must have smiled when he opened it for the American clerk said, "Good news?"

He read the first line. That was enough. "Nada" he said to the American clerk, hoping that would end the conversation. Annoyingly it did, so he threw the crumpled note in the basket and set out once again through the shimmering, breathtaking streets.

It had rained for twenty-eight consecutive days. The bean sprouts had rotted in the ground, the fodder was so moldy the cows refused it, and the road up West Hill to town was so gutted he couldn't even get the buckboard over it. They were still living on salt pork left from the winter's supply, but if he couldn't get the buckboard to town in another week, they would be out of kerosene for the lamps. They wouldn't starve, but he'd have to do the morning milking in the dark which was a sloppy damn business. And after a solitary winter mostly snowed in, he needed some voice to listen to other than Mildred's. So it was an occasion for him and the woman when Harry Miles rode up on his aging mare with a letter.

"A letter," Harry said, handing it down. Harry never was one for clever talk. He just sat there dripping in the rain waiting for the letter to be opened.

"Well?" he said. "Got some good news maybe?"

"Nothing."

The three of them watched the yellowed notepaper being crumpled into a small ball and then dropped into the clay-brown water which ran down the ruts.

The setting is important in all three of these passages, but in quite different ways. In the first, the "Sno-Blower" scene, the geographic setting is vague. We know it must be in America because nowhere else in the world do bankers operate equipment like that to clear their sidewalks, but beyond that we cannot place the town. It might be any American suburban community north of the Mason-Dixon Line. Temporal setting, however, is very exact: We know the decade since machines of that sort are fairly recent; we know the season of the year, the day of the week, and approximately the hour of the day. We also know a good deal about the social setting both from the sort of work he does and from the kind of equipment he can afford.

The second, the Madrid scene, swings the emphasis from temporal setting to geographic setting. Whatever happens in that story, the city of Madrid will play a significant part. The very fact that I found it natural to label it "the Madrid scene" even though the name of the city is used only once shows how vividly a specific, highly individualized city can flavor even a short fictional passage. The season is also important, but one tends to think of this as a *Madrid* summer, returning once again to geographic setting. Social setting is almost nonexistent, partly because the character is uprooted from his own world, but partly, we might assume, because the author considers it unimportant in this particular story. We know that he is not a bum because he has a job of sorts; and we know he is not a *Dolce Vita* aristocrat for the same reason. But there are many grades between, and this story, so far, makes no attempt to differentiate them. Compare this with the social emphasis in the opening paragraph of Fitzgerald's "Winter Dreams"—or with almost anything by Fitzgerald for that matter.

The third selection, the farm scene, makes little use of specific geography—the farm could be almost anywhere. But it is packed with rural details, so in this respect geographic setting is important. The real emphasis, however, is on social setting: the salt pork, the kerosene, the moldy fodder are partly a matter of the period—this appears to be nineteenth century—but they are also clues to the standard of living, which is primarily a social concern.

Turning now from examples to the specific characteristics of each type of setting, we can see that each contains not only different problems and dangers but different advantages as well.

One of the most common questions concerning geographic setting is whether to use and label cities and towns from real life or to create one's own area. But there is a fallacy in the question itself. Since all fiction is only an illusion of reality and, as Frye puts it, hypothetical, an author does not have a choice of a "real" area versus one of his own creation. All fictional settings are imaginary, and the difference between Henry Miller's "New York" in *Tropic of Cancer* and the unspecified city in Kafka's *The Trial* is only the difference between the creative imaginations of the two authors.

The author's choice is not, then, "Shall I set this story in a real city?" but "Shall I use the name and certain characteristics of a real city in the exercise of my imagination?"

There are two good arguments for drawing on a known city. First, it can serve as a kind of geographic shorthand. Many readers, for example, know that if a character is heading east from Third Avenue, New York, he will soon reach a river and that a clerk at Macy's who lives in Queens does not walk to work. Similar assumptions may be made in stories set in San Francisco, Chicago, and possibly Los Angeles. But no American city serves in quite the same way as London does for the British and Paris for the French. If a writer does not consider what the story will be like for the reader who has never been in that particular city, he is guilty of a kind of provincialism.

The other advantage has little to do with art directly. It is merely a matter of convenience. Some writers simply find it easier to let the geography of a real city provide the internal logic of a story. It saves making up one's own map.

The argument that using real place names necessarily adds vividness and credibility is suspect. An unimaginative and inconsistent use of a setting will be dull and unconvincing regardless of whether it is an unspecified city or called Chicago. As I have pointed out earlier, the reader's willingness to accept the story as if it were a real experience depends on such factors as variety and freshness of detail and, above all, real internal logic.

There are a number of questions which the author should ask himself before making the decision to name specific places. If one is tempted by a large city, for example, one should make sure that the story is organically suited to that city and not simply grafted on to it for the sake of resembling something recently read in *Evergreen Review* or the *New Yorker*. The author should make certain that he really knows something about the city or some part of it. If he does not, he may begin to depend on such standard conventions as a rainy night on Forty-Second Street, pomposity on Park Avenue, hysteria on Madison Avenue, rumbles on either the lower East Side or the upper West Side, and general perversion in the Village.

The same is true for Paris. If in blind ignorance the author spices his story with shots of the Eiffel Tower, cancan dancers, and prostitutes with hearts of gold, the fiction is bound to reflect the television programs and musical comedies from which this material was taken.

One should also be aware of the fact that binding oneself to the physical facts of a specific geographic area may stifle the process of metamorphosis as outlined in Chapter 3. The work may never be weaned from experience. This is particularly true of stories set in the town or city where they are being written, and it is more dangerous still when they are based on recent experience.

Turning now to the general concerns of geographic setting, we find that the same advantages and dangers stemming from the use of actual place names apply just as significantly when the setting is not linked specifically to the real world.

Purely fictional settings can also become a form of shorthand. Although one cannot depend on the reader's knowing that if a character walks east from a particular street he will reach a river, one can easily establish that bit of information and use it later. For example, the house in Graham Greene's "The Basement Room" is a complete geography of its own. The location of the rooms is important both in the construction of the plot and in the creation of symbolic significance. As soon as Greene had established the physical details, he was free to use the house as if it were previously known to the reader.

To achieve this freedom, the author must ask himself many more questions than will ever be answered directly in the story. He should know who lives next door or in the apartment above, what the street is like outside the house, what kind of town or city he is writing about, and where one would end if one walked in either direction on any particular road. If he fails to do this, the story may exist in a vacuum; the result is often intellectualized, sterile, and unconvincing.

Temporal setting is often less important than matters of geography.

Some stories are written without specifying the year (usually contemporary), the season, or even the time of day. But in other works any or all of these concerns can become highly significant.

A story such as Peter Taylor's "A Spinster's Tale" could perfectly well have been written in a contemporary setting. The author's decision to use the nineteenth century may have been partly due to the fact that sexual fears and repression were more pronounced in that period. More important, however, is the fact that because we have certain preconceptions about the Victorian and Edwardian periods, the author can imply aspects of the protagonist's character which he might otherwise have to state. This is particularly valuable in first-person narration told by a naive protagonist.

The season and time of day are also valuable aspects of temporal setting, but there are well-worn conventions here which one should remember. Winter is traditionally the time for poverty and death; spring is for love; summer is for passion. Evenings are quiet times; nights are for love or terror. Rather than avoiding the conventions with blind determination, the author is better advised to consider what season and what time of day seem natural to his particular story; if one of these should come to mind, he must develop it with freedom and inventiveness.

Social setting is like temporal setting in that it can be used or ignored with equal success. Fitzgerald's "Winter Dreams," for example, highlights the author's preoccupation with class structure by using in the opening sentence the following key phrases: "poor as sin . . . one-room houses . . . the second best grocery-store . . . the best one . . . wealthy people . . . pocket-money." From there on, the subtleties of the American class structure, which becomes more ingenious the more we deny its existence, are woven into a fascinating pattern. Interestingly, the "winter" of the title is extended in the story itself so that temporal setting, although minor, adds a symbolic overtone to the social setting.

Another example of social setting is Bellow's "Mr. Green," which I have described earlier. The protagonist in this story is socially "above" those with whom he is trying to establish contact—Fitzgerald's concern in reverse. Oddly enough, the use of seasonal cold is also used, echoing social setting with the temporal by making use of "The winter of our discontent."

All three types of setting can be avoided—though some minimal attention to geographic setting is almost always necessary. The point of this chapter is not to urge full development of setting in each of its aspects for every story; far more important is the ability to isolate the use of setting in a story which is still undergoing revision. It is at this point that one may either heighten, mute, or metamorphose aspects of the setting according to the needs of that particular story. It is impossible to predict all the situations which might warrant such revisions, but the following patterns deserve special attention.

Heightening or emphasizing the setting should be considered when the theme of the story seems to show through in a mechanical or contrived fashion. This is particularly true of stories which have had their origin in an idea or thesis rather than a personal experience of the author. Geographic setting deserves the first attention. But both temporal and social setting may add breadth or scope to an otherwise thin story.

Muting or playing down the setting is important whenever it has taken over as a blatant concern of its own. Excessive emphasis on geographic setting results in "local color" stories; a heightened concern for temporal setting moves the fiction toward the historical novel and "Americana"; and heavy-handed development of social setting can lead to the "businessman novel" or to the "proletarian novel" of the thirties. In each case the emphasis on setting has driven the story away from the sophisticated level and toward the simple.

Metamorphosing the setting is a possibility when the author is still too close to his material to be master of it. In Chapter 3 I described this method as one means of weaning the story from the experience which inspired it. The process of metamorphosis is as helpful in the three areas of setting as it is in plot and characterization.

Setting, like conflict and tension, is usually a catalyst. That is, it is not an end in itself but a means of developing thematic concerns and characterization. It is also like conflict and tension in that it is often developed quite unconsciously. There is nothing wrong with this as long as the author is then capable of analyzing what he has done and evaluating how it might be improved.

11

SELF-CRITICISM—FICTION

The importance of *rewriting;* the *mechanics* of using scissors and paste; the use of a checklist as a *review* of this section, a guide to *group discussion,* and *self-analysis;* the *checklist* itself.

When one examines the working habits of established writers as reported in *Writers at Work* (Malcolm Cowley, ed.) and elsewhere, it is extraordinary how few common characteristics there are. But there is one clear and significant point: The proportion of time spent on revisions compared with the time spent on the first draft is about three times higher for the professional than the beginner. As a general rule, both those taking college courses in creative writing and those struggling on their own spend far too little time rewriting.

One factor may be the nature of courses in writing. A college term is relatively short, and the effectiveness of the course demands a fairly high output of new material. Rewriting cannot in most cases be given as much credit as new writing, and credit is a fearfully important commodity for both undergraduates and graduate students. But the tendency to underrate extensive revisions is also found in those hundreds of informal writing groups and clubs which are made up largely of adults not driven by the academic struggle.

Another factor is a rather persistent belief that the writing of fiction is a great game of chance, with the roulette wheel spun either by the muses or the subconscious. This view was proposed by Plato, was recently pushed to its logical extreme by the Dadaists, and is still popular among some Beat writers.

More significant, however, is the fact that many writers simply do not know what to do with a first draft. Criticism from friends, teachers, and associates varies considerably, and the bewildered writer is apt to be left with the feeling that whatever worth there might be in the first draft would be damaged or lost if it were tinkered with. One of the functions of this text is to provide a way of looking at one's own work which will suggest a multitude of possible revisions.

After one has asked the right questions and answered them honestly, there are certain mechanical considerations in the task of revising a manuscript. Retyping stories takes time and as a purely mechanical act is to be avoided as much as possible. The best way to cut down time wasted is to use scissors and rubber cement. Changes in diction and syntax can be made in pencil until the paragraph can no longer be read easily. Then is the time to retype the paragraph and paste it over the old. When an entirely new paragraph is to be added, cut the page in two and splice the new material into the middle of the page. New pages may be incorporated into the original numbering scheme by adding letters such as 13, 13a, 13b, 14, and so on. Delete paragraphs with a clear line through the first and last sentences and an *X* through the material. Cut individual words and sentences with a heavy, soft-lead pencil. Sketchy, hesitant, and vague deletions and additions only postpone the final decision and make the working manuscript look hopeless.

For some reason, many beginners resist with emotional intensity any use of scissors and paste. Perhaps these tools remind them of primary-school activities, but for a writer to waste time copying entire pages unnecessarily is far more childish. The goal is to spend as little time as possible in the mechanical task of arranging words on the page, reserving as much as possible for the creative process itself. The technique of scissors and paste seems clumsy at first—as does the typewriter itself when one is learning; but when mastered, it becomes a natural and expedient part of writing.

The remainder of this chapter is in the form of an outline which may be used as a review of this section on fiction since the numerical headings refer to chapters. It may also prove helpful as a guide to the kind of topics which might be raised in group discussion of a particular story. Note, however, that the questions having to do with the experience behind the fiction (mostly under heading number 3) are no one's business but the author's. The New Criticism has wisely ruled out matters of biography in the task of evaluating literature. It is the writer in his private role of self-critic who must concern himself with *how* a story has been formed as well as *what* it has become.

The third and by far the most important use of this outline is as a checklist which a writer may use to analyze his own story. No matter what criticism an author may receive, the final decision of what revisions to make is up to him. This checklist is a formal presentation of the kind of questions most writers ask about their own work while in the midst of revision; it is an introduction to effective self-criticism.

1. Is this "sophisticated" fiction?
   a. Are plot and characters complex enough and subtle enough to interest a well-read adult?
   b. Has the story become so didactic that the thesis converts the fiction into a tract?
   c. Are there several thematic concerns?
2. Is the story based on a well-worn convention?
   a. Is it a warmed-over television plot?
   b. Is it based on adolescence or preadolescence overly sweetened with sentimentality?
   c. Does it depend utterly on a melodramatic gimmick or a trick ending?
   d. Is it just another version of the gray-flannel-suit convention?
3. Has experience been used imaginatively?
   a. Have interfamily relationships been developed with some subtlety?
   b. Is there a possibility of developing differences in attitude due to differences in age, sex, or personality?
   c. Should the original experience be metamorphosed to increase clarity of theme or to exclude irrelevant material?

   d. Or is it already too clear and direct?
   e. Is the author too close to the experience to see it with perspective?
   f. In general, has the story avoided the extremes of unaltered personal experience and pure invention?

4. Does the plot need revision?
   a. Has the story been freed from experience?
   b. Is there any advantage in having the plot follow a different sequence than the "story"?
   c. Does the story lend itself to an open-ended treatment or to the formal plot?
   d. Has the story been allowed to develop its potential through successive drafts?
5. Could the means of perception be shifted?
   a. Could the entire story be seen through the eyes of a different character?
   b. Should the story be shifted from first to third person—or from third to first?
   c. If first person, which is best: as-if-told narration or neutral style? What about the time lapse between the events and the telling? An hour? A week? Fifty years?
   d. If third person, which is best: means of perception limited to one character or divided among two or three?
6. Does characterization need further work?
   a. Do the main characters have some subtlety and variation in personality and attitude?
   b. Is there internal logic in the actions, dialogue, and thoughts of each?
   c. Do blocks of character analysis slow the story?
   d. Are the actions, dialogue, and thoughts of characters such that the reader can draw conclusions of his own from them? Could physical details and character change be used to the same end?
7. Is conflict used as an effective catalyst?
   a. Has the conflict become an end in itself or is it a means of developing theme and characterization?
   b. Is the conflict either too slight to keep the story moving or so heavy as to become melodrama?

  c. If the conflict involves a character against some external force like nature, society, or another individual, is there a possibility of developing an inner conflict as well?
  d. If the conflict is primarily internal, is there a way of adding some external threat to increase the dramatic impact?
8. Is there either a lack or an excess of tension?
  a. Does the story fail to arouse curiosity because too much information is provided too quickly?
  b. Has too much withheld information reduced curiosity to mere confusion?
  c. Does the suspense hold the plot taut or merely reduce it to a simple adventure story?
  d. Is there a possibility of developing irony or making use of paradox?
  e. Would satiric elements be effective?
  f. If shock is used, does it add to the story as a whole or is it simply a desperate attempt to awaken a dead story?
9. Is the dialogue effective?
  a. Does dialogue appear in long, solid blocks, unbroken by reply or action?
  b. Does conversation have the illusion of natural give-and-take?
  c. Do characters explain the theme of the story directly or do they show thematic concerns obliquely through what they say?
  d. In addition to developing theme, does the dialogue subtly reveal character, establish the tone of the story, and move the plot? In short, does most of the dialogue serve at least more than one function?
  e. Does internal dialogue serve the same function?
  f. Is it blended successfully with external dialogue?
  g. Do all forms of dialogue used help to create internal consistency of character?
10. Has any thought been given to the setting?
  a. If actual place names have been used, is there any literary justification?
  b. If New York or Paris is used, has the author ever been there?
  c. If a town or farm or particular house is used, has the author included enough details so that it appears genuine?

d. Have regional details been used to such an extent that the story sinks into "local color" fiction or an article from the *National Geographic?*
e. Should the year, the season, or the time of day be developed as an aspect of the setting?
f. Has an excess of temporal setting shoved the story into the area of the historical novel?
g. Should the social setting be developed?
h. Or has this concern turned the story into just another scholarship-boy-at-rich-boarding-school plot?
i. Would metamorphosing any aspect of setting improve the story?

11. What is worth remembering about this story?
    a. Is there any one aspect or specific scene in this story which is particularly effective? Why did it turn out that way?
    b. Is there any one aspect or specific scene which fails badly? How might it be revised?

PART TWO

The Writing of Poetry

12

POETRY DESCRIBED

Verse distinguished from prose by its use of *the line, rhythm,* other *sound devices,* the *stanza,* a tendency to *compress* expression, and a preference for individual *reflection;* simple verse distinguished from *sophisticated poetry* by complexity and originality of poetic techniques.

Composing a true definition of poetry is a task for critics. Leave it to them. It is an exceedingly difficult, continuing effort which is related but not central to the art of composing poetry.

An informal description of characteristics, on the other hand, may be extremely helpful for the poet. It serves as a base for what eventually should become a natural familiarity with the genre. The first step in such a description is to isolate those characteristics which differentiate what we call verse from what we call prose; the second is to distinguish sophisticated poetry, sometimes called "serious verse," from simple work such as jingles, doggerel, and greeting-card verse.

The one characteristic which differentiates *all* verse—including the works of Chaucer, Ginsburg, Eliot, and Edgar Guest—from all prose is the use of the line as a significant aspect of form. In prose, the length of a line is an incidental concern of the copyist, typist, or linotype operator; it is a purely mechanical decision which, when varied in different editions, does not alter the work as art. In brief, prose is continuous. With verse, on the other hand, line length contributes to such artistic concerns as rhythm, sound patterns, and even thematic elements. We do not allow the printer to make the slightest change in the length of the line because it is a part of the art form itself.

This is more than a technical distinction. The poet tends to *think* in lines, using them as a base for the construction of images, rhythms, and sound patterns. It is for this reason that many poems are begun with what eventually may become the fifth, the twelfth, or the last line. The poet adds lines the way the sculptor adds clay, far removed from the prose writer's concern for chronology.

The second characteristic of verse is the use of rhythm. This is discussed further in Chapter 14, but it should be described briefly here. Generally, rhythm is a systematic variation in the flow of sound. All speech varies the flow of sound, of course; the alternative would be a steady hum. But the key word here is "systematic." Such systems vary enormously. Traditional meter, a fairly regular repetition of stressed and unstressed syllables, is the most common form. The rhythm of *Beowulf*, however, and more recently of G. M. Hopkins is based, not on the total number of syllables in the line, but simply on the number of stressed syllables. Quantitative meter, rarely used in English, depends not on stress but on the length or duration in the pronunciation of a syllable. Varied as these approaches are, they all constitute systematic variations in the flow of sound.

But there are also nonauditory rhythms. Striking effects have been achieved by patterning the number of syllables in each line regardless of stress (Marianne Moore), by balancing syntactical elements (Walt Whitman), by repeating key words and phrases (Allen Ginsberg), and by arranging the length of lines (E. E. Cummings). These systems cannot generally be detected by listening alone. The definition of rhythm, then, must also include recurring patterns in meaning and in typography as well as in sound.

Prose also contains samples of rhythm, as is seen in the fiction of Thomas Wolfe and Dylan Thomas. Such rhythms, however, tend to be of the nonauditory type described above and are never established by line length.

The third concern in poetry is for sound devices other than mere interruption in the flow. Such techniques include matching final sounds (rhyme), similar initial consonants (alliteration), similar sounds within words (assonance and consonance), relationship between the sound of the word and the sound of the thing it describes (onomatopoeia), and others. The relationship between rhythm and what I am here calling sound devices can be seen in music when one compares the beat—that which one can tap out upon a table—with the harmonies.

The fourth general characteristic is the use of stanzas or other divisions of the text. In some respects, stanzas are similar to the paragraph in prose. Like the paragraph, the stanza is often a unit of thought or feeling or, in narrative poetry, action. But the stanza does much more. It is often the unit which completes a cycle of rhythmical repetition such as the ballad's sequence of tetrameter, trimeter, tetrameter, trimeter. Thus, it becomes a function of rhythm. More significantly, with rhymed verse it isolates a cycle of rhymed endings, clarifying the distinction between a sequence of *a,b,b,a* rhymes and, say, stanzas of *a,b,a,b*. This is more than a matter of simple identification, it is a method of intensifying the sound relationships within the poem. When this is done, the stanza serves as a function of sound in a way the paragraph never can.

In free verse, the stanza divisions often become fluid, varying in length more like the prose paragraph. But they still can serve as fundamental aids to both rhythmical patterns and sound devices, as seen in such widely divergent styles as T. S. Eliot (note especially "The Hollow Men") and Whitman.

Fifth, verse tends to compress its material by extending the meaning or suggestion of individual words and phrases. Both the simile and the metaphor, for example, are methods of linking what is often a complex set of associations with the subject at hand, sometimes providing in a phrase what would in prose take a paragraph. The symbol charges a single word or phrase with an almost limitless depth of meaning. An exhaustive examination of Eliot's phrase, "the hollow men," for instance, would result in an analytical text covering most of his early work and possibly the historical period as well.

Once again, the characteristic cannot be applied to all verse.

Epic poetry, for example, is not noted for its compression except in individual passages. And the short fiction of John Updike is far more packed with suggestive language than, say, the poetry of Kingsley Amis. For all this, one of poetry's significant characteristics is a concern for compression of statement and feeling, a kind of verbal shorthand intensely individualized by each poet.

Of these five characteristics, not one touches on matters of content. Indeed, it is impossible to make any generalization about *what* a poem may say. Some tell stories like fiction, some present theses like essays, and many express feelings like a journal entry. But if we narrow our sights to twentieth-century verse, we see a general tendency to avoid the long, narrative poem which pleased Byron's readers and an even more pronounced avoidance of the didactic poem such as Pope's accurately titled "Essay on Man." With significant exceptions, the poet has turned in on himself with special fascination for the intricacies of feeling, sensation, and personal reflection. Whether this is good or bad is an excellent question for articles in the *Saturday Review* and literate dinner parties, but it would serve no function here.

Verse, then, is distinguished from prose in its significant use of the line, its use of rhythm and other sound devices, its manipulation of stanzas or stanza-like divisions, its tendency to compress meaning, and, in our own century, its association with reflection as opposed to narration.

The next problem is to distinguish that which is sometimes called *serious* or *true* poetry from other types of verse.

The phrase *serious poetry* is misleading because although it is used simply as a synonym for *good,* it also appears to exclude work which is either humorous or witty. This would, of course, eliminate much of Chaucer, Shakespeare, Donne, Marvell, Pope, Eliot, and Dylan Thomas, among others. And if one avoids this error by insisting that the term refers to poetry which is serious *in intent,* one must accept as "good" any inept love jingle which was written with grim determination.

True poetry is no better as a descriptive term. Too often the antonym is simply that which the critic doesn't like. Greeting-card verses about ideal mothers and dear old dads are based on well-worn conventions, but so were Elizabethan love sonnets. Which is "true"?

Even that time-honored distinction between *verse* as anything written in meter and *poetry* as verse with substance fails to specify just what "substance" is.

This problem of terminology is similar to the one in fiction. And the solution is identical: Poetry is a broad term covering a wide range of expression from the very simple to most sophisticated levels.

Sophisticated poetry is by definition complex, but not necessarily cluttered or obscure. Varieties of complexity can be created in any or all of the characteristics of verse discussed earlier in this chapter: use of the line, rhythmical effects, sound devices, stanzas, compression, or subject matter. Further, complexity may involve refashioning an old convention, such as Coleridge's use of the ballad form in "The Rime of the Ancient Mariner" or Dylan Thomas' ironic use of the elegy in his "Refusal to Mourn the Death, by Fire, of a Child in London."

Joyce Kilmer's "Trees" has been used many times in battles over what is and what is not "good" poetry. I raise it here not for one last hatchet job but for purposes of an objective analysis in terms of simplicity and sophistication.

The following is three of six stanzas.

> I think that I shall never see
> A poem lovely as a tree.
>
> A tree whose hungry mouth is pressed
> Against the earth's sweet flowing breast;
>
> A tree that looks to God all day
> And lifts her leafy arms to pray; . . .

Setting aside all concern for evaluation, we can see certain specific characteristics which, first, indicate that it is indeed verse and, second, that it is simple verse. It uses meter, but the iambic tetrameter is without a single variation and no attempt has been made to integrate rhythmical patterns with tone or statement. It contains stanzas, but each is grammatically a complete sentence chopped off with an end-stopped line.

There are sound devices, but they are strictly limited to end rhymes, each of which is a single rhyme landing bluntly on a one-syllable word. There are no examples of assonance, consonance, double rhymes, slant rhymes, and other such devices.

The use of imagery varies. The first stanza is denotative, direct, and without any figure of speech. It is a good prose sentence. The second and third use two metaphors: The tree's roots are likened to one suckling at a breast; and the branches, to one lifting arms upward in prayer. Since only an unweaned contortionist could manage this, we must assume that we are not dealing with an extended metaphor. The use of two separate, visually unrelated metaphors in two adjoining couplets intensifies the separation between stanzas already established by the meter and the rhyme. Further, the images themselves are essentially unchanged and undeveloped borrowings from two well-used metaphors: Mother Nature and a tree as a man reaching toward Heaven.

By way of contrast, here is Ezra Pound's two-line poem, "In a Station of the Metro":

> The apparition of these faces in the crowd;
> Petals on a wet, black bough.

Because this is so short, many readers are tempted to make a quick judgment and pass on. But my concern here, as with Kilmer's poem, is not evaluation; the poem can be examined with the same objective sense the biologist uses when dissecting.

As with "Trees," the line is an intentional part of the form and not subject to variation by the typesetter. Assuming that the reader knows that "Metro" refers to the Paris subway, the poem consists of two major parts: the more or less literal statement of the scene in the first line (what I. A. Richards calls the tenor) and the metaphorical association (the vehicle) in the second.

But the first line is not entirely denotative in the sense that Kilmer's first stanza was. The word "apparition" has overtones which we do not normally associate with subway stations. First, it suggests that something has appeared suddenly or unexpectedly; further, it has the meaning of ghosts or phantoms. In some way, then, the faces of those in a crowded subway station remind the poet of apparitions.

The second line develops this in an intricate fashion. The image is one of petals presumably torn loose in a rain storm and plastered on a black bough. Each word is significant. "Petals" has a conventional association with youth (spring) and innocence; "wet" is our only clue that there has been a storm; "black bough" not only establishes a contrast with the lightness of petals but provides the picture of faces in the black subway car which rushes in with the suddenness of an apparition which viewed from the platform.

There's no moral here and not even a "message" such as some school children are taught to seek in every poem. But there is the sense of suddenness when the subway car rushes into a station, a touch of fear, and a highly original suggestion about the relationship between that solid, black metallic product of modern society and the faces one sees through the window, pale and fragile.

The first reason for calling this poem sophisticated, then, is the complex use of imagery and the subtlety of the suggestions which result. But the rhythm is also complex. The first line is iambic throughout. The second breaks the pattern with a trochee which stresses the first syllable (*Pe*-tals) and then abandons meter for the sake of those three heavy stresses which demand a pause between them: ". . . wet, black bough." Just why iambic followed by a trochaic foot moves the poem from light to heavy tone is a matter for Chapter 14, but it is enough to point out here that in this poem rhythm, with all its variations, is bound quite consciously with meaning and tone.

There is no true rhyme in this brief poem, but there are other samples of sound devices. The final words in each line are bound with similar vowel sounds (cr*ow*d and b*ou*gh) in what is called a slant rhyme or assonance. The second line is constructed with two linked pairs: p*e*tals and w*e*t joined with assonance, and *b*lack and *b*ough with alliteration.

Beyond the technicalities of composition, these two poems differ considerably in their apparent function or purpose. Kilmer's poem is predominantly assertive: It states at the beginning that trees are "lovely" and ends with the proposition that "only God can make a tree." Pound, on the other hand, presents no clear proposition. He makes use of what appears to be a fleeting and personal observation. The reader's concern is not so much whether he agrees or disagrees with a proposition but whether he sees what is described and feels what is suggested. And if he does, his reactions and insights may grow the more he reads the poem. If one begins with the sense of certain visual relationships coming abruptly (like an apparition), one has drawn a good deal from the poem. Later, however, the implication of these people who look like petals may emerge as a major concern. Or one may work out some of the implications of the "black bough"—the subway train and all it represents. In short, one does not "learn" a poem like this in the way one quickly memorizes a popular song; it is more like a Bach quartet in its ability to draw the trained and interested listener back for repeated and expanding interpretations.

Poetry, like every other art form, has its militant factions, and these two poems happen to represent two of the broadest. I have presented this analysis, however, not as a battle cry, but merely to suggest that beneath all the squabbling about the "value," "worth," and "spiritual significance" of poetry, there are certain objectively definable differences between composition which is, on the one hand, simple and unimaginative use of poetic conventions and, on the other, complex, original, or fresh use of conventions.

I should point out, however, that this division is not clear and distinct like that between two species in biology. It consists of two poles which, like the poles of fiction described in Chapter 1, draw on essentially the same body of literary conventions.

The following nine chapters will deal with the nature of these poetic conventions and the range of variation which can be imposed on them to create sophisticated poetry.

13

THE SOURCE OF A POEM

The danger of undigested *abstractions;* the use of *sense perception,* including sight, sound, touch, smell, and taste; the use of *specific emotions;* the fragmentation of *experience;* the fascination for the *sound* and *meaning* of words themselves.

If this were a text for fifth- or sixth-grade students, a chapter on where to look for poetic material would not be necessary. To an extraordinary degree, children of this age use such sources as sense experience, specific emotions, and verbal combinations which give pleasure in themselves just as mature poets do. They lack only a variety of experience to draw on and a breadth of language to explore it.

Those who have let their poetic talents lie dormant until the college years or after, however, have a special problem: Many of them tend to begin with broad, abstract concepts such as Love, Death, Life, Nature, War, Peace, Brotherhood, Hypocrisy, God, Beauty, and Truth. The results, at worst, turn out like newspaper editorials in iambic pentameter. Some of these poems manage to find their way back from the morass of conventional generalities to something approximating genuine feeling, but it is a long and perilous journey.

Established poets rarely begin with a broad abstraction which could best be analyzed logically by assertive prose. Instead, they tend to begin with a specific piece of sense perception, a feeling or emotion, an experience which one may fragment into manageable sensations, or a phrase which in itself gives some verbal pleasure. This list is not exclusive, but it covers some of the most fertile areas available to the poet. They deserve individual examination.

Sense Perception The human being is trapped in the dark confines of his own mind and makes contact with the outside world in five specific ways: by sight, by hearing, by touching, by smelling, and by tasting. It is possible to get through life fairly successfully by seeing and hearing only what is necessary, feeling nothing but pain, smelling only that which is unpleasant, and tasting nothing whatever. If there is any meaning to terms like "poetic sensitivity" or "poetic inclination," it is rooted in the ability—perhaps the compulsion—to see, hear, feel, smell, and taste more in this world than the average human. Usually this is coupled with a desire to share this awareness—poetry as communication. Occasionally there is no such desire—poetry as pure expression. For most poets there is a balance.

While the writer of fiction looks for events which might be rearranged into a full narrative, the contemporary poet seeks shorter, more fragmented units of experience. Most often these come in the form of things seen: birch trees bent over from winter storms, a dead colt, a Yiddish newspaper lying in a gutter, a piece of wrapping paper rolling down a windy city street, a river bank remembered in tranquillity, a dead cat floating in the East River, the patterns of frost on a poplar leaf, the veins running along an old man's hand, or the cracks in a cement playground.

Rarely is the poet content to describe the object as an end in itself. The original image was selected because it had certain qualities—feelings, associations, implications, and the like—which develop as the artist expands his first conception.

Occasionally large areas serve as the poet's starting point: a specific farm on which the poet was raised, the city of Chicago or Paterson, New Jersey. But in these cases, the poet moves almost at once to those small fragments of visual impression which shift the work from generalities to vivid detail. Without doing this, he runs the danger of remaining vague in diction (large, dirty, noisy, busy; or, conversely, calm, tranquil, peaceful) or of borrowing from conventionalized sources.

Sounds are also significant sources for the poet. The range is equally wide, including such details as the whisper of a scythe; wind through an oak grove; the roar of a pneumatic drill; the smashing of plate glass; or human sounds of crying, laughing, singing, chanting, and the like.

It is annoying, of course, when the sound which actually initiated a poetic sequence is sufficiently overused to be considered a cliché. Brooks babbling, gulls crying, and wind in the rigging have all reached the level of song lyrics. If the sound is truly an individual experience, one can include it in the early drafts and decide later whether to delete the image altogether or revitalize it as Howard Moss did in "Local Places" where the potentially dangerous babbling brook became "the stream's small talk at dark."

The other senses, touch, smell, and taste, serve less frequently as sources for the poet. But when one does experience such a sense perception, it is well worth a moment of contemplation, such as Proust gives to his taste of madeleine and tea. These may be mild reactions, such as the feel of grit on a dirty kitchen table, the coarse lick of a cow, the smell of a pine grove in August, the odd mixture of oil and hops outside an urban brewery, the taste of "fish and chips" combined with the smell of sweat, or the exhaust of a Diesel bus. Or they may take more severe forms, such as birth pains, the application of ether, or the burning taste of raw whiskey.

Once one has caught a specific piece of sense data in the memory and translated it into words, one has, by definition, an image. Whether to use it directly, employ it as a simile or metaphor, build it into a symbol, or expand it as the core of an image cluster is the subject of Chapter 16. I am concerned here only with the poet's need not only to keep his eyes open but to keep the other four senses alert and receptive to every stimuli about him—or as much as he can stand.

Emotions Important as pure sense perception is, emotion is equally valuable to the poet. One, of course, does not exclude the other; no matter which served as the starting point of a poem, the other will necessarily be used in its development.

The emotion of love is an extraordinarily popular topic in spite of the fact that it is artistically the most dangerous. The risk comes from the fact that no subject has a greater collection of poetic conventions. When Shakespeare begins "Sonnet 18" with the question, "Shall I compare thee to a summer's day?" he quickly answers it negatively, not just because his love was in fact "more lovely and more temperate," but because the comparison between love and summer had become even then a thoroughly overused convention. Yet three centuries later college sophomores are still linking their loves with summer days.

It is a mistake—or at least cowardly—to avoid a subject merely because it has been widely used. But one should be aware of the fact that it takes more skill to make it a fresh work. One solution is to instill in the love such high ambivalence that a tension is created between the love and the hate. W. D. Snodgrass' "A Flat One" is in one sense a kind of love song to a dying man called Old Fritz, but the love is matched with disgust and pure hatred to a brutal degree. Anne Sexton does much the same with her "The Division of Parts" in which her mother is the object of love and hate. Both these poems may be found in Hall's *The New Poets of England and America* (second series) and are worth careful study. Another approach is irony such as is found in Dylan Thomas' "A Refusal to Mourn the Death, by Fire, of a Child in London." The refusal is ironic in that the poem, fiercely bitter about the conventional method of mourning, becomes a deeply moving tribute. Another form of irony is used in Eliot's "The Love Song of J. Alfred Prufrock" where the emotion is essentially self-love.

There are other emotions which lend themselves to poetic expression: loneliness in childhood, in a foreign country, in a crowd; warmth of a family, a friend; loss of a parent, an old friend, one's childhood; discovery of nature, the city, hatred; wonder at the growth of a sunflower, the strength of an old man, one's own prejudices; anticipation of adulthood, war, love, dying.

These are, of course, all described here in the abstract. The poet is concerned with what he can make concrete through the use of vivid and fresh imagery. His first question might be, "Did I really feel this?" Such a query would eliminate a great many unconvincing love lyrics. The next question should be, "Were there any complexities, ironies, ambivalences in this emotion?" If there are none, it might be wiser to drop that subject and go on to another. The emotion which most naturally lends itself to poetry is not necessarily intense, but for most poets it must be genuine and fairly complex.

Experience Basically, both sense perceptions and emotions are forms of experience. I use the term here, however, to describe those broader portions of one's life, whole episodes including events and dialogue.

This is, of course, the material of fiction. But whereas poet and short-story writer may seize upon similar episodes for literary treatment, the two usually move in opposite directions from the very start. The writer of fiction dwells on characterization and event, combining the two to create some sort of dramatic tension. For this reason he is concerned with the whole episode, often enlarging or expanding on what may have been a rather simple sequence of events. He builds out from the center, adding the way a sculptor working in clay creates form.

The poet, on the other hand, usually selects a single aspect of the episode, reducing this by analysis and rejection of peripheral elements until he has a hard core with which to work. He usually abandons the dramatic elements and concentrates on a set of sense responses or images, which I offered as the first source for the poet, or a set of emotional responses such as those described as the second source. The actual experience has been metamorphosed as thoroughly as it would have been by a writer of fiction, but the poetic concern for incident usually involves fragmentation and concentration on the fragments.

By way of specific example, Richard Eberhart, discussing his poem, "Squirrel Crossing the Road in Autumn, In New England," has described how this was an experience which happened to him when driving and moved him sufficiently to jot the first lines down only minutes after it happened. The poem concerns an experience, a set of emotions, and several visual images. This was enough. But should a writer of fiction use the same incident, he would probably begin to add other characters in the car (dramatic interaction), a reason for driving fast (motivation), a destination (curiosity or suspense), and an entire set of details involving characterization. In doing this, he has moved back from the incident (what happened before), forward (what happens next), and stretched an occurrence into a chronology. Mr. Eberhart, whose imagination moves directly into poetry without flirting with fiction, perceived the event as instantaneous, and he concentrated on the subtlety of his reactions with microscopic attention.

Any generalization about the sources of poetic imagination is dangerous, of course, and here we must acknowledge truly narrative poetry. Certainly the longer poems of Frost ("Home Burial," "Two Tramps in Mud Time," and so forth) and most of Robinson Jeffers have expanded episode in almost the same way as might be done in fiction. But even in those cases the concern for sense data and the intricacies of emotional reaction are greater than we normally expect in fiction, a difference which can be readily seen if one types out a page of Frost or Jeffers as if it were fiction. Too, the tide of poetic concern has run against the narrative—the late R. P. T. Coffin is reputed to have written an epic longer than those of Homer, but no one will print it. If we recognize the exceptions, it is fair to say that the poet is generally committed to the lyric and has been for some time; and when the lyric is based on experience it tends to be a concentrated examination of a fragmentary portion of man's life.

Verbal Concerns This final source of poetic imagination is the furthest removed from that which writers of fiction are apt to use. It is, simply, a fascination for words themselves. The starting point may be merely a play on words—even a pun. Or it may be pure sound—even nonsense syllables. Such phrases may strike the poet as delightful, surprising, shocking, or merely clever.

Often, of course, such concerns result in light verse. Take, for example, these lines from Ogden Nash's "Portrait of the Artist as a Prematurely Old Man":

> One kind of sin is called sin of commission, and that is very important
> And it is what you are doing when you are doing something you ortant. . . .

There are two tricks here. The first is the forced rhyme of "important" and "ortant," and the other, closely related, is the shift in tone from the apparently serious to the absurd.

But tricks with sound and tone are not limited to light verse. T. S. Eliot's "The Hollow Men" is a grim condemnation of the age, and when he shifts directly from the lines, "The hope only / Of empty men" to:

> Here we go round the prickly pear
> Prickly pear prickly pear
> Here we go round the prickly pear
> At five o'clock in the morning

we do not laugh. The jolt is verbal as was Nash's, but the effect is shock.

Or take the punning in Thomas' "A Refusal to Mourn . . ." which in no way detracts from the seriousness of the poem:

> I shall not murder
> The mankind of her going with a grave truth
> Nor blaspheme down the stations of the breath
> With any further
> Elegy of innocence and youth.

"Murdering mankind" is high irony emphasized by alliteration; a "grave truth" is pure pun, and the Stations of the Cross is tied to the life breath in a way which would have gained the admiration of John Donne. The ingenuity here is rooted in a fascination for words; yet unlike light verse the cleverness is not an end in itself.

It is my impression that no aspect of poetry is more shabbily treated in secondary school than is word play. But the student who has come to believe that only grave truths incased in cautious diction can produce great poetry has murdered not only his creative talent but his ability to read poetry as well.

The sources of poetic creativity are clearly as various as those of fiction. But the poet's focus of attention is different. He should be acutely aware of that which he has seen, heard, touched, smelled, and tasted; he should dwell as long on a single emotional response as the biologist does on a drop of swamp water; he should be capable of fragmenting experience into manageable pieces; and he should take full delight in the sound and sense—either comic or startling—of words themselves.

14

RHYTHM

Rhythm defined as a systematic variation in the flow of sound; *meter* defined as one of several rhythmical systems; types of metrical *feet, lines,* and *stanzas; muting* of metrical rhythm by run-on lines, split feet, substitution, and shifts in line length; rhythm of *stress; visual* rhythm; *syntactical* rhythm; rhythm as a *liberating force* in poetry.

Rhythm in its broadest sense is used to describe any cycle of events, such as "the rhythm of nature" as seen in the seasons or "the rhythm of life" in the sequence of birth, growth, and death.

In its strict sense, however, rhythm is, as defined in Chapter 12, a systematic variation in the flow of sound. Even when used in this way it is a fairly broad term which may be applied to music and to prose as well as to poetry.

Meter is merely one method of creating rhythmical patterns in poetry, but it is one of the most elaborately evolved and intricately employed of all. It is a waste of creative energy to argue about the merits of meter with catch phrases such as not wanting to play tennis with the net down or, on the other side, with the charge that iambic pentameter is an anachronism which must be battled to the death. Individual editors, of course, have individual preferences, but there is no academy in England or America which suppresses either free or metered verse. This is clearly demonstrated in Donald Hall's excellent anthology, *New Poets of England and America,* the second series of which contains over 300 poems by 62 poets all under forty: Meter is as well represented by these younger poets as are other rhythmical devices.

Meter is our first consideration here because, first, it serves as a helpful description of rhythm just as both grammar and linguistics serve as descriptions of language. And, second, it is in such wide use by young poets that it cannot be viewed as the exclusive property of an earlier period. For all the heated editorials in little magazines, meter shows no indication of either dying out or, on the other hand, becoming the kind of tyrant it appeared to be before the first World War.

In general terms, meter is the element in verse which can be imitated by tapping one's foot. That is, the word "except" can be echoed with "tap-*tap*" and so can "she *might*" and "to *steal.*" "Midas," on the other hand, becomes "*tap*-tap" and so does "*swift*ly," "*spit*ting," and "*lost* it."

One can see from this that meter is based on the order of stressed and unstressed syllables. These units, known as feet, have been, in common usage, limited to four. The most popular foot is the iamb, a combination of one unstressed followed by one stressed syllable, as in the words "ex*cept*" and "she *might.*" The next most frequent foot is the trochee, which is simply the reverse: a stressed followed by unstressed syllable, as in "*Mi*das" and "*lost* it."

The other two feet each consist of three syllables. The anapestic foot has two unstressed syllables followed by a stressed syllable, as in "disap*point*" and "lower *down.*" The dactylic foot is the reverse of this, as seen in "*hap*pily," "*mer*rily," and "*sing* to me."

These basic four feet are common enough so that familiarity with them is sufficient to scan (analyze and classify) almost any sample of metered verse in English and related languages. And they provide enough flexibility for the poet to do almost anything he wishes without knowing some of the thirty other combinations used by classical poets. Conscientious scanning occasionally requires familiarity with the spondee—two equally stressed syllables, as in "heartbreak"—and the pyrrhic foot—two equally unstressed syllables, such as "in the" or "but the"; but the practicing poet normally reads these as softened versions of iambs or trochees.

By way of reviewing, the following chart shows the four basic feet with the conventional signs for stressed and unstressed syllables. I have also replaced the foot-tapping analogy with the traditional "ta-*tum*" as a way of illustrating unstressed and stressed syllables:

TYPE OF FOOT	ADJECTIVAL FORM	ITS SOUND	EXAMPLES
iamb	iambic	ta-*tum*	except; she might
trochee	trochaic	*tum*-ta	Midas; lost it
anapest	anapestic	ta-ta-*tum*	disappoint; lower down
dactyl	dactylic	*tum*-ta-ta	happily; sing to me

In addition to the types of feet, there is the matter of how many feet are used in each line. By far the most popular length in English is five feet, known as pentameter. Unrhymed iambic pentameter, known as blank verse, was Shakespeare's favorite form; pentameter is also the line used in the sonnet; more recently, Frost and such younger poets as X. J. Kennedy have made extensive use of this line.

The four-footed line, tetrameter, is a close second. And trimeter is also used widely. Lines which are longer than pentameter and shorter than trimeter are used far less frequently, but for the purpose of clarity, here is a list of types:

One foot to each line (very rare)	*monometer*
Two feet to each line (rare and usually comic)	*dimeter*
Three feet to each line (fairly common)	*trimeter*
Four feet (sometimes combined with trimeter)	*tetrameter*
Five feet (most common in English)	*pentameter*
Six feet (less used in this century)	*hexameter*
Seven feet (rare)	*heptameter*
Eight feet (a heavy, very rare line)	*octometer*

Finally, there are terms for the number of lines in each stanza. These are largely self-explanatory:

1. *Verse:* the technical name for a single line of poetry.
2. *Couplet:* a two-line stanza or poem (heroic couplet is two rhyming lines of iambic pentameter).

3. *Tercet or triplet:* three-line stanza.
4. *Quatrain:* a four-line stanza, as in a ballad and much contemporary verse.
5. *Quintet* or *cinquain:* five-line stanza.
6. *Sestet* or *sextet:* six-line stanza (and also the last six lines of a sonnet).
7. *Septet:* seven-line stanza, as in rhyme royal.
8. *Octave:* eight-line stanza, as in ottava rima; also the first eight lines of a sonnet.

It is at this point in an introduction to metrics that many students balk, sensing an overly rigid system imposed on what is rightfully considered an essentially fluid and musical form of expression. There is frequently the feeling that even vague familiarity with such classificatory terms will stifle one's ability to create. The point to remember is that this is a formal description of what for most poets becomes a fairly unconscious technique. By "fairly unconscious" I mean to suggest something like the rules of grammar or patterns of linguistics which one can learn laboriously but which, once understood, are not thought of consciously except when one comes to a particular problem, like whether to use "who" or "whom" in certain complex sentences. It is no more possible for familiarity with meter to stifle a poet's sense of rhythm than it is for a knowledge of grammar to damage one's prose style. The only reason this problem comes up at all is that an introduction to meter usually comes so late in life.

As soon as one moves from the abstract theory of metrics to specific examples it is clear that meter is almost always muted. That is, what would become a blatant, toe-tapping rhythm if developed with rigid regularity is intentionally softened.

Take, for example, this opening stanza of X. J. Kennedy's "First Confession." It is a fine example of regular iambic tetrameter.

Blood thudded in my ears. I scuffed,
Steps stubborn, to the telltale booth
Beyond whose curtained portal coughed
The robed repositor of truth.

In spite of the fact that the meter is not varied, it does not take over the rhythm bluntly. It serves only as a subtle overtone of the stanza. The muting here has been achieved by two methods. First, the use of run-on lines keeps the reader's eyes moving and gives the impression of continuous flow. A run-on line is one in which both the grammatical construction and the sense are continued directly to the next line. It is opposed to the end-stopped line in which there is a natural pause—usually the end of a sentence. Line two and particularly line three in the stanza quoted above are run-on lines. The fourth line is end-stopped. This is common at the end of a stanza, but quite often run-on lines are used even at that point, thrusting the reader's attention to the next stanza without interruption. The first line, which ends with a comma introducing a modifying phrase, is about halfway between, since the reader pauses slightly at that point.

The use of the run-on line does not, of course, destroy the meter. But it is one of the most natural ways of blending the rhythm into the sound of the entire piece. In almost every case of poetry which sounds "sing-songy" or monotonous, the end-stopped lines far outnumber the run-on lines.

The second reason Kennedy's meter remains in the background is that rarely does he use a word which is in itself an iamb. In fact, not until "beyond" in the third line can one find an iambic word. And that is the last one. All the other iambic feet, perfect as they are, are made up of two words or parts of words. Although this may not have been consciously in the poet's mind, it has a significant effect in the muting of the rhythm. Once again, poems which appear too regular in meter are often made up of an excessive number of words like "beyond," and "intoned" (the only two iambic words in this entire poem). The result is an excessive emphasis on meter as a consciously constructed device.

The third and most popular method of muting the metrical sound of a poem is substitution. Iambic feet can easily be substituted by trochaic feet since each has the same number of syllables. This is particularly effective at the beginning of a stanza or a line, either to stress a particular word (the trochee stands out as strong compared with iambs) or merely to break what may have become excessively regular. Take, for example, the third stanza of this same poem:

Hovering scale-pans when I'd done
Settled their balance slow as silt
While in the restless dark I burned
Bright as a brimstone in my guilt

The first two lines here start with trochees; the third line is iambic throughout; and the final line again uses an initial trochaic substitution. Note that in the three lines in which he has converted the first foot from iambic to trochaic, he quickly returns to the standard iambic form which has been established as the basic meter of the poem. It would have been easy enough to convert that entire last line to trochees had he left "a" out and added a two-syllable word at the end like this: "Bright as brimstone in my anguish." But in most cases, substitution is used sparingly so that the basic meter of the poem is still identifiable.

The fourth method of muting the meter is a simple matter of alternating the line length. The most common form of this is ballad meter in which each line of iambic tetrameter is followed with a line of iambic trimeter, as in this first stanza from "Sir Patrick Spens."

> The king sits in Dumferline town,
> Drinking the blude-reid wine:
> "O whar will I get a guid sailor
> To sail this ship of mine?"

Historically this may have come from a seven-foot form, for if you combine the first two and the last two lines you end with a rhyming couplet without changing a word. It is a simple matter for a printer, concerned with the size of his page, to cut each seven-foot line roughly in half, placing four feet in the first and three in the second. We don't encourage printers to take such liberties today, but the form has proved to be a highly popular use of meter, and the folk ballad has continued to exist as the literary ballad—notably by Coleridge and Keats.

John Donne, who is in some ways far closer to twentieth-century poetry than either Coleridge or Keats, makes extensive use of line variation to mute his meter. In "The Canonization" he uses a nine-line stanza in which the number of feet in each line is 5, 4, 5, 5, 4, 4, 5, 4, 3. This appears to be so varied as to be no system at all, but it is matched, with only slight variations, in the other four stanzas. In "The Flea" he again uses a nine-line stanza, this time alternating tetrameter and pentameter in this way: 4, 5, 4, 5, 4, 5, 4, 5, 5. This is repeated without variations in all three stanzas.

This much complexity in metrical scheme leads some to ask

"Why bother?" There are two immediate reasons and one which is more general. First, the poet is able to sustain his rhythm without ever having it turn into a monotonous chant. Second, by varying the line length he is able to mute an equally complex rhyme scheme. The casual reader, for example, may not notice that "The Flea" is made up of rhyming couplets with a rhyming triplet at the end of each stanza. Such regularity would sound like Pope if it were not for the fact that the rhyme cycle is carefully offset by the metrical cycle, burying both to the point where they are heard only in the way certain melodic patterns are detected in, say, a concerto. The third and basic reason is simply that Donne obviously adored the subtlety of sound and could no more disassociate poetry from complex rhythmical patterns than Bach could remove complexities of melody from his composition.

Meter, then, begins with the tapping of feet; but if it is not made subtle by ingenuity it is apt to reduce the poem to the mechanical regularity of a metronome. The first step is to master the terminology of meter so that it no longer is an awkward possession. The next step is to read enough of metered verse so that one has the feel of it. And the final step is mastering the techniques of muting it so that it becomes a part of the entire poem rather than a blatant, technical device. This can be done by using run-on lines, by distributing metrical feet over more than one word, by simple substitution, or by varying the line length. In each case, the goal is not to trick the reader but to give him the sense of rhythm as an overtone of the poem.

I stated earlier that meter is only one of several rhythmical techniques open to the poet. There are, generally speaking, three other techniques which are not metrical but which are effective and popular methods of creating a sense of rhythm in poetry.

The first of these is what we may call rhythm of stress. Rather than employing formal units like feet, the poet concerns himself only with the number of stressed syllables in each line. Most Anglo-Saxon (Old English) poetry is based on such a system. "Beowulf," for example, is made up of lines containing four stressed syllables and a varying number of unstressed. Although there is a definite pause (caesura) between the two halves of each line, there is no way to scan the poetry since it does not make use of conventional feet except by accident.

A recent and complex variation of this can be seen in Gerard Manley Hopkins' technique of "sprung rhythm" in which a foot is made up of one stressed syllable with from one to three or more unstressed syllables. The effect is not simpler than formal meter, nor does it resemble "Beowulf," but it does indicate that rhythmical effects can be achieved through stress even when one abandons traditional feet.

The second rhythmical device departs from our original definition of rhythm insofar as it is not strictly a matter of sound. As a general term, we can call it visual rhythm. It usually takes the form of systematized line length (horizontal patterns) and spacing (vertical patterns). E. E. Cummings did not invent it, but he developed the system with wit and ingenuity. In describing Buffalo Bill, for example, he presents his material like this:

> and break onetwothreefourfive pigeonsjustlikethat
>   Jesus
> he was a handsome man

Here the word "Jesus" appears to be linked syntactically with Buffalo Bill's shooting ability; but then it leaps forward to become linked with how handsome he was. It is essentially a visual trick, tripping our expectations through an unexpected shift in rhythm.

A more recent example can be seen in the last ten lines of David Ray's "On the Poet's Leer."

> But I merely
>   mutter
>   disconsolate sighs
>   and sip
>   the evening's last pale glass
>   wondering
>   how far the fat-cheeked
>   boy's hands
>   have plowed
>   by now.

The whole subject of typography will be discussed fully in Chapter 19, for it has uses which go much further than merely creating rhythmical effects. But it is worth noting here how the downward progression, a rhythmical descent, is created with little dependence on sound. The effect in Ray's poem here would be almost wholly missed if the poem were not seen on the page.

Just as more conventional uses of rhythm can slow the reader, emphasize key words or phrases, show relationships between words, or merely provide a lyrical element to the poetry, so can visual rhythms. But it is worth remembering that visual devices can easily become visual tricks. Once one poet has written a poem in the shape of a mushroom cloud, there is no point in anyone else trying. Partly because of this, and partly because poetry has been more traditionally linked with sound than visual patterns, this type of rhythm is declining. It reached a kind of explosive high point with Cummings and Williams; yet of the 300 contemporary poems collected in Hall's anthology, only two—both by David Ray—make extensive use of visual rhythm.

The final type of rhythm, syntactical, is one which poetry shares with prose. Here elements of the sentence—grammatical units—are arranged to create relationships. This is not strictly visual rhythm —one can respond to it without seeing the work on the page; but it is not rhythm of sound either—unlike meter it cannot be detected by one who does not know the language. This last sentence, by the way, is an example of syntactical rhythm in prose which can be described as: "statement—amplification; but second statement —amplification." Note that this involves both meaning and grammatical sequence.

The great master of syntactical rhythm in poetry is Walt Whitman. Now, after one hundred and eight years, we no longer take sharp issue on what he said, reserving our energies for the arguments for or against how he said it. It may take another hundred years before we can so concentrate on his most recent disciple, Allen Ginsberg. These two men have become patron saints for those who insist that syntactical rhythm is the essence of poetry and devils incarnate for those who do not. Seldom has the somewhat rarefied issue of rhythm in poetry taken on such frenzied passions or been so thoroughly confused with political and social issues.

Here is a sample from Whitman's "Passage to India":

> Ah who shall soothe these feverish children?
> Who justify these restless explorations?

> Who speak the secret of impassive earth?
> Who bind it to us? what is this separate Nature so unnatural?
> What is this earth to our affections? . . .

This is rhythm by syntactical repetition. The repetition of the word "who" is only a cue; the full interrelationship among these quoted lines has to do with the echo of each question with the one which precedes it. The key verbs are "soothe," "justify," "speak," "bind," and "is." One can see from these highly varied verbs that the *statement* is not repetitious; it is only the *form*. Whitman has replaced rhythm of metrical units with rhythm of grammatical units.

Ginsberg wrote "Howl" some hundred years after Whitman first published "Leaves of Grass," and here is a brief sample:

> who broke down crying in white gymnasiums naked and trembling before the machinery of other skeletons,
> who bit detectives in the neck and shrieked with delight in police-cars for committing no crime but their own wild cooking pederasty and intoxication,
> who howled on their knees in the subways and were dragged off the roof waving genitals and manuscripts
> who let themselves be . . . in the . . . by saintly motorcyclists, and screamed with joy. . . .

Syntactical rhythm can take much more complex forms, as seen frequently in Whitman and occasionally in Ginsberg, but it usually requires long passages to see the subtle repetition worked through. Another fine source comes from the fiction of Thomas Wolfe. This is one device which is shared almost without variation by the two genres—a fact which leads some to argue that Whitman is no poet and others to proclaim Wolfe as a poetic writer of fiction. I am more concerned here, however, with varieties of rhythm than with varieties of literary loyalties.

Some novice poets become convinced that concern for rhythm is a barrier against free poetic expression. Perhaps this comes from dull spasmodic drill in meter off and on from the seventh grade through college. But the fact remains that artistic freedom is rarely found in ignorance. It is found in choice. The poet who has mastered a variety of rhythmical systems is then free to select what suits his needs. Some, like Richard Wilbur and Robert Frost, find freedom through meter. Poets like Ginsberg and Gregory Corso find freedom through syntactical rhythms. The first is sometimes damned as pretty and the latter two as ugly, but none of them is ignorant of tradition nor would any be "better" if he were.

Armed with tradition, the student should feel free to "doodle" with rhythmical techniques, feeling respect but no undue reverence for the past. For the musician this is called finger exercises, for the artist it is sketching; for the poet it is a matter of random exercise of his rhythmical sense.

Take, for example, these first four lines from Shakespeare's "Sonnet 2."

> When forty winters shall besiege thy brow
> And dig deep trenches in thy beauty's field,
> Thy youth's proud livery so gazed on now,
> Will be a tattered weed of small worth held.

This sample of iambic pentameter is unusual in that there is not one substitution. For this reason, it serves as a fine base for rhythmical doodling. One might begin, for example, by converting it to iambic trimeter. There are many ways of doing this, but here is one:

> When forty winters shall
> Besiege thy brow and dig
> Deep trenches in thy face
> Thy youth's proud livery
> Will be a worthless weed.

The point of this exercise is not to improve on Shakespeare but to improve one's own ability to work with meter and one's inner *sense* of pentameter and trimeter. Line-length conversions are easy; shifting from iambic to trochaic requires a little more effort. It might come out like this:

> Forty winters shall besiege thy lovely
> Brow and dig deep trenches in thy beauty's
> Field and youth's proud livery loved so fully
> Soon will be a tattered weed of little worth.

The perceptive reader will notice that I have slurred "livery," a three-syllable word, to "liv'ry," two syllables; I also allowed an extra stressed syllable at the end of the fourth line. If this reader is also a poet, perhaps he can devise a more perfect rendering.

Moving from meter to visual rhythm, any number of translations might be tried. Here is one sample:

> When forty winters shall
>   besiege
>   starve
>   torment
> The rounded beauty of your brow,
>   then
> Your light step will
>   limp
>   pause
>   trembling before the last descent.

This, of course, verges on syntactical rhythm in that "shall" is followed by a series just as "will" is; but the relationships are highlighted by typography. If we shift to almost purely syntactical concerns, we might come out with something like this:

> Now your youth's proud livery
>   is our envy
> Now your smile's light courage
>   is our delight.
> But then some forty years will
>   wear you threadbare
> And then your darkened eyes will
>   show our fear.

All of this doodling requires enough terminology to see what one is doing and to describe what one has done. But with surprisingly little technical training, one is ready for both the reading and the composition which is essential if one is to feel at home with varieties of rhythm. Since almost all poetry contains rhythmical patterns of some sort, every anthology and little magazine serves as a source for study. It takes both extensive reading and random experimentation before rhythm in poetry ceases to be a burden and becomes—often with surprising speed—one of the most liberating aspects of the genre.

15

SOUND

The need to *listen* to language; a sample of *lyrical prose* illustrating *alliteration, assonance, consonance,* and *onomatopoeia;* secondary *sound clusters;* definition of *rhyme;* analysis of specific *stanzas;* the *importance* of sound devices in poetry.

Sound relationships are as important in poetry as are rhythmical systems. And they take almost as many forms. A great emphasis is often placed on rhyme, but a cursory examination of what is actually being written in our century reveals that rhyme is only one of many techniques.

The first step in discovering what sound can do in language is to listen. But one must discriminate. So much of what we hear at the theater and on television is devoid of subtle language that we sometimes forget to listen even when there is something to be heard.

For this reason I shall begin not with a technical analysis of rhyme but a sample of prose from Dylan Thomas' "August Bank Holiday." It contains no rhyme, but it is more fully packed with sound combinations than most poetry. It describes a summer holiday not through plot but through a succession of vivid images. The first paragraph is typical of them all. It is reprinted here with the linking sounds italicized.

August Bank Holiday.—A tune on an ice-cream cornet. A *s*lap of *s*ea and a tickle of *sand*. A f*an*f*are* of sunsh*ades* opening. A *w*i*n*ce and *wh*i*n*ny of bathers *d*ancing into *d*eceptive water. A tuck of dresses. A rolling of trousers. A compromise of paddlers. A sunburn of girls and a lark of boys. A silent hulla*baloo* of *balloo*ns.

There are two levels of sound present here. The first, a primary list, is clear, definable, unarguable, and graced with specific literary terms. The secondary list is vague, arguable, and without terminology; but it constitutes a significant part of what we commonly call lyricism in both prose and poetry.

Starting with the primary list of sound relationships, it is clear that words can be linked in only three ways: by the initial sound, by some sound within each word, and by a final sound. In addition, these can be based on consonants or on vowels. Moving in this order, we can group the sound relationships according to type.

Alliteration is the repetition of consonants, particularly those at the beginning of words. There are three groups of these:

slap–sea–sand
wince–whinny (a similarity, not an identity of sound)
dancing–deceptive

Assonance is the repetition of similar vowel sounds regardless of where they are located in the word. Some good examples are:

w*i*nce–wh*i*nny
sunb*ur*n–g*ir*ls (similarity of sound, not spelling)
hullabal*oo*–ball*oo*ns

Consonance is often confused with assonance, but the clearest definition limits the word to similarity of consonantal sounds with changes in the intervening vowels. It is differentiated from alliteration if we limit the latter to initial sounds. There are three sets of consonance in this passage:

wi*n*ce–whi*nn*y
gir*l*s–*l*ark
si*l*ent–hu*ll*aba*l*oo–ba*ll*oons

Onomatopoeia is often defined as a word which sounds like the object or action which it describes; but in point of fact, most onomatopoetic words only suggest a sound to those who already know what the meaning is. That is, we are not dealing with language which mimics life directly; it is usually just an echo. There are three good examples from Thomas' paragraph:

> slap of sea (the sound of a wave on the beach)
> whinny (an approximation of the horse's sound)
> hullabaloo (the derivation of this coming from "hullo" and "hello" with an echo of "babble")

The devices used in this single paragraph of prose represent the bulk of sound devices available to the poet. And yet there are still more relationships present in this passage. These so-called secondary sound combinations will be missed by many readers. Like subtle harmonies in music, they are difficult to detect.

In general, they take the form of related vowel sounds which are not close enough to be called assonances but which, when taken as a group, echo each other. The first group includes the cluster of sounds around *a* and *e;* the second link the "rounder" sounds of *u, o,* and *ou.*

Representing the first group we have "sl*a*p of *sea* *a*nd a tickle of *san*d." Here "and" and "sand" are clearly linked by assonance; but Thomas has also added the related sounds of *ee* in "sea" and the short *a* of "slap." This would be of no significance if we did not find other examples. We do in "f*an*f*are* of sunsh*ades*" where the sounds *an, air,* and *aids* are clearly not identical but distinctly related. As a third example of the *a* and *e* cluster we have "b*a*th*er*s d*a*ncing into d*ecep*tive w*a*ters."

The second cluster, that of *u, o,* and *ou* sounds is seen first in "t*u*ne . . . c*or*net." It is then seen in "r*o*lling of tr*ou*sers." And it appears once again in "h*u*llabal*oo* of ball*oo*ns," which is primarily a sample of assonance (*oo* and *oo*) but which also links the *u* sound with the *oo.*

Secondary relationships in the form of sound clusters like these are not essential to poetry—though they were to Thomas both in his prose and his poetry. I stress them here to indicate that sound in literature is not just a matter of mastering certain technical terms and struggling to sprinkle one's work with a representative sample for critics to play with. Sound is for most poets an integral part of composition, and the manipulation of sound takes place both consciously and unconsciously.

To this point, I have limited the analysis to a sample of prose to stress the fact that sound is not the exclusive property of poetry. But it would be a mistake to argue that prose is in general as rich in sound relationships as is poetry. Certain writers like Thomas and Wolfe are more lyrical in their fiction than certain highly dissimilar poets like Allen Ginsberg, Donald Hall, and Philip Booth; but most poetry is basically more lyrical than most fiction.

There is one sound device which is by definition the exclusive property of poets: rhyme. Only when composition makes use of prescribed line length can one have end rhyme. Since prose is written consecutively, there can be no regular rhyme scheme. This cannot be taken as an argument for using rhyme in all poetry (another one of those noncreative and nonproductive disputes), but it is a reason for knowing enough about it to make the use or avoidance a free choice.

Definitions of true rhyme can reach levels of incredible complexity. None which I have seen, however, contain more than this three-sentence description. *True rhyme* is an *identity* in *sound* in accented syllables. The identity must begin with the *accented vowel and continue* to the end. The letters preceding the accented vowel must be *unlike* in sound.

I have italicized the key concepts which seem to give the most trouble. First, we are talking here about true rhyme as opposed to slant rhymes or off rhymes, which are respectable and will be discussed shortly. True rhyme is not a general similarity in sound as are assonance and consonance, but an actual identity. Thus "ru*n*" and "co*m*e" are not true rhymes nor are "see*n*" and "crea*m*."

Second, rhyme is a matter of sound, not spelling. "Girl" and "furl" rhyme, but "to read" and "having read" obviously do not. It is often necessary to repeat the final syllable aloud several times before one is sure whether the rhyme is true or not—as do composers when testing the relationship between chords.

Next, there is the matter of continuing identity which must begin with the accented vowel and run through to the end of each word. This is only a problem with two-syllable rhymes (known as feminine rhymes). In "running," for example, the accented vowel is *u* and the only words which rhyme with it end with *unning* as in "sunning." The word "jumping" has the *u* sound, but the *mp* keeps it from rhyming with "running."

Finally, the letter which comes before that accented vowel

must differ from its rhyming partner. Thus, "night" and "fight" rhyme since the accented vowel (*i*) is preceded by *n* in one case and *f* in the other. But "night" and "knight" do not. These are technically known as identities.

Since rhyme, like meter, is based on the sound of syllables and has nothing to do with the division of words, the same principles apply when more than one word is involved in each rhyming end. "Bind me" and "find me" rhyme (the accented vowel is *i* in each case, and the rhyming sound is *ind me*), but neither rhyme with "kindly" because of the *l*.

Rules like these take on the artificiality of grammar when first met, but like grammar they become absorbed once one is used to working with them. An easy way to check each rhyme (and also review the principles of rhyme) is to ask these three questions of each potential rhyme:

1. What is the accented vowel sound?
2. Is the sound in each word identical from that vowel through to the end of each?
3. Is the consonantal sound preceding that vowel different?

These three questions become automatic; one's eye moves first to that key vowel, then forward to the end of each word, then back to the preceding sound. And in each case the eye is translating what is seen into what would be heard if the word were sounded—a fact which makes it almost impossible to work with rhyme without muttering.

It is important to move as rapidly as possible from the rules to application. The best method, of course, is actual composition. But the list on the next page may also provide a way of making unconscious what must begin as conscious effort.

All the sound devices discussed so far are mere verbal games until one begins to apply them. The rest of this chapter, then, will consist of specific samples taken from poets now living and under forty. I do not mean to imply by this that the contemporary student has nothing to learn from earlier periods—a conviction which is far too common in writing classes. In the area of sound alone, one has much to examine in such highly disparate poets as Poe, whose excessive zeal for auditory ingenuity is fascinating, and Pope, whose commitment to heroic couplets forced him to exploit

RELATED WORDS	ACCENTED VOWEL SOUND	ACTUAL RELATIONSHIP AND EXPLANATION
1. night fight	*i*	True rhyme (meets all three requirements)
2. night knight	*i*	An identity (preceding consonants are identical)
3. ocean motion	o	True rhyme (*cean* and *tion* have the same sound)
4. warring wearing	or and *air*	Consonance or off rhyme (accented vowel sounds do not match)
5. lyrical miracle	*y*	Off rhyme (the *i* in "lyrical" does not match the *a* sound in "miracle")
6. track to me back to me	*a*	True rhyme (a triple rhyme used by Hardy)
7. dies remedies	*i* and *em*	Eye rhyme (similarity only in spelling)
8. bear bare	*a*	Identity (preceding consonants are identical)
9. balloon hullabaloo	oo and *u*	Consonance and assonance (vowel sounds do not match nor do the endings)
10. then you see us; when you flee us	e	Quadruple rhyme—true (rare and usually appears forced—often comic)

every possible subtlety. But this is a text for writers, not critics; and writers have a special loyalty to their own century.

The first sample is the last stanza from Robert Mezey's "The Lovemaker." The poem is written in iambic trimeter with frequent substitutions (there are two in this quoted stanza). The rhyme scheme in these quatrains is a,b,c,b—the same as in most ballads, and most of them are true rhymes. My concern here, though, is not merely to illustrate a conventional rhyme scheme but to show how various sound relationships are worked together into a harmonious pattern.

> Unwilling to bend my knees
> To such unmantled pride
> As left you in that place,
> Restless, unsatisfied.

The rhyme here is only a minor aspect. In fact, it is not a true rhyme since the accented vowel in "unsatisfied" is *a*, requiring a word ending with *atisfied*. This, then, is a slant or off rhyme. But notice how each of these lines is linked with another with some sort of echo in sound.

The first line is linked with the second through alliteration and a secondary echo in the three syllables of "unwilling . . . unmantled." It is also tied to the fourth through "unsatisfied." Thus "unwilling . . . unmantled . . . unsatisfied" form a kind of miniature motif in this stanza.

The second line is linked with the third through the alliterative "pride . . . place," and the third is linked with the fourth through the clear assonance in "l*e*ft . . . r*e*stl*e*ss." The only combination left is the second and fourth: Here we have the slant rhyme in "pride . . . satisfied" as well as the alliterative "unmantled . . . unsatisfied."

One is never sure of how far to go with such an analysis—one critic's "significant relationship" is another's sample of pedantry. But this much is clear: First, to say that a stanza "has a nice sound to it" is a sloppy and pointless critical contribution unless it is followed by a more exact analysis; and second, it is absurd to limit one's list of sound relationships to those which were inserted by the poet intentionally. Just as a writer of prose may not be consciously aware that he is balancing a sentence with an independent clause and a qualifying phrase on one side of a semicolon with the same sequence on the other, a poet is often not aware that he is linking line two and line four with a combination of assonance and consonance. Much of his work is conscious labor; much is quite unconscious—explained only with the vague feeling that it "sounds right."

This stanza of Mezey is in no sense an elaborate or ingenious display of sound relationships; but the reason it "sound right" and "hangs together" and, the favorite phrase of noncritics, "works" is the result of several specific relationships in sound. And the reason they are worth analyzing here is that so much student-written poetry "sounds wrong," "fails to hang together," and "doesn't work" for reasons which must be analyzed if the poem is to be salvaged and the poet improved by the effort.

Quite often, a poet will decrease the number of sound relationships when dealing with a clear rhyme scheme and increase them when turning to unrhymed work. Such is the case with Carolyn Kizer. In "The Ungrateful Garden" she chose a rigid metrical scheme (iambic tetrameter with many trochaic substitutions) and rhyme pattern (a,b,a,b). The first stanza of four is as follows:

> Midas watched the golden crust
> That formed over his streaming sores,
> Hugged his agues, loved his lust,
> But damned to hell the out-of-doors

Here "crust"–"lust" and "sores"–"doors" are both true rhymes as are all but one pair of rhymes in the entire twenty-four lines. But there is hardly a sample of assonance, consonance, alliteration, or internal rhyme in the poem.

In her poem "The Intruder," however, she employs free verse (no meter and no regular rhyme scheme). Either consciously or unconsciously (it does not matter) she has used many other sound devices. The first four lines, for example, contain five pairs of linked words, three more than in the sample of rhyming verse quoted above.

> My mother—preferring the strange to the tame:
> Dove-note, bone marrow, deer dung,
> Frog's belly distended with finny young,
> Leaf-mould wilderness, hare-bell, toadstool,

The first line contains so strong an assonance that it appears to be an internal rhyme: "strange"–"tame." The second line begins with assonance in "note"–"bone" and ends with alliteration in "deer dung." And note that there is a vague link across that line, connecting "dove" at the beginning with "dung" at the end through assonance. The third line continues the alliteration of *d*'s with "*d*isten*d*ed" and adds one more sample of assonance in *dis* and *fin*. And the fourth line echoes "mould" with "toad" by assonance.

In the second stanza of this three-stanza poem the poet closes with a flurry of alliteration which is not matched anywhere in the first poem:

> Swiftly, the cat, with a clean careful mouth
> Closed on the soiled webs, growling, took them out to the back stoop.

Out of context, this run of four hard *c*'s (supported by two final *k* sounds) and three *s*'s seems contrived. Alliteration stands out even more blatantly than rhyme endings. But heard in the context of the whole poem and strengthened by the vaguely onomatopoetic association between the action of the cat and these sounds, the passage is natural and convincing.

At the beginning of this chapter I pointed out how the sound patterns in Dylan Thomas' prose can be grouped in two categories: a primary list of conventional relationships such as assonance, alliteration, and the like, and a secondary list of subtle relationships consisting, mainly, of similar but not identical vowel-sound clusters. For the final sample of sound in the works of younger poets, it is appropriate to return to this device. Donald Justice's poem called "Another Song" serves as a good choice. This is the first of three highly lyrical stanzas with strong echoes from Shakespeare's *A Midsummer Night's Dream:*

> Merry the green, the green hill shall be merry.
> Hungry, the owlet shall seek out the mouse,
> And Jack his Joan, but they shall never marry.

Primary sound devices are clear enough here. There is consonance in the *rr* of "merry" (repeated), "hungry," and marry"; there is assonance in "owl" and "mouse" as well as in "shall" and "marry"; and there is alliteration in "Jack" and "Joan" and in "shall seek." Finally there is a simple but inverted use of repetition in the first line which is arranged in a 1,2–2,1 sequence.

But the secondary devices are equally important here. The first line is dominated with a cluster of *e, i,* and *a* sounds without a single "round" vowel of the *o* and *u* sound. Taking just the vowel endings from the significant words we have a sound sequence like this: "erry, een, een, ill, al, erry."

The next line shifts almost the way music can shift from a major to a minor key without losing either the melody or the rhythm. The dominant sound here is *u* and *ou* (*ow*). When we convert this line to dominant sounds the result is "ungry, owl, out, ouse."

Close analyses like this one are the best way to isolate and understand such a wide variety of techniques in sound. But the apprentice poet cannot stop there. In addition, he ought to read a great deal of verse aloud, simply for sound, repeating lines over and over. Finally, he should take the time to experiment with poetic doodling like that which I recommended earlier in con-

nection with rhythm. Let this be loose, chaotic, and careless—written for the pure pleasure of sound.

By working in all three of these ways the writer finally reaches the point where sound has become both a natural and an integrated aspect of his poetry.

16

THE IMAGE AND WHAT TO DO WITH IT

Images of *sight* as dominant type; *sound* images; methods of combining *secondary impressions;* images as *similes, metaphors,* and other forms of figurative language; images as *symbol;* methods of *self-training* in the development of imagery.

In its purest sense, an image in poetry is any significant piece of sense data. Although we tend to think of images as objects seen, the term also covers sounds heard, textures felt, odors smelled, and objects tasted.

As was pointed out in Chapter 13, sense perception is one of the major sources of poetic creation. For this reason alone, the image becomes one of the most significant elements in the construction of a poem. But images are also the foundation of similes, metaphors, puns, hyperbole, and other types of figurative language as well as symbolic suggestion.

Because the term *imagery* is used so frequently in conjunction with similes and metaphors, it is sometimes taken to be a synonym for *figurative language.* In this text, however, *image* is used to mean any unit of sense experience regardless of whether it is employed literally, figuratively, or symbolically.

Images, then, tend to be concrete nouns or phrases which are readily identifiable through the senses. Much depends on how specific they are. "Bird," for example, is an image and "crow" a sharper one; but a vague term like "thing" is not. "Babbling brook" is an auditory image and "the stream's small talk" a fresher one; but "sound" or even "city sounds" is not. "A tart red wine" is a taste image, but the abstraction "tart" is only an adjective. "The whiff of fish left three days on the beach" is a highly odoriferous image, but neither "odoriferous" nor even "stink" is.

Of the five senses, sight is by far the most popular for the poet. This is natural enough when one realizes how much human beings depend on their ability to see. Blindness is a more severe loss than deafness, and the loss of touch, smell, and taste are mild oddities not even honored with words in common usage. Too, the dark is traditionally ominous. On the brighter side, humans gifted with sight link the sense with an emotion, as in the cliché at the beginning of this sentence, and consider it a "gift" unalloyed with displeasure as touch is with pain. Finally, sight is more fully subdivided in western speech than any other sense. We may speak of intensity (brilliant, bright, dull, dark), color (red, blue, aqua), shape (organic or geometric, the latter with many subdivisions), and have a particular name for almost every object seen. This may not seem so remarkable until one contrasts it with the limited vocabulary with which we describe sounds. There are a few specific terms like "whistle," "bang," "crack," and "sigh," but soon we turn to similes such as "like a song," "like a screech owl." And smells, even lower on our scale, are almost wholly described by association. It is only from whimsy or frustration with the language that we refer to "a blue smell" or a "round smell"; even such distinct odors as oil or flowers do not have words separate from the object that produces it.

Returning from the psychology of perception to the use of images, we can see how natural it is for the poet to seize upon something seen as the core of a particular work. Often it is a specific place, such as that area along the banks of the river Wye which Wordsworth developed in "Tintern Abbey." The full title of that poem, "Lines Composed a Few Miles Above Tintern Abbey, on Revisiting the Banks of the Wye During a Tour," is rarely remembered even in oral examinations, but it is germane here. It suggests that the starting point for the poet was not such abstract conceptions as "tranquil restoration" or "holier love" or even "Nature"; it was that specific visual image of the river Wye. Significantly, his first use of the image is quite literal, a description for its own sake. He then turns to a negative simile:

> These beauteous forms,
> Though a long absence, have not been to me
> As in a landscape to a blind man's eye:

From there on the image of "these beauteous forms" is variously used, in whole or in part, as simile, as metaphor, as personification, and as symbol. But the central image of "this green pastoral landscape" is never abandoned.

Place as the primary image has grown more popular as the traditional conventions of subject matter became more widely rejected. But one can go back to William Cowper's dreary little poem, "The Poplar-Field," written in the late eighteenth century, the second stanza of which reads like a child's version of "Tintern Abbey."

> Twelve years have elapsed since I first took a view
> Of my favourite field and the bank where they grew,
> And now in the grass behold they are laid,
> And the tree is my seat that once lent me a shade.

Contemporary and perhaps more familiar examples include Dylan Thomas' highly lyrical "Fern Hill" and Yeats' "The Wild Swans at Coole."

It is interesting to note that Yeats, so far removed from Wordsworth, begins this poem with lines which are on first reading almost purely descriptive.

> The trees are in their autumn beauty,
> The woodland paths are dry,
> Under the October twilight the water
> Mirrors a still sky;
> Upon the brimming water among the stones
> Are nine-and-fifty swans.

This initial image, of course, is soon developed as metaphor and finally as symbol; but the significant point here is how the poet has used a specific place—either real or imagined—as the foundation for the entire poem.

More frequently, some single aspect of nature or some object in the material world is used as visual image. Frost, for example, though thoroughly identified with nature imagery, rarely uses a specific place as the base of his poems. His narrative poems like "Two Tramps at Mud Time" and "Home Burial" contain vivid visual detail, but the root of the poem is a narrative, a sequence of dramatic events such as is usually associated with fiction. When he works more directly with nature, as in "Birches" and "A Hillside Thaw," it is an aspect of nature, not a specific place, that becomes the base of the imagery. In the first of these, for example, he is not concerned with a particular birch grove. He begins with "When I see birches bend to left and right / Across the lines of straighter darker trees," and this image could be seen in any area where birches grow.

It is a mistake to assume that visual images must necessarily be from nature. A poet, after all, has a perfect right to detest the country. Sandburg's "Chicago" is a far cry from "Tintern Abbey," but his use of that city, "Hog Butcher for the World," is as clearly rooted in visual experience as Wordsworth's use of the "sylvan Wye." And Hart Crane's "To Brooklyn Bridge" makes complex use of its mechanical image.

To this point, I have selected poems which use visual details as the central or primary image. Needless to say, almost every poem utilizes minor visual images fairly frequently. It is worth noting that often it was one of these which served as the origin of the poem even though this may not be apparent in the final version. As a general rule, the creative process of poetry is far less bound to chronological order than either fiction or drama; that is, the poet may have begun with the last line or at some midpoint and moved erratically, guided more by association than by orderly sequence. In this respect, the poet is closer to the painter, whose attention is drawn to first one part and then another of his canvas, than he is to those guided either by narrative order, as in fiction and drama, or logical sequence, as in assertive writing of the essay.

Sound images are far less used than sight, but they are extraordinarily effective both in the development of a poem and in its inception. Frost's "Mowing" is a good example. Note how five of the following six lines make use of the single image of a scythe's sound.

> There was never a sound beside the wood but one,
> And that was my long scythe whispering to the ground.
> What was it it whispered? I know not well myself;
> Perhaps it was something about the heat of the sun,
> Something, perhaps, about the lack of sound—
> And that was why it whispered and did not speak.

In the next seven lines, not one reference is made to sound—either directly or metaphorically. But the poem returns again with this final line:

> "My long scythe whispered and left the hay to make."

There are two incidental points in this selection which are worth noting. First, the word "sound" is both abstract and vague and frequently represents poetic laziness—the poet settling for the general because it takes time and effort to find the exact word needed. Editors and teachers grow weary of "sounds of the night," "sounds of the street," and "sounds of the sea" which recur with deadening regularity. But although "sound" is used twice in the six quoted lines, it is vividly contrasted with a single and highly specific sound image of the scythe "whispering," a metaphor which is used three times. This portion of the poem, then, is rooted in a single sound, not in the generality suggested by the word in the abstract.

Second, it is significant that Frost returns to the image at the end of the poem. This is a common practice for it adds to the verbal (not necessarily logical) unity of the poem.

This same pattern is seen in Louis Simpson's "To the Western World." He begins this fifteen-line poem with:

> A siren sang, and Europe turned away
> From the high castle and the shepherd's crook.

The following nine lines are based almost exclusively on visual images, leading naturally from "castle" and "shepherd's crook" in line two. But the last four lines of the poem return once again to a sound image, new but linked by opposition to the first one:

> In this America, this wilderness
> Where the axe echoes with a lonely sound,
> The generations labor to possess
> And grave by grave we civilize the ground.

The three remaining senses, touch, smell, and taste, are "lower" in the hierarchy of human experience in that we are not able to make as subtle differentiations in these areas. But their use in poetry is often highly effective. Occasionally they appear as single, isolated images which serve to amplify relationships already established. No matter how hidden they may be in the final version of the poem, they may have been the poet's starting point.

Another approach is combining several types of images in a single passage. The result is "sensual" in that sense data are being used with great variety and, usually, intensity. The poem "Local Places" by Howard Moss provides a fine example. The following stanza is the first of five and the italics, mine, have been added to stress the use of sound, sight, and touch.

> The song you *sang* you will not *sing* again,
> Floating in the spring to all your local places,
> Lured by archaic sense to the wood
> To *watch* the frog jump from the mossy rock,
> To *listen* to the stream's small talk at dark,
> Or to *feel* the springy pine-floor where you walk—
> If your green secrecies were such as these,
> The mystery is now in other trees.

The italicized words are not, of course, the images themselves but verbs which introduce and emphasize such images as song, frog jumping, mossy rocks, the sound ("talk") of a stream, and the like. Three of the five senses are used in this single stanza; only taste and smell are missing. The second stanza introduces the desert cactus, which is allowed "To perfume aridness," adding one more dimension of sense experience.

Each stanza of this poem is unified with a dominant visual image: the trees for the first, the desert for the second, the ocean for the third, and the rocks for the fourth. In the final two lines of the poem Moss recalls each of these visual images and links them with the same sound image used in the first line quoted above:

> The tree, the sand, the water, and the stone,
> What songs they sing they always sing again.

There is, of course, a logical development in this poem; and there is a "theme" or "statement" and something which might be called a "message." But what concerns us here is the degree to which the poet as artist has conceived of his work as the expression of sensation. These images of sight, sound, touch, and smell are not mere turrets and gargoyles added to an otherwise solid piece of logic; they are the bricks and timbers with which the piece is constructed.

Turning now from the types of images to their use, we may distinguish three main areas: literal, figurative, and symbolic use.

As pointed out earlier in this chapter, Wordsworth's opening description of "These waters, rolling from their mountain-springs / With a soft inland murmur" in "Tintern Abbey" is primarily descriptive even though this same image is used figuratively and finally symbolically later in the poem. In Cowper's "The Poplar-Field," his "favourite field and the bank where they grew" is an image used literally throughout the poem. Cowper apologists may argue that the mortality of the poplar trees suggests symbolically the mortality of man, but in the last line of the poem he points out directly that these trees have given some pleasure by being "less durable even" than man himself, a comparison which reduces the poplar trees from symbol in the usual sense to objects used quite literally as they might be in an informal essay.

Figurative use of an image most commonly takes the form of a simile or a metaphor. These two figures of speech are both comparisons, the first linking the two elements explicitly with "like" or "as," and the second implying a comparison. The following lines from Frost's "Birches" is a simile:

> You may see their trunks arching in the woods
> Years afterwards, trailing their leaves on the ground
> *Like girls on hands and knees* that throw their hair
> Before them over their heads to dry in the sun.

The italics, mine, indicate the simile. Had he chosen to write, "Trunks arching in the woods / Are girls on hands and knees," the statement would be literally untrue but truly a metaphor.

A simile is not just any comparison. To say that Bill is like Jim is not a simile; but to say that Bill is like an ox clearly is. The difference between the two examples is best seen through I. A. Richard's distinction between the *tenor*, the principal subject (bowed birch trees in the above selection), and the *vehicle*, the secondary subject (girls sunning their hair). In most cases, the vehicle is different from the tenor in all but certain significant characteristics. Quite often this difference consists of an abstract tenor ("love" for example) and a concrete vehicle ("rose" or "yacht" or even "Buick"). The strength of a simile comes from its surprise, and the surprise comes from the fact that the two objects are in all other respects so different.

The difference between a simile and a metaphor is more than just a matter of syntax. It is a shift from an explicit to an implicit or implied comparison; it is a shift from a statement which is literally true to one which is literally untrue but *figuratively* effective. Although all metaphors may be translated into similes, the conversion is not always a simple one. Take these lines from Thomas' "Fern Hill":

> Now as I was young *and easy under the apple boughs*
> About the *lilting house* and happy as the grass was green

There are three metaphors here which I have italicized. The final phrase, "happy *as the grass was green*" is a simile. To convert the passage so that it contains all similes requires more than the addition of "like" or "as." It might come out in this awkward fashion:

> Now as I was young and living *as if* all things in
> life were easy and *as if* I spent all my time in the
> orchard looking up through the branches, the house and
> the entire area of my childhood were *like* a gay and
> rhythmical song and I was *as* happy *as* the grass is green.

It should be clear from this brutal translation that a metaphor is not necessarily a simile with "like" or "as" removed. The metaphor is often highly compressed, with the vehicle carrying overtones which require entire phrases or clauses to explain. This should also serve to explain why the simile is the dominant form of comparison in prose whereas the metaphor is far more frequently used in poetry.

This is a particularly important point for the writer who, having spent most of his literary effort writing prose, tries to shift to poetic composition. The tendency is to inflate his lines with needlessly explicit similes and the result is a lack of compression which is apt to sound prosaic. The solution is to remember that the intelligent reader of poetry moves slowly and is prepared to make extraordinary leaps in his perception of imagery. Further, he is willing to go over the poem several times. Those first two lines from "Fern Hill," for example, don't truly reach the reader until after the entire poem has been read—preferably aloud—two or three times.

Most other figures of speech are forms of the metaphor, and their technical names are more important for the critic in his work of analysis than for the writer in his task of composition. Hyperbole, for example, is commonly defined as extreme exaggeration, but in most cases it is a metaphorical exaggeration. Andrew Marvell's "To His Coy Mistress," for example, is filled with hyperbole.

> My vegetable love should grow
> Vaster than empires and more slow;
> A hundred years should go to praise
> Thine eyes. . . .

Transposing this back to a simile, we would begin, "My love would be *like* a vegetable which *like* an empire would grow. . . ."

Synecdoche is also a specialized form of metaphor. In this case a portion of something (the vehicle) represents the whole (the tenor). In common speech we still hear the phrase, "A town of four hundred souls"; in poetry it can reach the complexity of Dylan Thomas' "The lips of time leech to the fountain head" (from "The Force That Through the Green Fuse Drives the Flower"). Here the intent is "time clings," but time is first personified and then one part of that personification is taken to stand for the action of the whole, adding the overtones of the bloodsucking leech.

Even the pun can be seen as a form of metaphor when one is able to separate the tenor from the vehicle. In the selection from Thomas' "A Refusal to Mourn . . ." quoted earlier, we have a play on "grave":

> I shall not murder
> The mankind of her going with a grave truth. . . .

The tenor here is "solemn truth," and he has, in effect, added "*as if* spoken at the grave-side." He uses essentially the same device in "Do Not Go Gentle into that Good Night" with the line, "Grave men, near death, who see with blinding sight. . . ." Once again, one has only to convert the pun to a simile in order to see it as a part of metaphorical construction.

Although many metaphors are used fleetingly and then dropped, it is important to remember the added strength derived from compounding them either through extended metaphors or through image clusters. Such is the case in Robert Mezey's poem, "The Wandering Jew." The poem is relatively long—124 lines in thirty-one stanzas—and its theme covers the changes in attitude over a lifetime. Yet although the poem is apparently scattered, it is linked by four lines each of which uses a taste image with religious overtones. Thus, in the first stanza we read:

> When I was a child and thought as a child, I put
> The Sabbath wine and prayer-shawl to my lips.

And in the fourteenth stanza:

> I sucked for milk and honey at her tongue

And in the seventeenth stanza:

> For years I ate the radish of affliction
> Until my belly sickened at its tang

And in the twentieth stanza:

> Tasting my bondage in the lives of others,
> I found it bitter, but my constant food;

And at the end of the thirty-first stanza:

> *Live,* says the Law—I sit here doing my best,
> Relishing meat, listening to music.

Linking metaphors in this way is extraordinarily effective both in short, tightly constructed poems as well as in longer ones such as this.

Turning now to image as used in symbolic language, we shift to a different emphasis altogether. In brief, the symbol is any detail—an object, action, or state—which has a range of meaning beyond and usually larger than itself. Our language is filled with public symbols, like Madison Avenue (wealth), the flag (the country), the cross (the church), which are widely accepted. But the poet more generally constructs his own private symbols. The process is a form of teaching in which "instructions" are given either in the course of a single poem or in several. Anyone familiar with Dylan Thomas' poetry, for example, has learned that "green" is not just a color but a symbol for youth, vitality, growth, and the like. Thus, the phrase from "Fern Hill" quoted above, "happy as the grass was green" is coupled with other uses of the word in the same poem such as "I was green and carefree," "And fire green as grass," "the whinnying green stable," and "the children green and golden." Once the symbolic association is made, any reference to the word (the vehicle) brings to mind the intended meaning (the tenor).

This private symbol of Thomas' is in sharp contrast, of course, with the public symbol of wealth as seen in the term "greenbacks" and developed so vividly by Fitzgerald in *The Great Gatsby*, where green lawns and the green light are the very opposite of youth and innocence. It is often difficult for a poet to reject public symbols like youth–spring, winter–age, nature–mother, God–old man. But when he does, as in Francis Thompson's "The Hound of Heaven," the result is often startling and effective. More often, the poet takes a word not already strongly identified as a public symbol or already vaguely associated with the quality described, such as T. S. Eliot's use of "dry" as sterility.

Symbol is often confused with metaphor. The simplest way to distinguish between them is to recall the terms tenor and vehicle. In the metaphor, the base or root is the tenor. That is, the reader has, in most cases, been introduced to the tenor or subject at hand. In the statement "Bill is an ox among bulls," the subject is clearly Bill and the comparison follows. This is not just a matter of word order; the root of the statement would not change if we shifted the sentence to read, "An ox among bulls is Bill."

The symbol, on the other hand, uses the vehicle as the root. Continuing with our unfortunate Bill, we might have a poem about an ox, describing its various characteristics and its mode of life in such a way that we gather a further or symbolic intent—the true tenor of the poem.

Eliot's satiric poem, "The Hippopotamus," begins in just this way. The tenor of the poem is the church, but the fact that this is made explicit does not convert the image into a metaphor. Although the tenor of a symbol is often left unstated, it is occasionally identified directly, as in this case. And conversely, although the tenor of a metaphor is usually made explicit, occasionally we are left to identify it indirectly, as in the case of Thomas' "the lilting house." So it is confusing and sometimes misleading to identify a symbol as a metaphor with the tenor left unstated. The significant difference is whether the base of the passage rests on the tenor or the vehicle.

Frost's poem "Birches" serves as a clear example of what, in the abstract, seems like a rather pedantic distinction. The poem is about birch trees. The title states this, and the opening lines appear to be a purely descriptive and literal image:

> When I see birches bend to left and right
> Across the lines of straighter darker trees,
> I like to think some boy's been swinging them.

The base is so clearly birch trees that the poem has been a favorite of those who like poetry "simple and about real things that we all see."

But as his description continues—with deceptive simplicity—these bent trees take on the qualities of old men bowed by the weight of a long and hard life. Here the image has become a symbol for age. Later in the poem he describes how boys climb up young and straight trees "*Toward* heaven, till the tree could bear no more, / But dipped its top and set me down again." Here the trees become a release from earthly concerns, a way of escape which is not like death for it returns one to earth again. The image of the straight trees becomes a symbol either of nature or possibly of imagination which allows the individual to rise beyond day-to-day commitments.

The work, then, is primarily symbolic with both similes and metaphors used secondarily. The base is birch trees and associative significance is drawn from them. But suppose the poem had begun with a description of old men wearied by life, unable to rise beyond the dull demands of their lives, "like birches bent by winter storms." The base in this case is "men" and the development is by simile or metaphor. If the comparison were sustained, we would have an extended metaphor, not a symbol.

This is more than a critic's descriptive distinction. It represents a choice which the practicing poet must make either consciously or unconsciously with almost every poem. Further, an ailing poem may be revived by converting metaphorical treatment into symbolic or vice versa. If, for example, a poem is begun with a feeling of strong ambivalence toward the city, the poet may come across an image such as the subway which would capture elements of his pleasure and his disgust. Such a poem would probably develop as an extended metaphor. It would be well worth considering the possibility, however, of beginning with the image itself and adding to it symbolic significance. And conversely, if a poem has begun with something seen which only after several drafts begins to take on real significance, it might be worth beginning with the new-found tenor and employing the image as metaphor.

The use of the image in poetry is so basic that it is infinitely variable. The poet must exercise his imagination in two areas if he hopes to make full use of this potential: First, there is the matter of responding to the kind of stimuli most people shrug off as inconsequential. He should stop and examine what others have missed, whether it be veins on a leaf or the surge of a mob; he should hear what others miss—not just skylarks but the breath of an old man or sleet against the window; he should respond to the feel of a rusted iron railing, a cut, or a gull's feather; he should identify the variety of city smells and country odors and consider what it is that makes an unoccupied house different from one lived in; and he should taste not only food but pine gum and smog.

But all this is only half a poet's training in the use of the image. The other half is what other poets have done. This requires analysis —reading poetry critically and even competitively, not as verbal Musak. It is worth lingering over a complex metaphor to determine not only the similarity but the differences between the tenor and the vehicle; it requires converting metaphors into similes, similes into metaphors, and both into symbols; it demands a constant search for the overtones in every image.

17

DICTION

Poetic diction: restrictive or free? The *four dangers* to fresh diction: *Clichés* described as dying metaphors, *hackneyed language* as "soft" expression, *sweeping generalities* as alien to the poet's language, and *archaisms* as needless aids to meter; fresh diction seen as the *stimulant* in poetry.

The question often arises as to whether there is such a thing as poetic diction. That is, is there a difference between the kind of words which lend themselves to poetry and those which we tend to use in prose? The only valid answer to this question is that some poets do make such a distinction and others vehemently do not.

When, for example, one reads the works of Richard Wilbur, it is difficult to find words which are colloquial and almost impossible to find samples of what might be described as base or vulgar. Although these descriptive terms are all highly relative, one has the feeling that there is within this poet either consciously or unconsciously a censor who passes judgment on each word used. Writing in *Mid-Century American Poets* (John Ciardi, ed., 1950), Wilbur insists that he has "no special theory of diction." But he does suggest a personal preference when he writes: "The Auden school of the thirties, which gave poetic language a refreshing infusion of slang and technical terminology, has also been aped quite enough now." And this feeling is reflected in his work which is described by his admirers as "beautiful" and by others as "pretty."

John Ciardi, on the other hand, opens his poetry to a wider variety of words. Writing in the same anthology, he states his position without qualification: "There is no subject not fit for poetry and no word not fit for poetry." And to make his point perfectly clear he adds: ". . . the language of common speech is preferable to enlarged rhetorical constructions, and the 'pretty' should be approached willingly but with caution." We are not, then, surprised to hear him pay poetic tribute to the human race by comparing it to that extraordinary insect which avoids extinction by perfectly resembling a "bird turd," nor are we unprepared for the opening lines of his "Elegy Just in Case":

> Here lie Ciardi's pearly bones
> In their ripe organic mess.

or his brutal fourth stanza:

> Here lies the sgt.'s mortal wreck
> Lily spiked and termite kissed,
> Spiders pendant from his neck,
> Beetles shining on his wrist.

It is interesting to note that, although Ciardi recently described the Beat Poets as "unwashed eccentricity" and "not only juvenile but certainly related to juvenile delinquency," he has shared with them this militant demand for the poet's right to use whatever diction he can find.

The fact is that for the past forty years there has been no "academy" dictating standards of diction any more than there has been one enforcing or restricting the use of meter and rhyme. For better or for worse, the literary scene has been highly fragmented for almost a half-century, with the extremes finding a voice in publications which are as varied as *Wings* on the one hand and *Pocket Poets* (publishers of Ginsberg's "Howl") on the other. This is disturbing for those who would like to have a single literary standard—and there are those in both camps who editorialize for this under the banner of "freedom"; but for the serious poet who is primarily concerned with developing his own art, it provides the luxury of exploration and experimentation.

The first rule of diction, then, is that there is no general rule demanding a single level of usage. One can concentrate on what John Frederick Nims described as "the language of men as used by an expert in men's language"; or one may employ language which is, as Ginsberg put it in "Howl," "obscene odes on the windows of the skull." The choice is an individual one.

Beneath this individuality and disagreement, however, is a shared belief in Ezra Pound's dictum: "Keep it fresh." This is no truism; it is one of the essential differences between poetry on the amateur level and genuine literary composition. It is not a matter of taste; it is a concern which is rooted in the definition of poetry.

The ambition shared by most poets is to break through to the consciousness of the reader or listener. To achieve this, the diction —like other aspects of the poem—must startle the reader either by its ingenuity, its beauty, or merely its effectiveness. This goal is in sharp contrast to such subliterary forms as greeting-card verse, which is designed to lull the reader by murmuring the familiar in much the same way that Musak is selected to soothe the restaurant patron without disturbing his meal or even his thoughts.

With this in mind, the poet must be on guard against diction which allows the reader to skip words or phrases without a single reaction. Regardless of whether the verse is light or serious, each element must make contact on some level—and preferably on several.

There are many pitfalls between the novice poet and this ideal. These four are the most dangerous:

The cliché is equated with sin from the seventh grade on, yet it remains a constant problem long after one's schooling is over. Part of the difficulty lies in the fact that few people bother to analyze just what it is about the cliché which makes it a literary sin. They memorize the tabooed expressions as if they were profanities—and revert to them in much the same way.

The cliché, as George Orwell pointed out in "Politics and the English Language," is actually a dying metaphor. That is, an expression which was once fresh enough to create a clear picture in the reader's mind has now lost its vitality. Thus, "sharp as a tack" has become dull; "free as a bird" no longer takes flight; "clean as a whistle" sets the reader wondering—if at all—whether he is to picture one of those bright penny-whistles or the sound of a "wolf"; and, as Orwell points out, "to toe the line" has drifted so far from the original metaphor that it is now frequently seen in print as "to tow the line."

Yet when these metaphors finally die—that is, become built into the language as single words which no longer appeal to a visual comparison—they occasionally regain respectability as utilitarian words. Thus a "current" of electricity has moved from metaphor to an independent word in its own right. In the same way, "stereotype" has moved from a metaphor based on the printer's term for the metal duplicate to an abstract meaning. The fact that it no longer serves as metaphor is proved by the number of people who use the word without having the slightest idea of its original sense. The tenor has been detached from the original vehicle and becomes good usage, just as "limelight" is freely used by individuals who are unaware of the fact that the word was once a metaphor referring to stage lighting which played an oxyhydrogen flame against a cylinder of lime.

The most dramatic example of a dead metaphor is the word "cliché" itself. It was originally a French word for a stereotype printing plate and it was an effective metaphor for standardized phrasing. Yet for those not in the printing business the word now clearly denotes the tenor without the slightest echo of its original metaphorical use.

The reader's attention is caught by a fresh simile or metaphor, and it is also held by words which have become denotative in their own right. The cliché is a word or phrase which is midway between these two—so overused that it no longer serves as suggestive language and not yet condensed into an independent, denotative word.

The cliché weakens a line of poetry because the reader skips over it rapidly without response. He draws from it neither the visual impression of a metaphor nor the denotative impact of a well-selected word. Further, because such expressions are associated with writing which makes no demands, the reader is lulled rather than awakened. The cliché, then, is a literary sin not because it is "bad taste" but because it converts intense, compressed, highly suggestive writing into that which is loose and bland.

There are three different ways of dealing with the clichés which appear in one's first draft. First, one can work hard to find a fresh simile or metaphor which will force the reader to see (hear, taste, and so on) the vehicle and make the startling association with the tenor. Second, one can merely drop the comparison completely and deal with the subject directly. Finally, one can twist the cliché so that it is reborn in some slightly altered form. This final choice is more frequently associated with comic verse, but there is no reason why it cannot be used with serious intent.

For example, if a poet discovers he has allowed "blood red" to slide into his verse, he can avoid this most ancient of clichés with such alternatives as "balloon red" or "hot red" or "shouting red," depending on the overtones he wishes to establish. If none of these will do, he should consider going back to just "red." Should the tone of the poem be whimsical, however, he might twist the cliché into "bloodshot red."

A good way to improve one's skill in dealing with clichés is to apply these three techniques to "sea blue," "rosy dawn," "tried and true," "mother nature," and "strong as an ox."

Hackneyed language is a general term which includes not only the cliché but the far more dangerous area of phrases which have simply been overused. Whereas clichés usually consist only of conventionalized similes and are easily identified, hackneyed language also includes direct description which has been seen in print too long to provide impact. A seventh-grader can compile a list of clichés as readily as he can recall names of birds; but only one who has read literature extensively can identify that which is literarily hackneyed. This is one reason why vocabulary lists which are emphasized so heavily in secondary schools are no substitute for wide and varied reading.

Certain subjects seem to generate hackneyed language like maggots. Take, for example, sunsets. The "dying day" is a true cliché, but perfectly respectable words like "golden," resplendent," "magnificent," and even "richly scarlet" all become hackneyed when used to describe a sunset. It is not the word itself which should be avoided—one cannot make lists; it is the particular combination which is limp from overuse.

In the same way, smiles are too often "radiant," "infectious," or "glowing." Trees tend to have "arms" and frequently "reach heavenward." The seasons are particularly dangerous: "Spring is "young" or "youthful," suggesting virginity, vitality, or both; summer is "full blown"; and by autumn many poets slide into a "September Song" with only slight variations on the popular lyrics. Winter, of course, leads the poet to sterility and death, terms which too often describe the quality of the poem as well.

Our judgment of what is hackneyed depends somewhat on the age. That which was fresh and vivid in an earlier period may have become shopworn for us. Protesting "But Pope used it" does not make a metaphor acceptable for our own use. But standards of fresh language are far less tied to period than most students believe. It is difficult to find lines in, say, Shakespeare's sonnets which would even today be considered hackneyed. Conversely, many of the conventions which he attacked as stale and useless have continued in popular use and reappear like tenacious weeds in the verse of college freshmen.

In "Sonnet 130," for example, he protests that

> My mistress' eyes are nothing like the sun;
> Coral is far more red than her lips' red. . . .
> And in some perfumes is there more delight
> Than in the breath that from my mistress reeks.

The poem is directed not so much at his mistress as at those poets of his day who were content to root their work in conventions which were even then thoroughly stale. Yet more than three hundred years later poetry is produced not only for class but for publication in which eyes sparkle like the sun, lips are either ruby or coral red, and breath is either honeyed or perfumed.

Hackneyed expressions can, of course, be twisted into new life in the same way that clichés can. This is what Shakespeare did in the sonnet which begins with a most contemporary question: "Shall I compare thee to a summer's day?" His decision in that poem was, as I have pointed out earlier, to shift the conventionalized comparison into a series of contrasts, stressing not the traditional associations of the season but the reverse. Thus, his next line inverts what would have been hackneyed:

> Thou are more lovely and more temperate.
> Rough winds do shake the darling buds of May,
> And summer's lease hath all too short a date.

The same inversion of a conventionalized association appears in Eliot's opening to "The Waste Land."

> April is the cruellest month, breeding
> Lilacs out of the dead land, mixing
> Memory and desire. . . .
> Winter kept us warm, covering
> Earth in forgetful snow, feeding
> A little life with dried tubers.

In both cases the poet has relied on our familiarity with the convention, but in neither case was he content merely to reinforce that familiarity. The vitality comes from drawing unexpected patterns from potentially hackneyed conventions.

Broad generalities in the form of overused abstractions are a third threat to the ideal of fresh, meaningful poetry. Some of the most dangerous are love, death, nature, life, liberty, sin, courage, fear, pride, patriotism, God, motherhood, and peace.

All of these, of course, have served and will continue to serve poets thematically; the problem arises only when the abstraction is treated as a single, indigestible lump. Love, for example, is a concern in Shakespeare's "Shall I compare thee to a summer's day?" but the poem is focused on a single and specific girl. Further, the poem also deals with the relationship between the mortality of the individual and the immortality of art. It is equally concerned with the transitory qualities of nature. It also suggests art exists only if men are present to see it. And, as pointed out above, it is a satiric jab at some of the literary conventions which he found trite. All this in fourteen lines. But which is "*the* message"? Which is "*the* statement"? Clearly the abstract quality of love is only one thread which is woven into not only other abstract concerns but a number of very specific things like "buds," "eyes," and, most important, "thee."

But when the subject of love is handled in a less sophisticated way we only learn that it is, for example, "a many-splendored thing" or "almost never never the same." Our first question tends to be "whose love?" And because there is no answer, our second question is apt to be "so what?" The difference is that love here treated in the abstract is only nebulous speculation. We have to add music to disguise the limitation of the lyrics.

In the same way, when death is the sole concern of a poem we wonder why the poet did not turn to assertive writing in the form of the essay. Before it becomes poetically manageable someone must either personify it as Donne did or relate it to a child in London as Thomas did or in some other way pull it down from the high level of abstraction.

Abstractions like patriotism, liberty, and peace have the same dangers plus an odd ability to attract clichés. The mind is so rutted with the language of unimaginative orators that what may have started out on an original course is apt to slip into one of these deep grooves and end, both figuratively and literally, in a political convention.

One solution is to shift the theme and attack rather than support all these concerns. I am convinced that at least some of the violently anti-everything poetry which we all wrote as college sophomores was not so much a political or even an emotional rebellion as it was a desperate search for fresh language. But this is no final solution; the anti-convention soon becomes conventional.

The more mature approach is breaking up the abstraction into manageable parts, reducing it from "concept" to images, and constructing figurative language which will give it life.

Broadly speaking, the generality is that which the reader, critic, and the writer of texts uses to *describe* patterns in poetry. The poet, usually, has not started with the high-level abstraction but a particular river near Tintern Abbey, a news item about a girl killed by fire in a London air raid, a bit of conversation in a Boston cocktail party, or a walk through a birch grove. From these he makes certain implications which, as we analyze them, are categorized as "nature," "death," "sterility," or "life."

The poet who begins with "Life is . . ." or "Love is . . ." should stop right there and ask himself just what a poet is and what a critic is, for he may well have confused the working procedures of each.

Archaic diction is the last in this list of four threats to fresh language. Quite often it takes the form of time-honored but dated contractions such as "o'er," and "oft" as substitutions for "over" and "often." But there are other words which now have the same musty quality: "lo!" "hark!" "ere," and even "O!" are the most frequently used.

The majority of poets writing today need no such warning, and some may be surprised that it must be included here. Yet the practice is seen repeatedly in college writing classes and is well represented in some of the less distinguished poetry journals.

There are two explanations for the persistent use of diction which the poet would never consider in speech or even in his prose. First, for one not used to the feel of meter there is a strong temptation to use any device which will allow the line to come out "correctly." Thus, if his first inclination is to work with a simple image like "The gull wakes the day before the sun," he may be bothered by the metrical confusion. Assuming that he is working with iambs, he has just produced a line which after the initial iambic foot is followed by four trochees.

It is at this point that some start reaching into the grave of archaic diction to force his meter back into line. If he is not careful, he may end up with something like, "Ere sun arises, lo the noble gull. . . ." He may be pleased that he has produced a line of perfect iambic pentameter, but his pleasure will be snuffed out as soon as he reads his work to a contemporary audience.

Were he a little more ingenious, he might have noticed that merely shifting "wakes" to "awakes" would also shift the entire line into iambic meter: "The gull awakes the day before the sun."

The second temptation which leads some poets to archaisms is far more serious because it appears to be based on logic. The syllogism runs like this: "Wordsworth used this sort of diction; Wordsworth was great; archaic diction is great." If one substitutes Keats and Shelley for Wordsworth, one has a valid explanation for the fact that many American poets manage to work skylarks and nightingales into their poems even when they have neither seen nor heard either creature.

These would-be poets have forgotten the essential fact that words have overtones. There is nothing "wrong" with any word per se. But if one uses words which are heavily associated with the nineteenth or eighteenth century, one must be prepared to have the reader's associations move back as well. Spenser used this technique effectively in "The Faerie Queene," and his readers are, if they are sensitive to language, moved back to an earlier period. But it is a difficult technique. In most cases, archaisms defeat the intent of the poem by establishing associations which are completely extraneous.

These, then, are the four practices which most frequently defeat the goal of fresh diction: clichés, hackneyed language, sweeping generalities, and archaisms. They are not absolute taboos. Each may, in certain cases, be used to create a particular effect. To succeed, the poet must be both conscious of the dangers he is running and skillful enough to avoid them.

Fresh diction, however, is not achieved merely by remembering the danger areas. The poet must be determined to prod the reader's consciousness. His goal is stimulation, be it intellectual, spiritual, or merely pleasurable.

In addition, he must probe the reader's unconscious rather than skim over it. To achieve this penetration, the poet must select each word on the basis of its denotative meaning, its connotations, its sound, its contribution to rhythm, and its capacity to establish an internal tension. This process is as necessary for the ballad as it is for the lyric, as essential to metered verse as for free.

If poetry is to be something more than a narcotic for the literate, then diction must be the initial stimulant.

18

POETIC TENSION

Verbal tension seen in *irony, satire, paradox,* and *puns; thematic tension* seen in *stated alternatives, implied alternatives,* and in intentional *ambiguity; tonal tension* described as an aid to the other types; *imagistic tension* analyzed in differing image clusters; *tension* summarized as essential in sophisticated verse.

A dull poem is a failure by any standard. Yet a good deal of technically competent work is unquestionably dull. What is one to do with a poem which was well conceived and developed with a good sense of rhythm, sound, images, and fresh diction, and yet for all this bores not only the readers but the poet himself? It is easy enough to blame such failures on the subject matter and to send the poet back to his typewriter. But in most cases the boredom was not due to a weak theme but to a lack of internal tension.

There are, generally speaking, four types of tension in poetry. *Verbal tension* is rooted in diction and includes such devices as irony, satire, paradox, and puns. *Thematic tension* plays one aspect of the theme against another, such as when the poem offers alternatives or intentional ambiguity. Closely related to this is *tonal tension,* in which the mood, tone, or level of usage changes within the poem. Finally, there is *imagistic tension*, in which one set of images (an image cluster) is played against another.

These four types are not, of course, utterly separate. In many cases the same element may be described as two different forms of tension. A contrast between two image clusters, for example, might also be described as tonal or even thematic tension. These terms, then, are not absolute categories like traditional verbs, nouns, and adjectives; they are differing *roles* played by poetic elements just as the role of the individual as father to his son differs from his role as son to his father.

Verbal tension is most frequently created in the form of irony. As I pointed out in Chapter 8, irony is essentially a reversal which in fiction can take the form of a statement that is the opposite of the intended meaning (verbal or conscious irony), a statement that is dramatically opposed to what the actual outcome will be (dramatic irony), or an event that is the reverse of normal expectations (cosmic irony). All three forms are also found in poetry, but what in fiction is generally presented through a character's statement or action is in poetry more frequently developed through the poet's own reflections.

Often poetic irony can be achieved with a single word or brief phrase. Anne Sexton, for example, when writing of her mother's death in "The Division of Parts" plays outward appearance against reality with these lines:

> . . . . I trip
> on your death and Jesus, *my stranger*
> floats up over
> my Christian home. . . .

The italics here are hers, thrusting the irony at the reader blatantly. Actually there are two samples of verbal irony in these lines. First, the phrase "Jesus, my stranger" is a jarringly effective reversal of the conventional "Jesus, my savior." She relies on the reader's familiarity with the conventional phrase just as Eliot relies on the reader's knowledge of the Lord's Prayer in "The Hollow Men" with the lines:

> For Thine is
> Life is
> For Thine is the
>   This is the way the world ends

The second irony involves a tension between the same phrase and one actually stated: "my stranger" and "my Christian home." Here the first phrase represents an inner truth and the latter, while no less "true," represents outer appearance.

These two examples from Sexton's poem and the one from Eliot's all establish tension through paired phrases which are, on the one hand, intimately related and, on the other hand, vividly opposed. In this connection it is worth noting that every example of irony involves a pair of items which are both linked and opposed even if one of these two items is implied rather than stated.

These examples are direct and clear, but often irony in poetry is so subtle that it is easy to miss. Take, for example, these lines from Denise Levertov's "A Solitude" in which she is describing a blind man in a subway:

> . . . . He doesn't care
> that he looks strange, showing
> his thoughts on his face like designs of light
>
> flickering on water, for he doesn't know
> what *look* is.
> I see that he has never seen.

There is a clear ironic contrast in the last line in which she *sees* his lack of sight. More subtle, however, is the example earlier which works as a kind of faint pre-echo: The face of a man whose world is total blackness is described as "designs of light."

Poets do not usually add irony to a poem the way a cook adds seasoning to a bland recipe—though the results may be similar. Instead, ironies suggest themselves to the poet either in the original conception or in the revisions.

Yet the poet cannot be entirely passive. He must be willing to probe his own ambivalences honestly, looking for elements of hate in love, hidden longings in hatred, or subtle desires buried in fears. He should consider potential reversals in each image he uses. Just as April is in some ways cruel and old age is in some ways beautiful, so also a love for the good life can be deadly, a war might be soothing, a serene dawn could be a deadly threat, and the roar of a jet a lullaby.

Irony is, as I stated earlier, the primary form of verbal tension in poetry. But satire is a close second. Basically, satire is a method of ridicule by means of either exaggeration or biased selection of detail.) The butt of the satire may be a person, a place, an institution, a historic period, or an attitude; quite frequently it is a combination of these.

Satire and irony are closely associated because, whereas irony frequently exists alone (all the examples given above are nonsatiric), ridicule is particularly effective when presented "with a straight face." That is, the cutting edge of satire is sharpest when the poet gives the illusion of presenting an unbiased view. It is the tension between the poet's apparent honesty and his actual intent which makes satire almost invariably ironic. In fact, when satire is presented without irony the result often appears rather crude. Such is the case with Kingsley Amis' "A Tribute to the Founder." In this first of four stanzas, the intent to ridicule is clear, but because the material is presented directly rather than ironically the attack lacks subtlety:

> By bluster, graft, and doing people down
> Sam Baines got rich, but mellowing at last,
> Felt that by giving something to the town
> He might undo the evils of his past.

There is, of course, irony in the title since "tribute" is not intended literally. But the first line destroys all chance of sustaining subtlety. As soon as we see the words "bluster, graft, and doing people down" we know exactly where the poet stands, which is no sin in itself unless one asks more of poetry than one does of a good newspaper editorial.

William Jay Smith describes essentially the same sort of individual in his poem "American Primitive," and he also is satiric. But notice how different the effect is when irony is sustained.

> Look at him there in his stovepipe hat,
> His high-top shoes, and his handsome collar;
> Only my Daddy could look like that,
> And I love my Daddy like he loves his Dollar.

The lines flow like the ripple which runs silently down the length of a bull whip; and with his final word comes the "snap" which is sharp enough to make the most sophisticated reader jump. This is still fairly light verse, but the satire, sharpened with irony, draws blood. The tension here lies in the contrast between the *apparent* tone of sentimental tribute and the *actual* tone of cutting protest.

Moving further—much further—in the direction of subtlety and complexity, we have a third example of satire in Eliot's "The Love Song of J. Alfred Prufrock." The poem is an entire course in satire and deserves much more careful scrutiny than I can give it here. One brief selection from 131 lines will have to serve as appetizer.

Like the other two poems, this one aims its attack at an individual who represents a general type. Unlike the other two, the attack comes not from the poet directly but from the character himself. As in the case of Browning's "My Last Duchess," the narrator damns himself. But unlike Browning's characters, Prufrock recognizes at least some of his weaknesses. He veers constantly from self-deprecation to self-defense, employing both in a pattern of self-deceit which almost deceives us, the readers, until we notice that in even a brief description of the man the word "self" is constantly repeated.

Take, for example, these lines in which Prufrock reflects on his own worth:

> Should I, after tea and cakes and ices,
> Have the strength to force the moment to its crisis?
> But though I have wept and fasted, wept and prayed,
> Though I have seen my head (grown slightly bald) brought in
> upon a platter,
> I am no prophet—and here's no great matter;
> I have seen the moment of my greatness flicker,
> And I have seen the eternal Footman hold my coat, and snicker,
> And in short, I was afraid.

The tension here is established in the strain between his apparent modesty and his extraordinary egotism; a more subtle form of tension is seen in the satiric irony of a man who reveals his egotism through the very phrases which he intended to be self-deprecating.

Specifically, we are tempted to see him as he sees himself: a man who recognizes the superficiality of his own society ("tea and cakes and ices"), a man who has tried to rise above it ("wept and fasted"), a man who is aware of his failure ("I have seen . . . my greatness flicker") and is, finally, uneasy about death ("I was afraid").

In the context of the entire poem, however, these lines expose an outrageous egotist. He is quick to blame the superficiality of his society ("tea and cakes and ices") when clearly he has himself selected that society by his own choice. The question he asks ("Should I . . . Have the strength . . . ?") implies a choice when in fact he clearly does not have the strength. His description of his efforts to achieve greatness ("wept and fasted, wept and prayed") are such an absurd hyperbole that we cannot believe him. His confession ("I am no prophet") disguises the fact that he is not even a whole man as does the line above ("I have seen my head . . .") in which he actually compares himself with John the Baptist. And the last phrase ("I was afraid") is the technique of a man who hides terror by confessing to uneasiness.

Notice that this satire is not based simply on one or two exaggerated characteristics. It is developed from the maze of a man's ironic observations about himself.

One can learn a good deal about poetic satire from these three examples. First, the function of irony is to disguise at least partially the poet's satiric intent. It is difficult (though not impossible) to hone a sharp edge without it. Second, the satirist should consider the value of surprise. The "snap" may come at the end of a phrase, a line, or a stanza; but no matter where it is placed, it should jolt the reader. Finally, the primary way to convert simple satire to that which is sophisticated is to broaden the base so that satiric elements are distributed over a wide area and touch on many aspects of the subject.

Closely related to irony and satire is paradox, the third form of verbal tension. Briefly, a paradox is a statement which literally appears to be a contradiction but which on a second level makes a specific point by implication. Some paradoxes have been embalmed in the form of clichés. "The trouble with women," comedians tell us with monotonous regularity, "is that you can't get along with them and you can't get along without them."

But the paradox need not be comic. John Donne, for example,

in his sonnet "Death Be Not Proud" ends with these well known lines:

> One short sleep past, we wake eternally,
> And death shall be no more; Death, thou shalt die.

The core of the paradox, of course, lies in the last clause. It is illogical to state that death can die, yet there is a poetic validity to the statement which rises beyond absurdity. It is worth noting that in this case the paradox is not simply a trick of logic added for entertainment; it provides the thematic core for the entire poem.

Even more dramatic is the paradox in his Sonnet 14, "Batter My Heart." At the end of this poem God is pictured as a violent suitor and the poet himself as the woman. Speaking directly to God, Donne ends the poem with these three extraordinary lines:

> Take me to you, imprison me, for I
> Except you enthrall me, never shall be free,
> Nor ever chaste, except you ravish me.

There are actually two paradoxes here, both charged with high voltage. The first suggests that he cannot be "free" unless he is "enthralled," a word which was then synonymous with "enslaved." Stronger yet is the final suggestion that he cannot be "chaste" unless he is "ravished."

Paradox is really a form of irony in that a tension is established between the apparent or literal meaning on the one hand and the intended meaning on the other. But what irony in its conventional sense does to tone and expectations, paradox does to logic. Effective paradox is a clash of logic from which some richer, fuller insight rises.

A fourth form of verbal tension is the pun. Once again we have a strain established between two forces, which are in this case two or more uses of the same word. As cited earlier in this text, Dylan Thomas used the same pun in two major poems: "I shall not murder / The mankind of her going with a grave truth" in "A Refusal to Mourn . . ." and "Grave men, near death, who see with blinding sight" in "Do Not Go Gentle into that Good Night." This particular pun was also used by Shakespeare in *Romeo and*

Juliet when Mercutio, a wit even while dying, says "Ask for me tomorrow and you shall find me a grave man."

Quite frequently the pun is not made up of perfect equivalents but approximations in sound, like this opening of Anne Sexton's "The Farmer's Wife":

> From the hodge porridge
> of their country lust

The pun here, which links their married life with a hodgepodge and a bland bowl of porridge, is particularly interesting because of the fact that "hodgepodge" comes from the Walloon "hosepot," which literally meant "house-pot" or the daily stew eaten by simple farming people such as those described in the quoted poem. Whether Miss Sexton was aware of this is of no importance; the point is that the much maligned pun can be made to reverberate with echoes of etymology and suggestive overtones.

Thematic tension extends this concept to conflicting or opposed elements to the theme of the poem. The clearest examples of this pattern are seen in those poems which offer alternatives directly. In Frost's popular "Fire and Ice," for instance, the alternatives are stated in the title and developed with apparent simplicity in the first four lines:

> Some say the world will end in fire,
> Some say in ice.
> From what I've tasted of desire
> I hold with those who favor fire.

The poem has more to it than seen by those who like to remember Frost as the friendly, simple, rural philosopher. A careful reading reveals that the poet *has* been destroyed by love (having "favored" fire) and, in the last five lines, *will* be destroyed by hate, elevating a casual bit of rural philosophy into an intense personal experience. But what concerns us here is the tension which is established between the destructive quality of love on the one hand and hate on the other. By eliminating the alternatives, one reduces the poem to flat statement either linking love with fire or hate with ice, both of which have been done in any number of unimaginative song lyrics.

This same technique appears frequently in Frost's poetry and is worth study because of the fact that what would otherwise be bland observation is given strength through such tension in thematic alternatives. "The Road Not Taken," for example, begins and ends with a choice, and the poem is equally concerned with each of these two paths. "Stopping by Woods . . ." would be nothing but a Grandma Moses print complete with quaint little pony were it not for the fact that the poet is caught between a longing for death (seen in such images as "frozen lake," "darkest evening of the year," and "woods . . . lovely, dark and deep") and the much less emphasized commitment to life (seen in "have promises to keep" and the somewhat fatalistic "And miles to go before I sleep.").

This type of tension can be found in a majority of poems for it is almost as fundamental to the genre as conflict is to fiction. But often it is less directly stated than it is in the samples given above. Take, for example, Denise Levertov's "To the Snake." In the first stanza she describes what it is like to hang a green snake around one's neck, feeling its scales and hearing its hiss. It is vivid but purely descriptive without a hint of thematic tension or even a suggestion of theme. Then the poem shifts as she opens the second stanza with these lines:

> Green Snake—I swore to my companions that certainly you were
> harmless! But truly
> I had no certainty, and no hope, only desiring to hold you, for
> that joy, . . .

Because this is the point at which one is first aware of how the snake is to be used symbolically, one is apt to miss the fact that this is also the introduction of tension into the poem: fascination for the snake and all it represents played against a kind of fear ("I had no certainty"). This ambivalence is made more complex by the fact that the fear itself becomes a desire: She had "no hope" that the snake was harmless.

Protest is also a form of tension. Usually one of the two "sides" is left unstated. Both Dylan Thomas' "Refusal to Mourn . . ." and Donne's "Death Be Not Proud," for example, are at least in part attacks on conventional attitudes. They are "debates" with only one argument stated.

When thematic tension takes the form of protest, it is usually combined with verbal tension. But certain poets concentrate almost wholly on theme, avoiding irony, paradox, and other such devices considered by them too clever for honest writers. This is the essential quality of the Beat movement. Those who defend such poets as Ginsberg and Corso almost invariably use terms like "vitality," "strength," and "fire," referring to the intensity of the protest. The real issue in the arguments for and against Beat poetry is not a matter of diction, taste, or even subject matter: It is a matter of whether thematic tension pressed to extreme can serve as a sole substitute for other types of tension.

These two types of thematic tension—alternatives and protest—are often left wholly undeveloped by novice poets. This is particularly common in poems which began with a simple observation, such as the look of bare branches against a winter sky, sticks floating in a rain-swollen brook, or the city sound of cars driving over wet pavement.

In some cases, of course, nothing more can be squeezed from those lines. The poem must remain blandly descriptive. But the poet should examine two areas before he gives up. The first is his own feelings about the scene. Why did he remember it? What impact did it have on him? Does it echo an earlier experience? These questions may lead directly or indirectly to thematic tensions. The other place to look is in the poem itself. Often the phrasing in a particular line or even a single word will suggest a thematic contrast which might instill new life into the poem.

The third and final type of thematic tension is by far the most complex—ambiguity. This aspect of poetry has been analyzed in detail by William Empson in his *Seven Types of Ambiguity* (now available in paper by Meridian Books), but what I am concerned with here is the distinction between ambiguity which is mere confusion and that which creates thematic tension.

Essentially, that which is ambiguous is that which suggests two or more different meanings. When these two meanings are unresolved and leave the conscientious reader baffled, ambiguity is usually considered a liability; but when they either join to suggest a blended meaning or provide two related and harmonious suggestions, they can become a poetic asset.

The clearest example of a resolved ambiguity is the pun. When Thomas writes "Grave men, near death" only a grave scholar would ask whether we should read this first word in the sense of "somber men" or "men nearing the grave." It is both, of course, and the two suggestions are harmonious. When the ambiguity is limited, as this is, to a turn of a phrase, it creates verbal tension; when it is enlarged to cover a broad or inclusive aspect of the poem as a whole, it is thematic tension.

The close relationship between verbal and thematic tension is seen in E. E. Cummings' "The Hours Rise Up." The second stanza, describing dawn in the city, is as follows:

> on earth a candle is
> extinguished   the city
> wakes
> with a song upon her
> mouth having death in her eyes

The ambiguity here leads us in two directions: First, we picture dawn in its conventional sense as a time for waking; we read "song upon / her mouth" as new hope and enthusiasm. Second, we note that a candle has been extinguished and that "death" is in the eyes of the city. The contradiction appears to be a hopeless confusion.

But the next stanza blends our two readings into one statement without losing the thematic tension:

> and it is dawn
> the world
> goes forth to murder dreams. . . .

Night here is far from the conventional association of dark fear, and day is far from its traditional bondage with hope and rebirth; Cummings links dawn with the realities of a harsh life, and what appeared to be baffling ambiguity is resolved. It is only on the basis of this ambiguity that he is able, later in the poem, to describe the faces of people as "contented hideous hopeless cruel happy." His lack of punctuation heightens the suggestion that these are not different faces in the crowd but the highly contradictory nature of man in a singular sense.

This same association between verbal tension and thematic tension is seen in Eliot's "Prufrock," though here the poet does not make the resolution of the ambiguity explicit. The heart of this tension lies in his ambiguous and frequently repeated question, "And how should I presume?" On the one hand we may read this as "Do I dare to take action?" and this is supported elsewhere in the poem with his own use of the word "dare." Yet it is also possible to read "presume" as "be so presumptuous as to . . . ," for "presume" also suggests taking liberties without proper justification. This much constitutes a verbal tension, a play on significantly different overtones of a single word. Yet this distinction is the root of the ambiguity in Prufrock as a man and in the type he represents. Part of him is coward, and part is merely aware that he has no choice. This ambiguity is never fully resolved—except in the realization that both views exist simultaneously in that part of us all which we share with Prufrock.

Tonal tension and the fourth category, imagistic tension, require little explanation here because they are almost invariably present in the caegories described above. One should not, for example, examine thematic tension in "Prufrock" without noting the more subtle but equally important tonal distinctions. On the one hand, there is the urbane and self-controlled Prufrock who can calmly satirize his circle with such quotable lines as:

> In the room the women come and go
> Talking of Michelangelo

and

> . . . would it have been worth it, after all,
> After the cups, the marmalade, the tea,

and can even satirize himself with "Do I dare to eat a peach?"

On the other hand, there is a distinct tonal shift when he breaks through with "And in short, I was afraid" and those last despairing lines:

> We have lingered in the chambers of the sea
> By sea-girls wreathed with seaweed red and brown
> Till human voices wake us, and we drown.

Much the same sort of tonal shift is present in Eliot's "Journey of the Magi" in which one of the three wise men describes his trip to see the Christ child. Of the trip itself, he is direct and vivid:

> Then the camel men cursing and grumbling
> And running away, and wanting their liquor and women,
> And the night-fires going out, and the lack of shelters . . .
> And the villages dirty and charging high prices: . . .

These are the details any businessman might remember of his trip abroad. Note how this shifts, however, when he speculates on how the birth of the Christ child was also a death of old ways for him and his people:

> . . . . this Birth was
> Hard and bitter agony for us, like Death, our death.
> We returned to our places, these Kingdoms,
> But no longer at ease here, in the old dispensation,
> With an alien people clutching their gods.
> I should be glad of another death.

paradox

The shift in tone is rooted in diction. The first quoted passage contains eight concrete nouns and no abstract concepts; the second contains eight abstract nouns, like "death," "ease" and "dispensation" and only two concrete nouns, "Kingdom" and "people."

But it is more than a simple matter of diction: The tone has shifted, establishing strong tension between petty complaint and somber reflection; and, further, the theme has changed as well. Incidentally, the second selection contains a complex example of verbal tension in the paradox of a birth which is equated with a death.

Imagistic Tension returns once again to the small unit such as was described under the heading of verbal tension. But what we are concerned with here is, not matters of irony, satire, paradox, and the like, but a simple contrast between image clusters.

Illustrations may be found in almost all the samples cited earlier, but the principle can perhaps be most vividly shown in the contrast between Donne's "The Flea" and "Batter My Heart."

"The Flea," a poem of seduction, has two image clusters, the first of which might be termed holy and the second secular. If we list the key words, excluding repetitions, we compile this list:

Holy images	*Secular images*
sin	flea
shame	blood
married	maidenhead
marriage temple	marriage bed
cloistered	
sacrilege	
innocence	
guilty	
honor	

Were we to look first at the lists of key words which establish images used in this poem, we might assume that the subject was a spiritual matter. But it most assuredly is not. Now, by way of contrast, let us do the same for "Batter My Heart," a holy sonnet in which a devout poet, a member of the clergy, appeals for acceptance by God.

Holy images	*Secular images*
three-personed God	an usurped town
chaste	viceroy
	betrothed
	enemy
	enthrall me
	ravish me
	reason

Not all of these words are true images, of course. But they establish image clusters which are significantly opposed. Donne has used sensual details predominantly when working with a religious subject and religious details when composing a sensual poem. Further, each poem, considered separately, establishes a tension through the vivid contrast between two sharply opposed image clusters.

These four types of tension—verbal, thematic, tonal, and imagistic—are found in a great variety of poetry. But it is a mistake to assume from this that tension is necessarily a part of poetic expression or that all poets are concerned with it. Earlier in this section I suggested that what sets a poem like Kilmer's "Trees" apart from poems commonly called "good" or "great" is primarily its lack of sophistication: Neither its method nor its conception has the complexity we associate with artistic (as opposed to crafty) productivity. It is now possible to sharpen this distinction by pointing out that this poem is utterly devoid of tension. In fact, one characteristic which links Kilmer's work with so much so-called newspaper verse is this very lack of tension. Works of this genus lie on the page limp as the protozoan which the biologist so calmly and without derision classifies as the least sophisticated form of life.

Tension, then, is not essential in verse; but its presence or absence is as radical a distinction as that between one-celled and multicelled organisms.

19

FREE VERSE

Free verse as an outgrowth of traditional verse; *rhythm* described as liberated meter; *sound* devices related to formal rhyme; *typography* defined as "fluid stanzas"; *"new" subject matter* seen as a recapturing of traditional freedoms lost during the nineteenth century; *traditional techniques* remain: dependence on the line, metaphor, linguistic compression, symbol, and the suggestive image.

There is no sharp division between so-called traditional verse and free verse. As one moves away from a strict adherence to metrical patterns and rhymed endings, one slides into what we call free verse. And for this reason, all the preceding chapters on poetic technique have touched on free verse at some point.

Free verse deserves a special chapter here, however, because so many students view it negatively, as merely a departure from tradition. It is essential to understand that sophisticated free verse is not linguistic anarchy. It is in no sense free of technique. It merely makes use of new conventions which in every case have their roots in some aspect of traditional poetry.

Failure to understand this often results in a "poem" which is actually prose chopped up into short lines. There is no advantage whatever in writing prose this way: One loses the tools of both genres and gains nothing.

It is, of course, possible to compose free verse without a thorough knowledge of meter, rhyme, stanza forms, and the like—just as it is possible to use a word without knowing its derivation. But the easiest, most natural, and most effective way to master this relatively new form is to see it as a development of the old.

Rhythm Traditionally, rhythm in English verse has been expressed by the arrangement of stressed and unstressed syllables and by unifying the number of syllables, as described in Chapter 14. These metrical systems—iambic pentameter, tetrameter, and so forth—have become as much a part of our consciousness as harmonious chords in music.

Free verse abandons meter, but it clearly does not abandon rhythm. The formal intricacies of metrical patterns are replaced with a looser but equally intricate collection of rhythmical devices. There are at least six common methods of doing this.

Variation in line length is the most common technique. In metered verse, line length refers to the number of syllables. A perfect line of iambic pentameter, for example, must have ten syllables; anapestic trimeter must have nine, and so forth. But free verse makes almost no use of the syllable, and line length becomes a largely visual element. The short line, like the short sentence in prose, has more impact and is usually read faster than the long line. A free verse poem written entirely in short lines tends to have some of the lightness and the sparkle of a formal poem in trimeter; conversely, the long-lined poem tends to become either flowing or solid and is apt to be read more slowly, as one reads hexameter verse.

In addition, the short line can be alternated with longer ones to highlight key images or used periodically to suggest a refrain or grouped in clusters to keep a poem from becoming ponderous.

It is, of course, almost impossible to discuss rhythm without considering content. Meter can be treated as a separate science (like harmonics), but rhythmical patterns in free verse come in the writing. Take, for example, the last three lines of Cummings' "Buffalo Bill's":

"and what i want to know is
how do you like your blueeyed boy
Mister Death"

The impact of the last line is partly a matter of diction, and partly rhythmical. The poem would not fail if "Mister Death" were added to the preceding line, but the rhythm would be altered and the dramatic quality reduced.

Indentation of words, phrases, or a set of lines is a rhythmical device which is simply an elaboration of line length. Extreme typography is not as popular now that it is perfectly acceptable as it was when it was a kind of anti-Edwardian rebellion. But it still has certain advantages.

One loses, of course, the natural left to right flow of eye motion and therefore the feeling of steady progression. The more extreme the typography, the more fragmented the poem becomes.

The advantage, on the other hand, is more control over the reader's speed and attention. Everything that can be done by altering line length can be done to an even greater degree by altering the position of the line on the page. Recall, for example, these three lines quoted earlier from the same poem:

> and break onetwothreefourfive pigeonsjustlikethat
> Jesus
> he was a handsome man

The admiring expletive is given impact by standing alone and serving as a short line. This effect is increased by extreme indentation.

Stanza length is equally valuable in creating rhythmical effects. Because one is free to group lines according to need rather than any consistent pattern, the stanza is simply another aspect of typography. What one can do by moving words or phrases left or right across the page, one can also do vertically by means of irregular stanza length. Since typography serves many functions beyond manipulating rhythm, it will be discussed by itself later in this chapter.

Punctuation may also be used to establish rhythmical patterns. The range of how much and how little punctuation is needed in verse is far wider than it is in prose. One can follow the lead of Cummings and William Carlos Williams, who generally use none, or one can study men like Pound and Eliot for whom punctuation is often a significant key to rhythm and sometimes meaning as well. But it remains one of the lesser-used devices of rhythm largely because the freedom in typography often serves the same function as punctuation marks. Whereas commas are necessary, for example, to distinguish a nonrestrictive clause from a restrictive one in both prose and conventional verse, the writer of free verse may make the same signal to the reader by indenting the nonessential element or isolating it as a brief stanza.

The fifth and most subtle means of creating rhythm is by *using the natural stress of the word*. This is not the same as meter because it is not necessarily sustained throughout the line. It is related to onomatopoeia in that meaning is derived from sound, but the suggested meaning usually comes from the context rather than from the sound of the word itself.

Eliot's oft-quoted last line of "The Hollow Men," "Not with a bang but a whimper," is a fine example of this. Grammatically the line falls neatly into two clauses (each, incidentally, with the same number of syllables). The first clause ends with a strong stress, "bang"; the second ends with the unstressed last syllable of "whimper." The poem is "free" because it cannot be classified under any metrical heading, but this technique of employing the natural stress of words is taken directly from traditional verse.

The sixth and final rhythmical device in free verse is *repetition*. This may take the form of particular words, but more often it appears as similar phrases. The effect is heightened when it appears at the beginning of lines or stanza-like divisions. Repetition has its roots in the prose rhythms of the Bible ("Genesis" is a particularly good example) and was developed poetically by Whitman and, lately, by Ginsberg and others.

Rhythmical patterns in free verse are more elusive than strict meter. They vary from poet to poet and from poem to poem. They even vary within a single poem. But they remain, as in traditional verse, one of those characteristics which distinguish poetry from prose.

Sound End rhyme can be used effectively in free verse, but rarely is it used regularly. The tendency is to use it sparingly if at all.

But this does not suggest any slackening of interest in sound devices. In fact, the free verse of Dylan Thomas is as rich in pure melody as any sample of traditional verse one can find.

Slant rhymes (off rhymes) are popular now, though it took a generation to retrain the ear of the poetry-reading public. This re-education was similar to that which went on in symphonic music during the twenties when that which was traditionally considered dissonant began to appear in the works of men like Copland. For the Victorian, rhyme implied an identity of sound; for many contemporary readers, similarity in word endings are not only good enough, but more varied and therefore preferable.

Burying the rhyme within the line is not a new device, as I have pointed out in Chapter 15, but it has become particularly popular with such poets as Robert Lowell. Like slant rhymes, it mutes the sound itself, makes it recede so far that often the reader is only subconsciously aware that the device is being used.

Strict onomatopoeia is another sound device which is frequently employed. But more popular still is the kind of vague association between the sound of the word and the object it represents. When Dylan Thomas referred to death in "Over Sir John's Hill" with the phrase "clear as a buoy's bell," he not only avoids the cliché, "clear as a bell," but he adds certain overtones through the actual sound of a bell buoy. No non-English speaking individual would guess that a bell was being described here; the sound association is a complex combination of the alliteration in these two words and the sense itself. But for the English speaking reader, the effect is essentially the same as the onomatopoetic association.

The most important sound devices in free verse, however, are the closely related trio; assonance, consonance, and alliteration. It is fairly easy to find samples of good free verse which contain none of the sound techniques already discussed; it is difficult to find any which do not make use of these three.

The uses, advantages, and disadvantages of these sound devices have already been discussed in Chapter 15. But it is worth noting here that these particular techniques have become significant aspects of free verse for precisely the same reason that slant rhyme became more popular than true rhyme: The technical aspects of the poem can more easily be disguised. This is particularly true of assonance. A poem can "absorb" an incredible number of assonances without sounding contrived. Rhyme and alliteration are more easily spotted and identified simply because they appear at the extremities of the word; excessive use of either (such as in Poe's "The Raven") makes the reader consciously aware of a technician at work. Assonance, like consonance, is usually buried within the word and the sound relationships become background rather than foreground, like subtle harmonies in music.

Typography Typography has already been touched on as a technique for suggesting rhythm, but it also has a far wider application.

There are essentially two ways of rearranging words on the page: vertical spacing and horizontal spacing or indentation.

The conventional stanza is simply one example of vertical spacing. The quatrain, for example, leaves a space after every fourth line. Seen in this way, the technique of poetic typography is a liberated version of the stanza. It is free in that one can set off any number of lines at any point in the poem, just as one can indent lines either singly or in groups.

The only function of the traditional stanza which free verse typography does not also fulfill is to define a regular rhyme scheme. For the rest, there is a direct correlation.

Typography as a rhythmical device as described earlier in this chapter is well illustrated in Eliot's "The Hollow Men." Take, for example, the following two lines which the poet has set off as a kind of couplet:

> Shape without form, shade without color,
> Paralyzed force, gesture without motion . . .

There is no clear meter in these lines. At best, they might be described as alternating trochees and iambs, but even this clumsy definition does not conform to any consistent metrical system in the poem as a whole. Yet clearly there is rhythm. It is "sprung rhythm" in the sense that there are unmistakably four heavy stresses in each line. But even this does not conform to any consistent rhythmical system in the poem. By isolating the two matching lines as a kind of "couplet," the rhythmical pattern is made precise and unmistakable.

More important, typography can be used to organize subject matter. Just as the sonnet often shifts its argument or view at the end of the octave, often beginning the sestet with "But," or "Yet," so spacing—either vertical or horizontal—can suggest a new topic, a shift, a turn, or a contradiction.

The refrain, so much a part of the traditional ballad, survives in free verse by means of typography. In Eliot's "The Love Song of J. Alfred Prufrock," for example, there are a number of significant refrains. "So how should I presume?" is repeated three times—each indented for emphasis. So too is the two-line refrain, " 'That is not what I meant at all; / That is not it, at all.' " Doubtless, the careful reader would be aware of these repeated lines as refrains even if the poem were written in a solid block of print; but the spacing and indentation serve as cues.

Finally, typography can be used to emphasize single words. As one begins to break lines up and indent them more radically, it becomes increasingly easy to isolate single words. This, of course, provides a sharp and vivid effect. The exact opposite effect is achieved when one runs the words together without spaces as Cummings did in the lines from "Buffalo Bill's" already quoted.

In spite of all these advantages, however, the use of extreme typography is waning. The best examples, such as those by Cummings, were written in the twenties. Recent works by poets still under forty, such as those in *New Poets,* are by contrast markedly conservative in arrangement.

There are many reasons for this new conservatism which will be discussed at the end of this chapter. But the one that applies to typography can best be described as a poetic law of diminishing returns: Typography can only be justified when it increases the worth of the poem as a single, organically unified work; yet as one increases the rearrangement of words and lines on the page, the poem becomes proportionally fragmented and, as a result, less of an organically unified work. It is for this reason that the most bizarre experiments in type arrangements are remembered for curiosity value rather than literary worth—they are mostly the two-headed horses and one-eyed cats of poetry. Typography, then, has returned to the position it held in the seventeenth century at the hands of men like Donne: It is a device worth cautious consideration.

The "New" Subject Matter The term "free verse" actually refers only to technique: verse written without the use of meter or a regular rhyme scheme. But liberation in subject matter has been identified with the form so consistently and with such fervor that it deserves mention here.

The roots of twentieth-century free verse are in Whitman, whose personal rebellion, launched during the ascendancy of the Victorians, was half technique and half subject matter. All the "free" techniques discussed in this chapter can be seen in his work; but equally important to him—and equally shocking to his contemporaries—was his contention that the poet could use such images as ". . . the old drunkard staggering home from the outhouse," "The suicide sprawls on the bloody floor," and ". . . their white bellies bulge to the sun." In singing of "The Modern Man" he not only insisted on new rhythms but new notes as well. Many were quick to agree with him when he wrote "Nor will my poems do good only, they will do just as much evil, perhaps more." But his lines helped to free the poet from the Victorian contention that certain words were appropriate to the genre and others were not.

Once again, however, one cannot view this as a wholly new departure from the history of the genre. Like the new rhythmical patterns, new methods of expressing sound, and the look of the poem on the page, the new subject matter is a natural development of the poetic tradition.

The right to use images which are appropriate to the poem, rather than to the genre as a whole, is a return to the freedoms valued by the metaphysical poets like Donne and Crashaw in the early seventeenth century. One can go further back, of course, to Chaucer and even the classical poets for "modern" diction and subject matter, but the impact of the metaphysical poets on such major twentieth-century figures as Eliot is unmistakable.

For example, we think of Eliot's description of the evening "spread out against the sky / Like a patient etherized upon a table" and Ciardi's description of death as "Where the land crabs run unmourning / Through a night of jungle skies" and John Heath-Stubbs little ode to a toothache, ". . . tell the attendant gnomes / It is time to knock off now" as being "modern" in diction and subject matter. Yet these are no more bizarre or shocking to the twentieth-century sensitivities than Donne's comparison of his love with a hungry flea.

This is not to say that the diction of contemporary poetry is imitative. But it is equally dangerous to view this new freedom as detached from the poet's literary heritage. The writer of poetry must listen to his own most honest inner self and to his age as well; but he cannot afford the kind of temporal provinciality which comes from ignoring the roots of his own poetic technique.

Traditional Techniques For all that is new in free verse, there is more which it holds in common with all poetry. It is in no sense a new genre. Unlike all other forms of literary expression, and like all forms of poetry, it makes full use of the line. It is through the arrangement of lines, as has been discussed in Chapter 12, that this form achieves rhythm, highlights sound patterns, controls the attention of the reader, and dramatizes the development of theme.

In addition, free verse shares with all but epic poetry a concern for the compression of statement, a concentration of expression. To do this it relies on the multiple use of words and phrases through metaphor, symbol, and suggestive image. Finally, it tends to translate abstractions into that which can be absorbed by the reader through one of the five senses.

It is very easy to write unsophisticated, formless free verse. These failures cannot be attributed to disobeying any rule because there are no precise rules. Yet fail they do, clearly and unmistakably.

In nine out of ten failures the cause can be attributed to the tendency to think of free verse as more closely related to prose than to poetry. The result is often a fuzzy essay scattered either decorously or chaotically across the page. Only when the poet perceives free verse as a development of the oldest and richest literary genre can he hope to create a sophisticated work of art.

20

SELF-CRITICISM—POETRY

The tendency to be *satisfied too early;* the characteristics of poetry which make *revisions essential;* a *checklist* for purposes of review, group discussion, and *self-criticism.*

This chapter, like the one which completed the section on fiction, has three functions. First, it may be used as a review of the material discussed in the preceding eight chapters. Second, it should suggest ways of discussing a particular poem either in class or informally. Most important, however, it is intended as a guide for the poet who has reached that point where he must evaluate his own work.

It is not easy to determine just when a poem is "finished." As a general rule, inexperienced poets feel that they have reached this point far sooner than do those who are more experienced. This is due primarily to the fact that novice poets, like novice fiction writers, are not sure what questions to ask. It is for this reason that the checklist which concludes this chapter is written in the form of questions.

There are a number of different ways of going about revisions. Most poets work with pencil rather than the typewriter, leaving wide spaces between lines for changes. A few, on the other hand, work directly with the typewriter as do most writers of fiction under forty. In either case, the final draft usually bears little resemblance to the first.

One reason for these radical transformations is that the poet is far less bound to an over-all sequence than is the writer of fiction. By the time one begins to write a story, the plot is usually established and serves as a guide. But a poet may begin with only a line or, more frequently, just an image. As explained earlier, he is free to move back or forward from this point. He is not, of course, quite so free when working with narrative poetry; but in the case of lyrics, he often begins without more than a hazy idea of what the finished work will be.

Put another way, the poet often revises more than the writer of fiction because he usually begins committing his work to paper at a much earlier point.

One keeps on revising until one is satisfied with each line and each word. This list of critical questions is designed to keep one from being too satisfied too early.

1. Does this poem make use of the devices we associate with poetry? (See Chapter 12.)
   a. Does it really make use of the line, or are sentences merely chopped up in random fashion?
   b. Are there rhythmical patterns?
   c. Are there any sound devices?
   d. Are there stanzas or stanza-like divisions showing some sort of internal structure?
   e. Is there enough complexity and originality here to justify calling the work "sophisticated," or is it "simple" in treatment?
2. Was the poem rooted in fertile ground? This is, of course, a question only the poet himself can answer. (See Chapter 13.)
   a. Was it founded on some undigested abstraction not truly felt or understood by the poet?
   b. Has the poem made use of details actually seen, heard, felt, smelled, or tasted by the poet?
   c. Are the emotions expressed genuine, or merely sterile conventions employed without imagination?
   d. If experience has been used, has the poet broken it down to some aspect which can be dealt with poetically?

e. Would the poet have an easier time of it had he chosen fiction as his medium?
f. Does the poet really show concern for the sound and meaning of words?

3. Assuming that there are rhythmical patterns, have they been employed effectively? (See Chapter 14.)
a. If meter is used, is the type of foot and line selected the best for the tone and thematic patterns?
b. And has the meter been muted so as to avoid the sing-song effect of simple metered verse?
c. If not, could the poem be improved by such devices as run-on lines, substitutions, and shifts in line length?
d. If rhythm of stress (as distinct from meter) has been used, does it come through successfully when read out loud?
e. If there are visual rhythms, are they meaningful for the reader as well as the poet himself? Or are they so obvious that they are only "tricky"?
f. If there is syntactical rhythm, is it meaningful or only a monotonous repetition of sentence structure?
g. Has the poet reached the point of liberation through rhythmical patterns, or is he merely struggling with them as necessary requirements of poetry?

4. Assuming that there are sound patterns, have they been employed effectively? (See Chapter 15.)
a. If there is alliteration, is it so obvious that it trips the reader's attention?
b. Did the use of alliteration tempt the poet into using stock pairs like "tried and true" or "sailed the seas"?
c. Have assonance and consonance been used to link words which are associated? If not, would such a device help to add a sense of sound to the poem?
d. Are there any samples of onomatopoeia? If not, would a few help to give life to the poem?
e. Are there any secondary sound clusters which would serve as subtle echoes?
f. If rhyme has been used, was the poet consistent in his use of the true rhyme or off-rhyme?
g. Is the rhyme ever used to stress key words or link paired words?

h. Has the poet strained normal syntactical patterns or his choice of diction in order to complete his rhyme scheme?

5. Are the images effective? (See Chapter 16.)
   a. Are the images of sight vivid to the reader or are they merely personal details from the life or dreams of the poet?
   b. Are they isolated or linked with some association?
   c. Are there auditory images? If not, would some help to broaden the existing dependence on things seen?
   d. Has the poet considered images of taste, feeling, or smell to enrich those already used?
   e. Have these images been employed for the sake of mere description or as similes, metaphors, or symbols?
   f. If similes have been used, would it be more effective to convert these into metaphors?
   g. If an extended metaphor was used, has the poet considered using the vehicle as the base of the poem, thus converting his extended metaphor into a symbol?
   h. If the poem is based on one central and complex symbol, would greater clarity be achieved if this were converted back to an extended metaphor?
   i. If none of these were used, wouldn't the poet be wise to convert his work to prose?
6. Is the diction both appropriate to this poem and effective as well? (See Chapter 17.)
   a. Are there any clichés in the poem?
   b. Is there any language—words or phrases—which is sufficiently close to a convention to be called hackneyed?
   c. Are there archaisms used to aid the meter or to make the work "poetic" in the worst sense?
   d. Has the poet selected words which are sufficiently fresh and appropriate so that the work breaks through to the reader's consciousness?
7. Does the poem make use of internal tension? (See Chapter 18.)
   a. Has the lack of tension resulted in a poem which is simply dull?
   b. Even if the poem is not dull, could it be improved by an increase or development of tension?
   c. Specifically, have methods of verbal tension such as irony, paradox, or puns been used?

d. Is there some sample of mild irony which could be expanded upon?
e. Should the irony be made more subtle?
f. Is there some sort of thematic tension such as alternatives or an opposition to some general belief?
g. If there is ambiguity, is it the sort which may be resolved either in the poem itself or in the reader's mind?
h. Would it be effective to reinforce thematic tension with tonal tension?
i. Or, further, with imagistic tension?

8. If the poem is free verse, is the poet aware that this convention is rooted in poetic tradition? (See Chapter 19.)
   a. Is there nothing which distinguishes this from prose chopped into short lines?
   b. Are the rhythmic techniques the best for this particular poem? Would others be more effective?
   c. If the poem employs special typography, is it effective or arbitrary?
   d. If the subject matter is unusual, does it give the impression of battling for a cause already won or is it a meaningful issue in its own right?
   e. Generally, would a great deal be lost if the poem were written out in the consecutive lines of prose?
9. What one characteristic stands out as being effective in this poem? What will one remember long after reading it? Will the reader be drawn back to reading it again?

PART THREE

The Writing of Drama

21

RESPECT FOR THE STAGE

Influences on the playwright; *fiction* and *film* distinguished from legitimate stage production; *examples* of faulty planning; *seven characteristics* of serious drama.

A playwright should have as deep a respect for his language as a poet. But in addition, he must respect the stage itself. Only through such an attitude will he appreciate the fact that he is creating a *performance* which will be presented "live" in a theater and observed by an audience.

For many, this acknowledgment is more difficult than it appears. One's definition of drama is necessarily influenced by related art forms, and it is easy to see how strong an influence these may have when one compares the number of legitimate plays one has actually observed in full production with the hundreds of novels, stories, and plays one has read and the even greater number of film dramas one has watched.

Begin, then, with a clear understanding of what a play is *not.*

First, a play is not a novel. It is more compressed. *Oedipus Rex* is one of the finest examples of this dramatic compression. The *story* of King Oedipus is a full biography running from his infancy to his maturity and eventual disgrace. But the play from which we discover this story is limited to the events of a single day. Quite a day! Most of us would prefer Shakespeare's less rigid interpretation of the unity of time, but the fact remains that the playwright must find the significant moments and build them into scenes which imply through dialogue, action, and mood what has gone before. The novelist may wander through his story; the dramatist must select and compress.

A play is not a short story either. The poetic fiction of John Updike's "The Crow in the Woods" or "Wife Wooing" is enormously compressed, but his art depends on the nuances of words, on finely etched descriptive passages, on subtleties of reflection. It would be almost impossible to translate these stories into an art form which depends on actors performing and speaking lines. Dramatic impact, then, is a necessary part of the play. Some plays like *Waiting for Godot* have extraordinarily little action, but they maintain dramatic interest through tension among characters and through constant anticipation.

Even stories with high dramatic impact are not readily adapted for the stage. Fiction often makes use of setting in ways which are almost impossible to reproduce on the legitimate stage. Steinbeck's "Flight" and Conrad's "Youth," for example, utilize the desert and the sea, respectively, almost as fully as if these aspects of nature were characters.

There is another important distinction which separates the play and all forms of fiction. The writer of fiction has a direct and singular relationship with his reader. The author's work is never altered by another artist. Not so with the playwright. His script is only the beginning of a long process. It is read and interpreted by a director whose work is creative and may profoundly influence the result. Further, the script is modified by the imagination of the set designer, the lighting manager, the costumer, and, most important, the individual actor. What the audience sees is the collective work of many. The playwright must in the act of writing visualize his work as a corporate performance.

Third, a play is not to be confused with cinema or television drama. These recent art forms allow extraordinary freedom: Scene shifts are no longer a limitation. We can move from Rome to Reno in an instant. We can move from reality to a dream, or from here to the moon without even lowering a curtain. Further, we can make use of visual details like a hand on a doorknob or the flicker of an eyelash with a simple twist of the zoom lens. And that which has to be only suggested on the stage can be created literally: The ingenious but limited scenes in which Shakespeare suggested a battle by having messengers dashing on stage and princes meeting in hand-to-hand combat can in film become an extraordinary spectacle with full armies firing real longbows en masse. The film version of *Henry V* is a fine example.

Finally, a play is not primarily a script to be read. We do, of course, study drama as literature on the page, but it was not until the nineteenth century that the dramatist thought of including material in his script which would be of interest only to readers. Publishing plays as material to be read proved to be a financial boon for men like Shaw and Barrie, as it has to every successful playwright since then, but the play as an object of art remains a performance. It is harsh criticism to say of a play, "It reads well but. . . ." Drama which borrows too heavily from the two other genres often turns into either shallow verse or defective fiction. In both cases, the playwright has deprived himself of certain specific advantages found in each genre and runs the risk of producing an artistic hermaphrodite.

The play, then, is not a novel, a story, a film, or a literary manuscript. But this is a negative approach to the genre. The playwright should examine the advantages he has.

The most important asset of drama springs from the fact that it is a "live" performance. Ever since the advent of the "talking movie," critics have prophesied the end of legitimate theater. Television has reawakened this talk of doom. But the fact is that new theaters are being built not only by municipalities but by colleges and universities, and there is a constant growth of little theaters converted from ballrooms, movie houses, and even warehouses. If there were not a genuine craving for performances given by actors on the stage, legitimate drama would have given in to celluloid long ago.

Theater, however, does not depend wholly on the "realism" of actors. The second advantage is that the small production can be aimed at a small audience. Even a Broadway production makes use of a specialized audience, minute compared with the multitude which must appreciate a nationally distributed film or television show before the costs of such a production can be met. It is perhaps for this reason that so much activity has been going on off Broadway and in municipally sponsored theaters. It is a simple formula: Low budget + sophisticated (that is, small) audience = sophisticated art form. For "=" one must read "may" rather than "will," of course.

Third, the stage play continues to stress the spoken word. The magnificence of *The Virgin Spring* and *La Dolce Vita* is largely visual. A close examination of the script in translation reveals little which the viewer did not already grasp. Playwrights like Pinter, Ionesco, and Beckett have moved increasingly toward the verbal. The word is essential. In this respect, cinema and drama seem to be moving in opposite directions rather than competing.

Finally, the very limitations of the stage work in favor of the playwright in a number of ways. He must suggest by symbol and inference what otherwise is only literally presented. He must concentrate on significant moments rather than wandering through his material. He must hold the audience's attention through his art, not through technical stunts.

Failure to respect the stage can be disastrous. But like a cancer, it can be cured if detected early enough. The playwright should test his work long before the dialogue has been composed. As soon as the play has been "blocked out" in scenes, one can begin to see the danger points. Basic revisions at this early point may save hours or even days of script writing. Here are some sample scenes which may well lead to trouble simple because they ignore in various ways the natural demands of stage production.

Scene: The protagonist stands in front of the fireplace, drink in hand, and tells his guests the story of his life. He begins with early memories of his father, a sadistic alcoholic, and describes a number of grim incidents with wry humor. He then describes his life at Chicago's P.S. 33 and, later, at Northern Indiana State Teachers' College. With increasing enthusiasm, he traces his career from streetcar conductor in Los Angeles to the president of a major airline.

Criticism: Wry humor and ingenuity of material not withstanding, this scene will drag the entire play to a stop. The protagonist has turned the other members of the cast into an extension of the audience and has killed all forms of dramatic interaction. Biographical accounts like this occasionally lend themselves to novels, but when they appear in plays it is usually because the playwright has been thinking in terms of fiction.

Scene: A dinner party with articulate, sophisticated characters discussing the aesthetics of architecture. Through the course of this brilliant conversation it becomes apparent that each character is revealing his own personality in highly symbolic terms. Further, the disagreements regarding the merits of certain schools of design suggest fundamental conflicts between these characters.

Criticism: Like the scene with the solitary talker, this one ignores that aspect of drama which demands movement on the stage. But it has one distinct advantage: It allows for the development of conflict between characters. This is a step forward.

The real weakness, however, lies in the fact that the playwright has constructed a complex verbal system which would probably require a careful reading to interpret. The lack of action here is coupled with intricacies which we normally associate either with fiction or poetry.

It is true, of course, that some contemporary dramatists—particularly those associated with the so-called Theater of the Absurd—have reduced action to a minimum and have relied heavily on symbolically complex dialogue. In almost every case, however, these plays contain a *dramatic question,* a technique which is the subject of Chapter 23. It is this essentially nonintellectual element which holds the audience.

Scene: Four men and a collie are adrift in a large life raft. The shortage of food raises various ethical and dietary problems.

Criticism: In spite of the fact that this is a rather blatant theft from the movie *Lifeboat,* this scene keeps reappearing in writing classes with monotonous regularity. Sometimes it is disguised in the form of desert islands, sunken submarines, or the ever-popular bomb shelter. But the most damning criticism is not its lack of originality but its lack of dramatic practicality. A life raft on the stage is so difficult to suggest that the audience will quite naturally take the scene as comic. Second, the restricted action will paralyze the playwright's imagination. Exits and entrances are impossible and even an occasional dunking such as enlivened the film version cannot be made convincing. And it is extremely difficult to find dogs who can act.

One way to save this scene is to break lose from the limits of realism. Ionesco, Pinter, and others have taken this course and have converted what would have been an unintentionally comic setting into an intentionally absurd one. But absurd drama is for these playwrights neither meaningless nor formless. Without thematic elements and dramatic form, the play would descend from a sophisticated to a simple work.

Scene: An escaped convict is making what is traditionally called "a dash for freedom" through a forest, hides behind a boulder, finds a small cabin, and faces the agonizing problem of whether it is a deserted refuge or headquarters for the deputy sheriff.

Criticism: Like the life-raft scene, this comes from an imagination steeped in film. Forests and boulders are difficult to create on stage, and there won't be room for more than a tree or two after one finishes constructing that cabin. About the only way to achieve such a setting would be through a highly suggestive design—either expressionistic or a bare stage as described in Chapter 25.

But there are other weaknesses as well. This is a scene based on action and deprived of dialogue. Subtle pantomime is often effective, but a flight is extraordinarily difficult. It takes an actor about nine seconds at the most to travel from stage left to stage right; and even this allows for furtive glances into whatever foliage the stagehands have been able to create. Then he must return. Although O'Neill managed to solve this technical problem in *The Emperor Jones,* it remains an exceedingly difficult task.

In most cases, the novice playwright who tries this sort of scene has turned his imagination to that which can be achieved in film. The solitary flight through woods, swamps, city streets, and across deserts has become a standard cinema device, mainly because it does lend itself to that medium. The fact that audiences are used to seeing the chase in a variety of forms makes it that much more difficult for the playwright to compete on the stage.

The solution, once again, is to give up attempts to emulate film techniques when writing for the stage. Respect for the stage involves exploring whatever devices and techniques are better suited for legitimate theater than they are for other genres.

These four scenes represent commonly repeated weaknesses in plays written by novices. They all represent a misunderstanding not of taste or even tradition but of how drama on the stage differs inherently from fiction, poetry, and cinema.

Turning now from warnings to a more positive description of what drama is, we can isolate seven characteristics of the genre. One can find, of course, plays which ignore one or more of these principles—but they are rare indeed.

1. Drama is by definition a dramatic art. Conflict of some sort is essential. Although it may take almost as many forms as it does in contemporary fiction, it must be strong enough to keep the audience committed to the work.

2. Drama is a visual art. The action must be significant and an organic part of the whole production. It is not usually enough in the twentieth century to have characters simply walk back and forth as they did in the highly stylized traditions of Greek theater. In most cases, the set as well as the actors must be considered as a part of this visual impression. There have been only a few exceptions to this.

3. It is a structural art form. Although a one-act play may have only one stated scene, it is usually divided into informal scenes by means of exists and entrances. A new set of characters usually suggests a new scene. Lights or curtains are not essential as cues; but when they are not used, the play still requires some form.

4. Drama is a continuous art. The audience, unlike readers of fiction or poetry, must maintain the pace set by the playwright. They cannot linger over a sage observation or a moving episode. They cannot turn back a page or review an earlier scene.

5. It is an auditory art. The audience is a listener as well as a viewer. The very fact that one cannot rely as heavily on visual effects in a stage production as one does in film not only makes the playwright more dependent on words but prods the audience to listen more attentively as well.

But the script should not be confused with "pure" poetry.

Dialogue can have complexity, but because it is the product of a particular character, it continues to echo common speech. A poet may work directly with his own feelings and his own thoughts; a playwright, on the other hand, works through his characters like fate speaking through that confused old woman at Delphi.

6. Drama is a physically produced art. A stage is a finite area. Sets are constructed with wood and nails. The playwright cannot ignore the task of the set designer and the stage crew.

7. Finally, drama is an art. If it is sophisticated, it does more than entertain. "Instructive" is a dangerous word because it leads away from drama toward the illustrated essay and the tract. But sophisticated plays, like novels and poems on the same level, contain insight, discovery, and lead to growth. The theatergoer may not learn anything intellectually or be morally changed, but he is usually more aware for having participated vicariously in this staged experience.

22

THEME VERSUS THESIS

Definition of each term; concern for *theme* seen as the mainstream of drama; *thesis-drama* seen in satire, morality plays, and social consciousness of the twentieth century; terms analyzed as "*literary*" and "*assertive*" aspects of all writing; *dangers* in both approaches; *value* of these terms.

The *theme* of a play is its primary abstract suggestion. It is sometimes referred to as the *central concern.* It is that underlying significance which often does not come to the viewer until after he leaves the theater and begins discussing the play in abstract terms. Quite often it is necessary to use the term in the plural since a complex drama is rarely based on a single thematic concern. *King Lear,* for example, is concerned with egotism of the individual, power both on a family and a national level, and the existence or absence of order in the universe; but the play as a whole does not take an assertive position in any of these areas. It is a play of exploration, not argumentation—a play of themes, not theses.

Thesis, on the other hand, is a much more precise term. It implies a proposition of policy. The thesis-play is, at least in part, a dramatic argument. The thesis of Ibsen's *Ghosts,* for example, may be described as a proposition that the sins of the father are passed on to the children, and from this we may draw certain specific lessons concerning moral behavior. No matter how many other implications we may see in this play, the thesis remains the foundation of the work.

These two terms, developed in some detail by Walter Kerr in *How Not to Write a Play,* are enormously important here not just because they represent two fundamentally different approaches to drama but because each presents a separate set of problems for the playwright.

The primary danger in thematic plays, for example, is lack of dramatic impact. In addition, it is often difficult at first to strengthen the major theme with others which are either parallel or minor echoes. And there is always the danger of having characters state the theme directly.

Problems arising from plays of thesis, on the other hand, almost all stem from the single, and for some, almost overwhelming temptation to convert the drama into a simple proclamation. The solutions, which I will discuss later in this chapter, include such techniques as shock, irony, wit, and the like.

Before dealing with these practical problems, however, one must understand the true nature of both theme and thesis and the differences between them.

The mainstream of drama from the classical period to the present has been thematic. But because it is easier to teach a play as a moral lesson, many students have been led to believe that drama is primarily didactic. *Oedipus Rex*, for example, is sometimes thought of as an argument against opposing fate or, in still simpler terms, against pride.

One could with equal logic suggest that the play's "message" warns us not to indulge in patricide and incest. Converting the play in this way from one of themes to one of thesis not only destroys the subtlety of the work but in many cases initiates a misapprehension about the traditional pattern of drama.

A more careful reading of the play reveals a number of themes, not one of which provides a specific piece of advice. We see that there are certain aspects of life over which we have no control, that certain men struggle against this limitation of their freedom, and that there is both a blindness and a greatness in such struggle. Then there are secondary themes, such as the suggestion that love for mother is in some cases something more than sweet sentiment, that resentment for one's father may suggest in some cases a desire to "take his role," that there is an irony in the sight of a man who struggles to reveal the very truth which will destroy him, that sometimes the blind "see" more than those whose literal vision is perfect, and that the brutal determination of parents to mold the future of their child may lead to the very events they were hoping to avoid.

Through the production of the play, we come in contact with all this and more. But we cannot say that man in all cases should or should not battle fate, that parents should or should not try to direct the future of their children, that the individual should or should not seek out the truth about himself. The play does not give handy instruction; it only makes manifest certain aspects of human experience.

In the same way, *Antigone* is frequently presented as a thesis-play arguing for the rights of the individual over the state. In this view, Creon becomes almost wholly evil. Such a reading misses the point that Creon is clearly the spokesman for civil law, and he defends the state as the only alternative to anarchy and chaos. He is seen, at the beginning of the play, as a reasonable man defending the law on rational grounds. What develops is not wrong pitted against right, but the rigid interpretation of governmental law pitted against an equally rigid interpretation of a higher law. Sophocles' tragedy is not about the individual's death at the hands of the fascist, but the destruction of both individualist and legalist when they find themselves unwilling to compromise.

There is some evidence for the argument that Sophocles admired Antigone more than Creon. But we are not justified in treating the play as an early version of Thoreau's "Civil Disobedience." Sophocles makes it quite clear that a nation of Antigones would be no nation at all; it would be chaos. Nor does the play propose the thesis that compromise is the "best" behavior for man. The vehicle of compromise, Ismene, is not presented as the heroine or even as a highly admirable character. In short, there is no thesis. But the themes are strong: the necessity for the state and for individual conscience and the agony when the two conflict.

This same preference for theme over thesis exists in contemporary drama. Miller's *The Crucible* may help us to understand the psychology of witch hunts and the dynamics of the so-called McCarthy era better, but we would dilute the play if we reduced it to a single moral "message." *Death of a Salesman* implies a great deal about the relationship between the social system and the individual as well as the corrosive qualities of deceit, but we are not provided with a sole cure-all for injustice and self-destruction. Both Tennessee Williams and Edward Albee have strong views on the nature of man and the dangers of self-delusion, but neither provides his audiences with simple solutions.

Turning now to thesis-plays, we see a tradition which is equally long though it is not as broad. Often it takes the form of satire. Aristophanes' *Lysistrata,* for example, although rejected by most secondary schools and some libraries as obscene, is rooted in three highly moral propositions. First, it suggests that war is absurd and can do nothing but make men ridiculous. Second, it quite blatantly suggests that both men and women become grotesque when they give in to sexual passions. And finally it attacks the egotism of both males and females who believe that they can manage perfectly well without the opposite sex. In purely ethical terms we are urged to reject war, control our passions, and recognize our need for the opposite sex. Thematically, if not in treatment, it is a morality play.

And in varying degrees, plays of satire have continued to be didactic. The satiric and nonreligious portion of *The Second Shepherds' Play* is, in essence, a mild jab at deceit and fraud. Jonson's *Volpone* is a sophisticated elaboration of the same ethical position. He broadens the ethical base by adding love of power to love of possessions, and he compounds the pattern of deceit by making the victims as despicable as the villains, and he keeps his audience laughing; but the thesis is clear enough.

And if we move down to the present with a work like Albee's *The American Dream,* we see once again a strong ethical statement. Here too, society is taken to task with sharp irony. The American Dream, both a character and an abstraction like Everyman, is a heartless, gutless, soulless shell, and he has been made so not by fate or chance but by society—by us. We are judged guilty and told how to correct our ways.

The apprentice playwright who is drawn to thesis-drama should study the long tradition of satire first. But he should not ignore those works which are serious in tone and direct rather than ironic in treatment. The clearest early examples are the morality plays.

It is significant fact that although *Everyman* is scorned and derided by students taking a course in English literature, it is imitated at least once a year in creative writing classes. The thesis is stated in the opening scene by God himself: ". . . every man / In my glory should make his mansion," and developed forthwith by Death and all the other allegorical characters such as Kindred, Goods, Strength, and the like. Modern critics have done much to draw other significances from this play, but the didactic base remains.

Christopher Marlowe makes use of these same devices in *Dr. Faustus.* Though the thesis is far more complex, he still sets Good Angel and Bad Angel on the stage to present, periodically, the moral alternatives.

Moving to the nineteenth century we can see a further development of the thesis-play in the works of Ibsen. It is a mistake to sum up plays like *Ghosts* and *The Wild Duck* with a simple thesis-statement without qualification and elaboration, but the thesis is there none the less. There are moral ambiguities similar to those in *Antigone*, but the final position of the play remains assertive.

The same is true of Shaw's work. Occasionally, as in *Heartbreak House,* he develops his thesis through allegory. In this play Captain Shotover is the head of a household which represents England as a whole. Hesione Hushabye suggests England's home scene or domesticity; and Addie Utterword, England abroad or the empire itself. The blatant use of abstractions for the names of characters has gone, but the link is made through comic associations and puns which are apparent even from this brief description.

More often, however, Shaw presents his thesis through plots which are not allegorical. His theses are based not only on moral convictions but on social, political, and economic beliefs as well.

During our own century, the thesis-play is often more serious in treatment. Clifford Odets used it to preach political liberalism in *Waiting for Lefty*, and Bertold Brecht blasted at the broader problems of social injustice and the horror of war in plays like *The Caucasian Chalk Circle* and *Mother Courage.* These last two are particularly worth study because of the fact that they so purposely and blatantly defy the conventions of so-called realistic drama. As with *Everyman*, the message is not hinted at but shouted out; and the use of ironic wit is not intended to soften the didactic function of the play but to intensify it.

There is not always a sharp division between a play of theme and a play of thesis. Albee's *Who's Afraid of Virginia Woolf?*, for example, is both. It makes assertions about the ideal relationship between men and women and, even more basic, about the sterility (quite literally) of self-deceit; it also deals with these and other concerns in ways which do not provide specific answers. But the distinction is fundamentally important for the playwright because of the fact that although *blending* the two can be successful, *confusing* the two can be disastrous. Only by reading a number of plays which clearly represent each approach can one see just how different the techniques and the basic assumptions can be, and it is for this reason that I have, so far, defined these terms mainly from an historical point of view rather than from an analytical one.

It should be clear at this point that analytically the difference between a play of theme and one of thesis is the difference between literary writing and that which *approaches* assertive writing. This is not to say that the thesis play *is* purely assertive or descriptive like an essay; it is still in the realm of literature. But the split between the basic premise of each approach explains why each has a different set of problems.

The primary problem in developing theme, as I mentioned earlier in this chapter, is making it strong enough to carry the weight of drama. Too often, the writer begins with a story which would lend itself best to fiction and then converts it to drama on whim or to satisfy an assignment.

Plays usually have stronger themes than do stories, partly through tradition but largely because of the nature of the art itself: It is continuous and must seize the attention of an audience for the whole of its performance.

Although the simplest way to meet this need is to select material which is naturally dramatic, any theme can be amplified by means of careful plotting. Frequently this is done by constructing parallel elements. In both *Period of Adjustment* by Tennessee Williams and *Who's Afraid of Virginia Woolf?*, for example, the thematic concerns (crises in identity) are developed through the protagonist and his wife and then rephrased through a second couple. The range and variety of thematic suggestion is more than doubled in this way.

Themes can also be strengthened through minor echoes, though this usually requires a fairly complex plot. Shakespeare's *The Merchant of Venice,* for example, draws what little unity, coherence, and significance it has from a dazzling array of loyalties which represent almost every possible type and degree. Similarly, Miller's *Death of a Salesman* amplifies the theme of self-deceit by echoing the protagonist's problems with those of his two sons.

The other problem in developing a theme is the temptation to "strengthen" it by converting it into a thesis.

These plays often begin with a subtle introduction of thematic concerns, develop naturally, and then, about two-thirds of the way through, explode with didactic lines like "The trouble with you rich people is . . ." and "Basically, the artist's role is . . ." and "Freedom is won only by. . . ." It is not just the line itself which is at fault. The damage comes from the fundamental shift in the playwright's conception of his work. The most noticeable effect is a jarring shift in tone. More serious, however, is the fact that the very premise on which the play was based has changed. In short, the author has now begun a thesis-play without either preparing his audience or guarding against the particular dangers inherent in this approach.

Turning now to the problems which are peculiar to thesis-plays, one must begin with the unalterable fact that argumentation and art do not mix well. The producer can phrase this in terms of profit: "No one pays money to hear a sermon acted out"; and the critic can phrase this more objectively: "Assertive writing and literary writing are at opposite ends of the verbal scale"; but the dramatist is the one who must solve the problem.

One approach, of course, is to leave assertions to those who write essays, speeches, sermons, and manifestoes.

But if the playwright feels compelled to try the thesis-play, he should remember that the only way to mix oil and water successfully is to add some sort of emulsifying agent; and when trying to mix art with ethical assertions, the blending agents which work best are irony, wit, shock, and frequent qualification.

Irony and wit, usually employed together, serve as more than mere sugar coating. Just as wartime humor and ghetto jokes are means of facing reality without despair, so the satiric play often speaks truths which audiences would refuse to hear in any other form. Brecht's *Threepenny Opera*, for example, contains a number of bitter theses about the nature of social justice—or the lack of it —yet a prosperous, well-fed America gave the play one of the longest off-Broadway runs on record.

Brecht's technique depends less on wit than on irony. What would otherwise be weighed down with "message" is made buoyant with internal contradictions, paradoxes, inversions, and visual surprises.

Shock has recently become a popular emulsifier for thesis-drama. Alcoholism, drug addiction, homosexuality, and racial injustice have all served—some with great effectiveness. The statement, "Drug addicts are human beings who need help" is a slogan which in itself is no closer to literature than "Drive as if your life depended on it. . . ." But if the impact of the drama is made overwhelming, the result can be truly hypnotic.

Shock of this sort, however, is one of the less enduring qualities in drama. When the very life of a play is based solely on a specific, contemporary social injustice, one can with all due respect predict what will become of the work when that social problem is finally a dead issue. Much depends on just how narrow the thesis is. Compare, for example, Odets' *Waiting for Lefty*, which now reads like a faded period piece, with Miller's *The Crucible*, which has grown in stature now that we no longer associate it solely with the McCarthy era.

The final means of developing a thesis-play as a sophisticated drama is the use of frequent qualification. Note well that strong as Brecht's convictions are, his dramatic statements (theses) are never pure. As Harold Clurman put it, "There is always a small 'No' or 'Maybe' in Brecht's larger 'Yes!' No one triumphs easily or irrevocably in his plays." * This is enormously important, for it is by exactly this type of qualification that the thesis-play maintains a strong hold on the essence of literature.

* "Brecht Is Global, Except Here," *The New York Times Magazine*, November 3, 1963.

One warning is needed here: If a playwright begins to feel that his characters, plot, and dialogue have become mere barriers between himself and the thesis he wishes to proclaim, he should turn to the essay. The more blatantly a thesis-play becomes thesis-dominated, the further it moves from drama as an art form. There comes a point when the cause being defended *deserves* direct, honest treatment in the form of assertive writing.

This general distinction between theme and thesis is one which the playwright should consider as soon as a dramatic situation begins to take shape in his imagination. All plays, of course, are self-contained systems in the way that stories and poems are; each develops its own unique world. But from the very start the playwright can sense whether he is more concerned with *exploring* an area of human concern or *asserting* his convictions. Only when he is certain of his approach will he be prepared for the pitfalls and ready to develop the potential of whichever form of drama he chose.

23

THE DRAMATIC QUESTION

The *dramatic question* defined; *examples* from classical, Elizabethan, and modern plays; *seven types* of dramatic question; certain *exceptions;* reasons for its necessity; *techniques* of developing a dramatic question.

A poem can survive on theme alone. A short story or a novel must have not only theme but characters. A play must contain both these elements and must also provide a dramatic question.

Briefly defined, the dramatic question is the emotional element which holds the attention of the audience long before the theme or thesis becomes clear. It is the question unsophisticated theatergoers ask during the first intermission; it is the unuttered question in the minds of the others; it is the question which draws them all back to the second act; it is the source of such critical clichés as "exciting," "provocative," "compelling," and "suspenseful." It is the core of that which is dramatic.

Students of drama often ignore the dramatic question because it tends to be simple, direct, and beneath their artistic sensibilities. It is what children see in a play which thematically is beyond them. It is one of those base elements which serious drama holds in common with melodrama, the adventure story, the detective story, and pulp fiction. Yet for all this, it is an ingredient which playwrights from Sophocles to Ionesco and Albee have respected and used. It may be a "low" concern in the sense of being unrefined, but it is also "low" in that it is the very foundation of a dramatic performance.

Almost any play in the Western tradition can serve as illustration. Take, for example, *Oedipus Rex*. The theme, as described in the previous chapter, has to do with man's attitude toward that which is beyond his control, the nature of freedom and determinism, psychological aspects of pride and desire. But the dramatic question is simply, "Who killed King Laius?" We are introduced to this question rapidly via news of the plague; as soon as we know that the plague is connected with the unsolved mystery of Laius' death, we are emotionally committed to the play. In this sense, *Oedipus Rex* is a murder mystery with the master detective unwittingly gathering evidence against himself.

It would be absurd to say that this play is *only* a detective story. On this point, the editors of *Classic Comics* are as blind to reality as was Oedipus, and their treatment of their source material is nothing short of patricide. But, on the other hand, to treat the play as pure poetry, as pure theme, is "comic" in the same grotesque sense. The dramatic question in all its simplicity works *with* the complex thematic concerns. Without the first we have boredom and sterility; without the second we have a melodrama.

The same relationship can be seen in *Antigone*. Students have spent hours discussing such complex themes as the relationship between individual freedom and the laws of the state, between absolute conviction and the spirit of compromise, between national loyalty and a "higher law." But the writer who wants to be more than a critic should take a close look at what actually happens in the first five minutes of playing time: A woman has committed a crime; will she get away with it? From the days when Greek audiences sat on stone amphitheater seats and watched drama cycles from sunrise to sundown, to the present, over a span of two thousand years, audiences have asked "Will she get away with it?"

The Platonic dialogues contain themes of equal significance and complexity. They are "dramatic" in the sense that they are written in the form of spoken discussion. But they do not generally contain a dramatic question. It is worth noting that neither Greek nor American audiences have been asked to sit through an evening of Plato. No matter how much we respect the dialogues as philosophy, we must admit that as drama they would be a box-office failure.

Again, however, I must stress the fact that it is not the dramatic question alone which makes *Antigone* appear year after year in full production. The works of Seneca and Shakespeare's *Titus Andronicus* also contain strong dramatic questions, but their lack of thematic subtlety classifies them as melodrama, and we view them, if at all, as historical curiosities.

The tragedies of Shakespeare each contained at least one dramatic question. In *Macbeth,* for example, it is simply, "Will he succeed?" The fact that the same question has been used a thousand times since does not make the play hackneyed, for the stature of the work rests in the themes, the characterizations, and the subtleties of language. We do not damage the work by pointing out how the dramatic question resembles that in Marquand's *Sincerely, Willys Wade.*

In *Hamlet* we ask, "Will he avenge his father?" In *Othello,* "Will he discover the truth about Iago?" In *King Lear,* "Will he survive?" And for *Romeo and Juliet* we might ask the soap-opera question: "Will this girl find happiness as the love of handsome, passionate Romeo, member of the hated Montague family?"

These analyses will appear to degrade Shakespeare's work only to those who misunderstand the nature of the dramatic question. Although it is the core of that which is dramatic, it is only one element in a sophisticated play. The fact that at least one fundamental technique is shared by the simplest soap opera and the most complex drama should be no more surprising than the biological fact that, say, calcium is essential for both the toad and the human.

To this point, all my examples have been taken from the past. But modern dramatists have a right—even an obligation—to be suspicious of tradition. Some, like Ionesco, have explicitly declared war on the past. It is extraordinarily significant, however, that this rebelliousness has not removed the dramatic question from drama.

Take, for example, Ionesco's *The Chairs.* We call this *theater* *of the absurd* partly because it has pushed the expressionism of O'Neill and Rice to the point of surrealism: There is no more connection between the situation and what we take to be "real life" than there is between the dream and waking life. This is Kafka put on the stage.* We also see in the play an existential suggestion that life is "absurd"; that is, our system of values is assumed to be beyond proof and thus may not even exist. All this is not entirely new, but it does represent a violent rejection of the "as-if-real" conventions which we associate with the works of Arthur Miller, Ibsen, and much of Shakespeare—and even Sophocles.

But what is retained? *The Chairs,* opens with the question "Where are we, and what are we doing here?" as do most plays in this school. But the real dramatic question arises as soon as the Old Man reveals his ambition to give the world his "message." From that point on, the audience is concerned with the query: "Will the Old Man finally deliver his message?" Like *Oedipus Rex,* like *Macbeth,* the play develops through a man's desperate attempt to achieve a certain end which, we suspect, will either be beyond him or will destroy him. Following the time-honored tradition, Ionesco increases the intensity of the dramatic question until it reaches the ultimate of human experience: death. The double suicide and the final message of the orator, acting as chorus, are filled with thematic significance; but in an even more basic way, they are the direct results of a carefully developed dramatic question.

The fact that conventional problem-plays of our own period contain dramatic questions is not surprising. It is natural enough to see *Tea and Sympathy* revolve about a kind of social trial ("Will he be acquitted?") or *Period of Adjustment* tied to two domestic problems ("Can these marriages be saved?"). It is, however, extraordinary to see how the device has been retained even by the most pronounced rebels like Ionesco, Beckett, Pinter, and Albee. In *Zoo Story,* for example, the patterns of dramatic structure are as traditional as that already described for *The Chairs.* A Christ-like bum struggles to convert his antithesis to love and self-awareness. The theme is complex, but we keep asking ourselves the simple ques-

---

* See Chapter 26 for a development of the distinction between realism and expressionism.

tion: "Will he succeed?" In spite of the brevity of this play, there are two other dramatic questions. At the start, we tend to identify ourselves with Peter, the conservative. Our question at that point is, "Will he be harmed?" And later we are encouraged to ask the question: "What *did* happen at the zoo?" This is achieved by repetition in much the same way Beckett's *End Game* is dramatized with the repeated question, "Will he leave?"—which in turn is just the opposite of *Waiting for Godot* where we ask "Will he come?" or "Will He come?" depending on our determination of the theme.

This long list of examples suggests an infinite variety of dramatic questions. The suggestion is valid. But one can also discern certain common types in plays which may be thematically quite different from each other. There is no need for the playwright to memorize a list of dramatic questions, but he should be aware that such classifications exist. Here are seven of the more common questions used in drama:

1. *Will he come?* The usual version of this involves a character who is expected to arrive throughout the play. As I pointed out above, this is seen in the highly dogmatic thesis-play, *Waiting for Lefty*, and the thematically obscure *Waiting for Godot*. The Greeks generally avoided it, preferring to see their Leftys and their Godots on the stage. Whether the recent uses of this echo the Christian promise of a second coming or a search for the "magic helper" is of more concern to the critic than the playwright. My point here is simply that it is a difficult question to sustain throughout a full-length play.

2. *Who did it?* This is, of course, the literary version of "Whodunit?" We find it running the full length of drama from *Oedipus Rex* to Williams' *Suddenly Last Summer*. The trial scenes in *The Caine Mutiny Trial* and, in a loose sense, *Tea and Sympathy* and *The Crucible* are simply variations of this. In many cases, of course, the audience knows who is guilty; the dramatic question arises out of the attempt on the part of the *characters* to determine guilt. It is a highly variable device, though the trial scene, when portrayed literally, has become overused.

3. *Will he succeed?* This is, cumulatively, the most used of all dramatic questions. It lent itself admirably to the classical tradition of great men performing great tasks, and it applies equally to

characters whom we take to be largely noble (from Antigone to Halvard Solness in *The Master Builder*) and those who are evil (Macbeth, Richard III, and Caligula). It has been used less during the twentieth century, partly because of our increasing tendency to view the hero as victim of such forces as society, the economic system, and his own neuroses. There is a weak but interesting echo of this dramatic question in the businessman novels, but few of them have achieved literary stature.

4. *Will he discover what we know?* As we have seen, this is the dramatic core of *Oedipus Rex,* particularly toward the end. It is even clearer in *Othello,* where the truth is revealed to the audience almost from the start. It is easily adapted to our own concern for psychological self-discovery in such diverse plays as *Tea and Sympathy* and *Death of a Salesman.*

5. *Will a compromise be found?* Such a question appears to be lacking in dramatic voltage, but as I have already pointed out it is one of the more compelling questions in *Antigone.* It was repeated with almost wooden fidelity in Galsworthy's *Strife.* We see the same pattern much more subtly developed in Tennessee Williams' *Streetcar Named Desire* where the remains of the old order (Blanche) are pitted against the brutality of the new order (Stanley); or in less social terms, excessive sensitivity is met with blunt insensitivity. It is worth noting that in all three of these examples the dramatic questions encroach on the theme itself—a far different relationship than is seen in the other four types.

6. *Will this end in violence?* This, together with the one which follows, is a highly contemporary concern. We know that there will be violence in a Greek or Elizabethan tragedy, and this assumption keeps it from being the central question. We make no such assumption in contemporary drama. As a result, playwrights such as Williams, Albee, Ionesco, and even Saroyan have employed it as the initial and often central dramatic question. The threat of a lynching, for example, holds our attention in Williams' *Orpheus Descending* and Saroyan's *Hello Out There.* The ominous stranger is the initial chill in Albee's *Zoo Story* and Ionesco's *The Killer.*

7. This final type should be used with restraint. It might be expressed as *What's this play all about anyway?* Dependence on this dramatic question is one of the primary causes of failure in student-written plays. There is a two-fold liability here. First, the

question is based, not on a controlled withholding of certain key facts, but on an all-inclusive obscurity. It is a fundamental breakdown in communication. More serious, it is the only dramatic question which is aimed not at the situation within the play but at the author's intention. It is critical and intellectual rather than emotional, and as such is really not a dramatic question as I have defined it. Yet for all this, it is the major reason audiences sit through Beckett's *End Game,* and it is the most frequently repeated question during the first intermission of Pinter's *The Caretaker.* The second of these two plays comes closer to making this question truly dramatic; the characters are sufficiently credible and the situation convincing enough to make us *want* to know what is happening, not just as drama critics or as cultured theatergoers, but as human beings who have, from time to time, been in situations which force us to ask this question of life itself.

I began this chapter with a statement which has the whiff of dogma: ". . . a play must . . . provide a dramatic question." For many this will necessitate writing a play which disproves the thesis. There is a hostility to literary rules in all of us. But before instigating a rebellion, one should examine just what happens when the dramatic question is removed from a play. There are several good examples.

Certain dramatic dialogues such as the works of Plato (*Phaedo* excepted) and the "Don Juan in Hell" scene from Shaw's *Man and Superman* have almost no dramatic question. But it is significant that we think of such works as "discourses" and treat them either as works to be read silently or to be given a dramatic reading. They are on the fringe of what we think of as true drama.

Second, political reviews such as are currently having a revival in England and the United States and satire such as Picasso's *Desire* contain no single dramatic question. But once again, few would classify them as drama in the full sense. The very term "review" suggests a series of scenes or skits which may be related in theme but which do not constitute a single drama.

Finally, such verse plays as Richard Eberhart's *Prologue I* and *Prologue II* lack a dramatic question and action as well. They have been produced as plays, but the defense which has been made for them is that they are fine samples of witty *verse.* When they are performed we listen, not because of an inner commitment and involvement with a situation, but because of the words themselves. For most, a reading would suffice.

It is clear from these exceptions that the necessity of a dramatic question is not based on tradition alone—though that in itself is impressive. The fact is that such a question is implicit in our definition of drama. As soon as a work acted upon a stage appears to be without a dramatic question, we find ourselves using such terms as *discourse, review, skit, reading,* or *verse.* These words are not evaluative; they do not suggest something inferior. But they are quite descriptive; they suggest something other than drama.

In addition to our definition, there is a highly practical and non-literary reason for including a dramatic question in any serious play: the audience. The playwright is asking a group of people to sit still and become involved in a performance lasting from two to three hours. He denies them the right to smoke, drink, comment, or turn back a page. When he dims the house lights, he is asking for full concentration.

Even a good audience will not offer such concentration to a serious work if it does not contain that emotional magnet, the dramatic question. This is not a reflection on our own audiences; it is a statement about people. It appears to be as true for the Greek of the fifth century B.C. as it was for the Elizabethans, as it is for London, Paris, or New York audiences in our own decade.

Should a good playwright consider the demands of his audiences? It is true that few poets or novelists are willing to change a line of their works as a result of critical reaction. Such purity of artistic expression, however, has not generally applied to drama. Playwrights often listen to audience reaction and they, or their directors, are willing to revise extensively after opening night. Compare, for example, the script of *Period of Adjustment* as it appeared in *Esquire* with that used in the Broadway performance.

Our reaction to the dramatic question depends largely upon what sources we have based our definition of drama. The playwright who moves into this field from a strong literary background (poetry, fiction, and drama as literature read on the page) is apt to underrate it. It is significant that some forty per cent of an average college writing class begins with play outlines wholly lacking a dramatic question. If, on the other hand, the individual has been saturated with, say, four years of television drama (remember that casual viewing provides some 1,300 separate productions during the four high-school years), one is apt to overrate it.

There is no single formula. Each playwright determines his own proportions, and most are willing to remain flexible. There are no rules to follow or break. But the nature of the art suggests certain techniques which might be summarized as follows:

1. Distinguish in your own mind that which is the dramatic question from that which is the theme or thesis of the play. Differentiate the function of each.
2. Blend the two so that each depends upon and echoes the other. Notice how this is done in the various examples cited in this chapter.
3. Consider the value of introducing the dramatic question early. Notice how this reduces the temptation to state the theme bluntly just to keep the play alive.
4. Notice how much easier and more natural it is to present the dramatic question through the relationship between two or more characters.
5. Remember that if the dramatic question is allowed to become an end in itself, the play is liable to become melodrama or bombast.

Generally speaking, a nondramatic drama is not only a contradiction in terms but an imposition on an audience. But the range of possibilities within the genre is vast; the playwright is free to exercise his imagination and ingenuity as fully as the poet.

24

VISUAL EFFECTS—ACTION

Dramatic action analyzed in its four forms: *exits and entrances* which set off secondary scenes and provide dramatic structure, *relocation* of characters on the stage, *"business"* as solitary but significant activity, and *physical contact* between characters; the *need* for action in drama.

Action is embodied in our very conception of drama. "I *saw* a good play" we say, whereas for its sister art we are more apt to say "I *went* to the opera."

Before turning to the reasons for this, we should examine just what is meant by action. There are four general types: exits and entrances, relocation of characters, "business," and physical contact. These are, of course, all related. But since each serves a somewhat distinct function, it is helpful to consider them separately.

Exits and Entrances The first, exits and entrances, is the most important form of action for the dramatist. It is as basic a device as chapter divisions are for the novelist and in a sense serves the same function: It is the primary means of finishing one scene and beginning the next.

The word *scene* is deceptive. On the theater program it refers only to those formal subdivisions of an act which are separated unmistakably either by a brief lowering of the curtain or dimming of lights. These are also marked on the script and are minor acts within an act. I shall refer to these as *primary scenes.*

For the dramatist (and the actor), however, a scene also refers to each unit of action which begins with an entrance or an exit and ends with the next shift of characters on the stage. Those whose introduction to drama has been wholly literary are apt to miss the significance of these *secondary scenes.* But anyone who has had any experience in the production of a play knows how important they are both to the actor and to the playwright himself.

Occasionally, a secondary scene may have a strong dramatic unity. That is, it may build to a climax which is dramatically punctuated by the departure of one or more characters. Often, the unity is more subtle. It establishes the almost unnoticed rise and fall of action which distinguishes the play which is "interesting" from the play which appears to be "flat" or "dull."

Strindberg's *Miss Julie,* for example, is a one-act play in one primary scene. This much is stated in the script. But a close examination reveals that the action is divided into a series of sixteen secondary scenes.

One is hardly aware of these divisions when one sees the play for the first time. But from a writer's point of view, it is clear that they establish the structure of the play as significantly as the skeleton determines the human form.

The play contains three characters: Jean, the valet; Julie, his mistress in both senses; and Kristin, the cook. If we let the letters *A, B,* and *C* stand for these three respectively, we can see that there are only four possible combinations of characters on the stage: *ABC, AB, AC,* and *BC.* The actual combinations of characters Strindberg uses for his sixteen scenes is as follows: *AC, ABC, AC, C* (pantomime), *ABC, AB C* (sleeping on stage), *AB, AB* and chorus, chorus alone, *AB, AC, AB, ABC, BC, ABC, AB.* It is not necessary even to have read the play to see from this analysis that the playwright has used every combination of characters available. But those familiar with the play will notice that there is a pattern here. The most important relationship is that between Jean and Julie (*A* and *B*). There are six such scenes. Almost as important is the interrelationships among all three. There are four such scenes. Less important is the relationship between Jean and Kristin. Three scenes are devoted to this. The least significant relationship is Julie and Kristin, and for this we have only one scene. Clearly what appears to be the "natural" and therefore arbitrary coming and going of characters is a carefully controlled exploration of the relationships among three characters. Art has, once again, concealed art.

This kind of analysis can become rather academic—that is, removed from the practical concerns of a practicing playwright. But the fact remains that about eight out of ten unsuccessful student-written plays contain no secondary-scene construction at all. One can see just how serious this failing can be by imagining Strindberg's *Miss Julie* with all three characters on stage for the length of the play in one long, unbroken scene. Looking at this device in positive terms, it is significant that so many successful plays do employ rather complex secondary-scene construction.

Sartre's *No Exit,* for example, is thought of as a one-act play with one scene. The title can be taken theatrically as well as thematically. But even here, each character is brought on singly to provide an *A, AB, ABC* grouping at the start. And then the lack of exits is compensated for by having each character in turn ignore the other two or even feign sleep to provide a sequence of secondary scenes almost as complex as that in *Miss Julie.* This technique is employed just as frequently to subdivide primary scenes within a full-length play, and occasionally it is used as the only subdivision of an entire act. It usually takes a careful reexamination of the script to sort out these secondary scenes.

Entrances and exits are not, obviously, the first consideration of the playwright. No one begins with the premise, "I am going to write a play with three acts each of which is divided into two primary scenes each of which is subdivided into four secondary scenes." Plays are usually conceived from two or more characters in a particular dramatic situation. And in the first draft of writing, scenes are apt to begin and end as the development of plot demands that they do—the way one determines the length of a sentence in first-draft writing.

But with revisions, a thorough understanding of scene construction is not only a practical skill but a necessary one. If, for example, the play seems to "sag" in the middle, the problem may be lack of a dramatic question; it may be a character who has taken to preaching the theme of the play; or it may be that the rhythm of action has been made monotonous by a lack of secondary-scene construction.

And the diagnosis is only the first step. Equally important is the prescription. It is not enough to get a character off stage simply to answer the telephone, to take a nap, or to mix a drink. The exit must be a part of the dramatic fabric. It must be natural enough (that is, credible) so that the playwright's intention does not show through. Sometimes this effect is created simply through preparation: A telephone call is expected, fatigue and need for rest has been shown, thirst or nervous exhaustion has been established. More often, an over-all plan is needed. The ebb and flow of characters is most natural when it appears to be demanded by the plot itself.

Just as the artificially motivated exit is weak, so is the excessively dramatic exit. The exit lines with which Ibsen concluded most of his acts are the sort which we now associate with Hollywood films: We can almost hear that swelling, electronically vibrating chord from the organ. The secondary scene in drama is usually as subtle as the shift from the octave to the sestet in a sonnet or the end of a chapter in a contemporary novel. Once again one must return to the essential fact that art (the work as a whole) should conceal art (the craftsmanship). A good play should be able to convert at least momentarily the best drama critic into an absorbed theatergoer.

Relocation of Characters The second form of dramatic action is the relocation of characters on the stage. Often this is left to the actor or director. Long speeches are broken with a moment of silent pacing; a manic speech (such as in *Richard II*) is dramatized by a leap onto a table; a father's speech about infant-care is punctuated by removing a sopping diaper and silently wringing it dry out the window. The emergence of the director as a collaborator (lamented by such playwrights as Somerset Maugham) allows for all kinds of fundamental revisions simply through action on the stage.

Historically, movement of characters in drama has had some radical changes. The Greeks, who associated drama with a religious service, formalized and stylized almost all movement. The chorus chanted the strophe while progressing across the stage in one direction, and recited the anti-strophe while returning to their original position. Even major characters probably held specific positions, as was the case in grand opera before the reforms of Rudolph Bing and others.

Although the reawakening of drama in England and Europe with the miracle plays was also church connected, there was no link between action and religious ritual itself. Action was as free and natural as it was later in Elizabethan drama, but stage directions were nonexistent. The last attempt to stylize action on the stage (opera and ballet excepted) was the nineteenth-century cut versions of Shakespearean tragedy in which the plays often became a kind of oratorical display.

Only since the advent of play scripts which were intended to be read as well as performed have natural movements of the characters been carefully described by the playwright. What was once left largely to the actor has now been taken over by both the playwright and the director.

The main use of such movement is somewhat similar to exits and entrances. It provides even more subtle divisions of the plot. Long speeches—particularly those which are philosophical and abstract in nature—are deadly if not relieved by some form of action. The same is true of dialogue which on at least one level can be interpreted as idle chatter. The dinner party conversations which Proust strung out with such brilliance for upward to fifty pages in fiction would be hopeless on the stage. The same cleverness, the same insights into character, the same ironies which are used in *Remembrance of Things Past* are simply not enough to hold an audience's attention. The fault does not lie in the audience; the real cause is seen in the fact that one reads fiction two or three times faster than one can speak it, one is free to rest whenever one wants to, and one's favorite reading chair is far more comfortable than a theater seat. All the reasons for including a dramatic question in a play also argue for movement on the stage.

But if this were the sole reason for having characters move about, it would be perfectly acceptable to have random activity, such as endless lighting of cigarettes, going for drinks, or pacing. This is not acceptable simply because meaningless activity is as boring and nondramatic as no activity.

The other function of mobility, then, is statement. That is, the good playwright utilizes action in the same ways he uses dialogue: to further plot, to develop theme, to highlight the dramatic question, and to define character. Each of these deserves a quick examination.

Plot is not thought. It is not intention. It is essentially action. The poetry of Hamlet moves us, but it is his sword thrust through the arras and the poisoned drink drunk and the final duel fought that moves the plot. The monologues of Willy Loman bring us understanding, but it is the theft of a desk pen, the playing of a tape recorder, and the desperate planting of seeds that drives the plot to its culmination. Even in a play as plotless as Beckett's *End Game,* it is the ritualized moving of a stepladder to first one window and then the next that makes up for the lack of coherence in dialogue.

And each of these samples of action on the stage serves equally well to develop both theme and the dramatic question. Fiction can substitute solid blocks of description, thoughts, and even author's reflection for action; drama cannot use these. When action is lacking, the theme and the dramatic question are left almost wholly to dialogue. There are, of course, subtle and indirect ways of having dialogue develop both these aspects, but the tendency for the novice is to force his characters to become philosophers, spouting the significance of life in the most implausible fashion. Action which *implies* aspects of theme and the dramatic question (as does every example given above) is the best safeguard against the "talky" play.

But it is with characterization that action takes on its most subtle role. Lady Macbeth's handwashing is a favorite example, involving both movement on the stage and individual "business," but almost every contemporary play requires either explicitly or implicitly that characters move in a way which reflects both their mood and their character generally.

Sometimes it is enough for the playwright simply to state that this character is "nervous and high-strung," or that one is "phlegmatic." A competent actor can take it from there. But a good playwright visualizes his character speaking each line, and it becomes natural for him to add such directions as "jumps to his feet and throws the book on the table" or "slumps in the chair as if exhausted" or "remains on the couch, feet up, arm dangling throughout the entire scene."

Too often, action is thought of as being necessary only to further plot. This can be avoided only if the playwright has a clear understanding of his character as he is writing the dialogue. One type of character demands high mobility, both in movement about the stage and in individual mannerisms. Another can be developed by taking stances, coupling action with heavy or pompous diction. A third may almost never move, and the lack of action will be in itself significant if played against others who are more lively.

Stage "Business" The term *business,* our third type, is often used to describe any bit of action including mobility on the stage. More specifically, however, it refers to activity which does not involve relocating characters at all: sewing, rearranging hair, biting fingernails, picking nose, scratching ear, examining a shoe, blowing a bugle, worrying a pimple, buttoning and unbuttoning a blouse, adjusting machinery, taunting a caged mouse, ironing shirts, looking for a lost purse, fingering a bottle, holding one's breath, or building a motorized toothpick ferris wheel.

It is an extraordinary fact that a great majority of plays written by college students are wholly devoid of fresh and original stage business. So much time and energy has gone into the theme, the significance of the whole statement, that no imagination is left for those little bits of action which can make a character come alive or save a long scene from sinking with its own weight. So marked is this lack that students who *do* concern themselves with such details find themselves praised for works which in other respects are quite inferior.

Before filling one's script with trivia, however, one should watch out for a number of dangers. *It is very easy to let business become a cliché:* the executive practicing golf swings in his office, the teenager curling around a telephone, the major slapping his riding boots with his riding crop (borrowed, by the way, from Hollywood, not life), or the Italian mother stirring spaghetti. All of these are but one step from the villain curling his mustache. It is much wiser to have the executive showing off his new wire recorder as in *Death of a Salesman,* or the teenager sweeping out a jail as in *Hello Out There,* or the military leader showing off his one-shelf "library" as in *Arms and the Man.* I leave the Italian mother to you.

Stage business often becomes detached from the play itself. This is particularly common in weak scripts which have been doctored with bits of action. Business may be thought of as dramatic seasoning, but it is a poor cook that adds garlic to the ice cream or fudge sauce to the salad. This does not mean that a playwright must be bland. By "detached" I mean unrelated, not unusual. To have Hamlet fondle the skull of a man he once knew is a bizarre bit of stage business, but it is not detached or unrelated to the lines he is speaking, the mood of the scene, or the thematic patterns of the play. He is, after all, discussing mortality and the scene is a light pre-echo of the heavily dramatic grave scene which is to follow. And it is as true a reflection of Hamlet's deep but controlled melancholy as Nora Helmer's dance scene in *A Doll's House* is a reflection of her wily naiveté.

Excessive repetition of the same mannerism is also a danger. Students of literature rarely err in this fashion, but students of television often do. Alfred Hitchcock's works contain excellent examples because this, like all his dramatic techniques, are blatant and undisguised with concerns for theme or characterization. To have a brutal and ruthless character seen clipping and filing his nails periodically might be, in a serious drama, an insight into an ironic aspect of character. But if he engages in this bit of business *every* time he appears, the action no longer suggests character, it *becomes* character. We leave the theater saying "remember the man with the nail clippers?" We remember him not as a man but as a cartoon. Here the technique is no longer a means to an end but an end in itself. Art has not concealed art and we respect the production as great entertainment, which is a compliment to a craftsman but not to a dramatist.

If one avoids these three dangers, there is no limit to the kind of business one can use on the stage. It may serve all the functions discussed under the general heading of relocation of characters, but the primary one is the development of character.

Physical Contact Physical contact between characters is the fourth and final type of action on the stage. It is not, of course, a wholly separate classification. Characters must move about on the stage to prepare for a fight or a kiss. But the contact itself has a dramatic impact which has become a kind of convention in itself. And like all conventions, it has its assets and its dangers.

In most cases, physical contact in drama suggests the ultimate degree of a human relationship. Aggressiveness is pushed, finally, to a fight; hatred culminates in murder; love on the stage must, for cultural reasons, be symbolically consummated with a kiss. These are the fundamental types, and they are seen throughout the entire history of drama. The same human relationships are also treated in poetry and fiction; but it is drama which has most consistently translated them into these visible and often almost stylized forms of physical contact.

Variations in cultural attitudes and the direct insistences of audiences have had, of course, a profound influence on the way drama employs this convention. The Greeks, because they were acting on holy ground, kept violence off stage. And kissing with masks is short of effective. But what they lost in dueling scenes, fist fights, and love scenes they made up for with off-stage combat and reports of love-making.

The Romans and the Elizabethans wanted their physical contact on stage and got it—in ways which appall modern audiences. It is not enough to say simply that Shakespeare's conception of tragedy insisted on the death of a great man. Elizabethan plays are filled with an endless array of physical combat—particularly duelling, stabbing, and choking.

Love was expressed more in terms of language and self-sacrifice partly because the women were played by boys but more significantly because drama was not such an intimate affair as it is for us. Picture, for example, Hamlet's bedroom scene played without a bed or other props under the glare of the afternoon sun. It was not until the theater moved inside, the props were made essential, and the audience was plunged into darkness that the silent embrace and climactic kiss became a really effective bit of dramatic action.

The contemporary audience shows an odd combination of prudery and sophistication. The primary scenes of hatred and violence in Eliot's *The Cocktail Party* and Williams' *Suddenly Last Summer* and *Orpheus Descending* are kept off stage and used dramatically by reference in the tradition of the Greeks. Adults, it is felt, cannot take such extremes of human emotions straight—such undiluted violence must be left to the adolescent horror film.

But serious drama continues to utilize physical contact to express such emotions as aggressiveness, hatred, and love. The real problem for the student-writer is to determine when he has missed a chance of employing the technique and when he has overused it. Although there are no rules as such, it is possible to distinguish physical contact which is organic to the play and that which has been added either as an end in itself or as a means of artificially bolstering an otherwise undramatic play.

A fist fight, for example, is a natural climax for an antagonism which has been building up for a number of scenes. Such varied playwrights as Williams, Miller, and Albee have used them for just this purpose. But they tend to be brief skirmishes, sometimes a single blow. They are not to be confused with the long and elaborate barroom fights which occur with such regularity in Westerns. Sophisticated drama avoids these gymnastic rituals because they provide only the simplest sort of dramatic impact, adding little if any insight into character or theme. Most dramatists find that a single, well-motivated jab to the chin or stomach provides all that is needed without the risk of becoming melodramatic.

The same applies to the love scene. The miles of celluloid Hollywood has contributed to recording the kiss were never intended to provide insight or understanding of the human condition. On the contrary, they were a form of entertainment by means of which the individual could escape into the dark, warm, womb-like confines of the local movie theater. The very basis of this brilliant craftsmanship is contrary to what the playwright as artist is trying to do.

Neither embraces nor fights are employed by the serious dramatist as a come-on, like free dishes on bank night; they are symbolic and emotionally charged aspects of life which can suddenly give us fresh insight or shatter previous assumptions about character or a situation.

The value of such physical contact is apparent. But as I mentioned earlier, the dangers are equally important. The almost overwhelming tendency for the student-writer is to employ action which is either conventional or excessive for the situation—or both. Here is a sample.

> *A college setting:* the protagonist is inwardly worried about his academic work but puts on the guise of sophisticated unconcern. The antagonist, on the other hand, has no desire to be at college, has no internal drive for excellence, but has adopted the guise of the "grind." *The situation:* an all-night study-session in which the "grind" keeps up the pretense by chattering about how much he has to do and by asking questions; the protagonist must adopt the casual approach, but is revealed through conversations home and a few monologues that he is scared and frustrated almost to the point of hysteria. Finally he takes down an ornamental M-1 rifle from the wall and pretends to clean it while his roommate watches and the audience waits grimly for the inevitable. The final, "accidental" blast provides the dramatic climax.

Now there are a number of reasons why this play will probably fail. First, the playwright, if he is a college student himself, is too close to the situation. He has no perspective. Also, although the play suggests some complexity of character, it does not present a naturally dramatic situation. It might have a better chance as a short story than a play. And the final murder, a mechanical version of the fight, is probably more than the play can take; that is, it runs the risk of being melodramatic. True, such murders do occasionally take place in real life; but we are talking about the construction of a one-act play, not case histories.

The real significance of this play—and the thousands of attempts which it represents—is that the potentially melodramatic ending was probably not accidental. If the playwright had a slight suspicion that he was too close to his subject, his natural inclination would be to "make it more dramatic"—which often means more like Tennessee Williams. And if he had doubts about the inherent dramatic qualities of the situation, this would increase his need to provide fireworks at the end. Thus the dramatic ending has not grown from a naturally dramatic situation. It has been added for precisely the opposite reason: to salvage a rather mild situation.

To test your own play you must be willing to ask, "What is the nature of this work?" The answer in this case would have to be, "A mild and rather conventional situation." This might have led him to salvage it by producing a mild, conventional, but perhaps sensitive (or perhaps satiric) short story. And it certainly would have warned him against adding a ruthlessly dramatic ending.

Summing up, we can see that action in a play is not just "what happens." As exits and entrances, it becomes the basic structure of the play through secondary scenes; as movement on the stage, it becomes intimately connected with plot, theme, the dramatic question, and characterization; as individual business, it becomes a particular form of character insight; and as physical contact it becomes a method of establishing emphasis.

One should be aware of all this while writing the first draft of a play. But the time for a really thorough evaluation of the demands and the potentials of dramatic action is during the rewriting. This is the time for comparing the nature of the work as written with the intention and the ideal. These are questions which will continue to be important even after actual production.

It is possible to write a play with almost no action. It is also possible to produce a painting with only two shades of white. Action is an essential part of the play not simply because tradition has decreed it. The genre demands it. "I *saw* a good play," we say, and quite unconsciously we state that visual effects are fundamental in this art form.

25

VISUAL EFFECTS—SET AND COSTUME

The *set defined;* the *realistic* set; the *expressionistic* set; the *combination* set; the *bare stage; costuming* analyzed, including realistic, expressionistic, and street dress; *lighting* effects; the playwright's *visual imagination.*

The term *set* is used here to include everything the audience sees excluding the actors themselves. Its greatest impact comes at the very beginning of the play: The house lights dim, the curtain rises, and the audience is plunged into a wholly new world. In this instant, even before the first line is spoken, the audience is preparing itself on the basis of what it sees for high tragedy, for comedy, for a realistic social problem, or for the mystery of a dream sequence.

As the play develops, action, dialogue, and the impact of the plot take over the audience's major interest. But the set—combined with lighting and costume—continues to influence the tone and the mood of the play.

There are three main approaches to set designing: realism, expressionism, and bare staging. Although there are no precise lines dividing these three, each has its own unique characteristics. More important, each has separate advantages and disadvantages. If the playwright does not decide fairly early which vehicle is most appropriate for the particular play he is engaged in, he will not be able to visualize his scenes as he writes. Worse, he cannot develop the full potential of any one approach.

Realistic

Sets The realistic set is so common today that we tend to think of it as the traditional approach. But it is interesting to note that if the 2,500-year history of drama were seen as a week, the length of time dramatists have even considered the realistic set would come to an insignificant half-hour. And already many dramatists have dropped it as too limited.

If we look at the realistic set with some historical perspective, we can see that, although it is not the only approach, it has offered and continues to offer the dramatist a valuable vehicle for his work.

When Ibsen's plays were first introduced to England in the late nineteenth century, the audiences gasped with amazement at the sight of a perfectly reproduced living-room scene, complete with real books in bookcases, real portraits on the walls, and doors that opened and shut. Soon the stage directions for the plays of Barrie and Shaw began to reflect this new realism by including the most minute descriptions—even to the title of a book left "carelessly" on a coffee table.

But the contemporary playwright cannot hope to impress the audience with such a device. This is, after all, an age when television can produce the Atlantic Ocean complete with gulls and a luxury liner for a drama lasting only three minutes, merely to suggest that a particular brand of cigarette is not harmful to the lungs.

Clearly no set designer can hope to make his stage look more realistic than a film shot of the real thing. It is naive to try. Nor should he compete by using tricks. Opera never became more realistic by bringing live horses and even elephants on the stage. A play called *The Kidders* was not made more realistic by having the protagonist shoot a bottle of whiskey from its perch on the newel. (For three successive nights the pin in the post, which was to crack the bottle as the gun fired a blank, failed to operate. On the fourth night the play itself failed.)

But the realistic set has not been abandoned. When it is used with skill and imagination it can establish the tone and even add to the thematic content of a play. Here are four examples of plays which have made creative use of a strictly realistic set.

T. S. Eliot's *The Cocktail Party* concerns characters who are members of the British upper-class society. Although the theme of the play is in no way limited to this group, our understanding of their attitudes, their values, their humor, and their immediate problems depend on identifying them socially. The set could consist of an unimaginatively designed living room with the usual indications of affluence. In the New York production, however, a side table with silver tray, glasses, ice bucket, and liquor bottles became a glittering focal point. And the last bottle, the one nearest the audience, was Vat 69, the only good Scotch on the market with a label large enough to be read from the balcony.

Part of this was suggested in the original script. Further, the side table is used repeatedly in stage directions. The set designer made full use of the directions by selecting objects which glittered and caught the eye. This is "realism" in that nothing has been blatantly distorted from what we might expect to see in an actual living room of this sort. But it is a creative and imaginative use of realism.

Tennessee Williams makes use of the same sort of focal point in his play *Period of Adjustment.* Here the characters clearly represent the middle class. The focal object is a television set. Because it is often on, it is placed with its back to the audience, upstage center. This way the characters can watch it, can comment on it while speaking toward the audience.

But the creative and imaginative use of the traditional set is not limited to selecting a significant focal point. In Robert Anderson's play, *Tea and Sympathy,* the mood of a boarding school master's living room is caught with a clutter of significant details, from dark woodwork to the furnishings themselves. And the playwright included at stage left a stairway whose primary function was to allow students to run up and down on their way from classes to their dormitory. This periodic thundering of feet was extraordinarily effective in suggesting a kind of restless energy among the students which was directly, though subtly, connected with the theme of the play.

In the recent adaptation of James' *The Aspern Papers,* the audience applauded the set before the first line was spoken. This response was not wonder at its "realism," but at the degree to which the set caught the decaying elegance of a Venetian living room. Here again it was the sum total of details like tall windows, peeling green wall paint, and faded tiles that created the mood.

Each of these sets could, of course, be dramatically reproduced in film. And the camera would have added the further dimension of exterior setting. But the roving eye of the camera loses one advantage that the stage offers: concentration on a single set of objects. The side table in *The Cocktail Party* would appear in any filmed version of that play, but it would be seen only momentarily in the great collection of scenes. Because the play is usually limited to one or two sets, each physical detail the playwright or the set designer decides to use becomes magnified in the minds of the audience. It is this concentration of attention in the stage play that makes even the realistic set a creative challenge and an opportunity.

Expressionistic Sets The basis of the expressionistic set is distortion. Its function, in most cases, is psychological realism. Just as Kafka created fantasies in fiction which were as "real" as the most vivid nightmares, so did such playwrights as Elmer Rice and Eugene O'Neill in drama. One of the best examples is Rice's *The Adding Machine.* More will be said about this play in the next chapter, but it is worth noting here some of the expressionistic devices as they apply to set design.

The protagonist, a Mr. Zero, is a pathetic cipher of a man whose world is dominated by the endless clutter of figures from his job as bookkeeper. The first scene, his bedroom, could be presented by means of a realistic set. We all know the kind of details which would suggest such a man. But Rice's expressionistic set calls for a room wallpapered with a vast collection of numbers ready for addition, subtraction, or division. In a sense, Rice is shifting the objective means of perception, which is traditional in drama, to Zero himself. We see the room as he sees it.

The same technique is used in the set described by O'Neill in *The Hairy Ape.* As Yank, the brutish representative of the lowest social order, passes an elegant jewelry store, he sees the price tags with magnified importance. And we don't have to take his word for it through what he says; we can actually see the price tags from our seat in the second balcony. Here again the set has become the view of the character himself.

O'Neill pushed this technique even further in *Emperor Jones,* where the flight of the Negro leader through the jungle (and symbolically back through the levels of civilization) becomes a true nightmare which the audience most readily accepts as "real." The only way this play could be rewritten realistically would be for film production. But even with all the technical realism of the Florida Everglades as background, one would not achieve exactly the kind of identification with this character as one does from the stage version as O'Neill wrote it.

The term *expressionism* can also be applied to those works which have recently and somewhat illogically been called Theater of the Absurd. This is a point which I will develop in the next chapter. I should mention here, however, that the sets which have been used for the plays of Ionesco and some of Albee are highly expressionistic. The room in *The Chairs,* for example, is completely surrounded with doors, and the "home" for the old parents in *End Game* consists of two ash cans.

Expressionistic sets can, of course, be used in plays which were not written for them. Shakespearean tragedies, for example, lend themselves to experimental set designing particularly well because the playwright was never limited by the demands of visual realism. In 1955 in a London production of *King Lear,* the sculptor Noguchi made dramatic use of the symbolic set: The stage was bare except for a number of multisided triangular and rectangular forms some thirty feet in height. Each side was a different color so that by rearranging the forms for each scene, they were made to suggest a palace scene, a forest scene, or "another part of the forest" in a matter of seconds. And because of the varied colors, the mood of a scene could be changed simply by revolving the forms.

The dangers of the expressionistic set are similar to those inherent in expressionism itself. If used carelessly, it can add obscurity to an already clouded play. In this respect, it is like free verse. The very freedom often leads to pure expression (as opposed to communication), which no matter how interesting or original, is something less than art. The other danger is that the technique itself can become so emphasized that the audience cannot accept the production as anything more than a technician's stunt. There will always be musicians who insist on playing the "Flight of the Bumblebee" on a trumpet, poets who will write poems without the letter "e," and playwrights whose expressionistic devices serve only to dramatize a private nightmare; but the experimenters we remember, like Rice, Strindberg, O'Neill, and more recently, Beckett, Ionesco, Pinter, and Noguchi, use technique as a means of developing the artistic creation as a whole.

Combination

Sets I am using the word *combination* in two senses here. First, it combines two or more scenes on the stage at the same time—usually two or more rooms of a house or an interior and an exterior portion of a home. Second, it combines aspects of the realistic set with those of the expressionistic set.

In *Death of a Salesman,* for example, we are shown an upstairs room, two rooms downstairs, and a portion of the yard outside. It is realistic in that the rooms themselves are fairly accurate representations of what we would expect in real life. Yet it is expressionistic in the sense that the audience must use its imagination in separating what is outside from what is inside. An *actor* in the kitchen can obviously see what another actor is doing outside; but it is soon made clear that a *character* must come to the "door" in order to see. This is not as complicated as it seems when one remembers that children at the beach can work the same magic with a "house" which consists only of lines drawn in the sand.

A more extreme use of the split stage is seen in William Ritman's set designed for Harold Pinter's *The Collection.* Working closely with the director, Alan Schneider, and the playwright, Ritman managed to present the illusion of three entirely separate scenes on the relatively small stage of the Cherry Lane Theatre in New York. I have included illustrations (drawn by Richard Tuttle) because it is such an excellent example of what can be done with an imaginative combination of realistic and expressionistic techniques.

When the lighting emphasizes what to the audience is the left side of the stage, we are in a sparse, modern living room. Simply by shifting the lights, however, we are moved to an elegant living room which, because the furnishings are so different, suggests an entirely different mode of living. There is no question in the mind of the audience that these two portions of the stage represent two entirely different homes. Beyond this, there is a third area represented: an outside scene with a telephone booth which is, in our imagination, separated spatially from either home. When this is lit, the audience moves to a third scene as easily as if the curtain had been lowered and the stage crew had worked for a frantic fifteen minutes to break down one set and build a new one.

This is more than a trick. It represents the combined imaginations of playwright, director, and set designer working under the influence of what I referred to in Chapter 21 as respect for the stage. It is solid proof that what is called "the limitations of the stage" is no more limiting for some than were the constrictions of the sonnet form for Shakespeare.

The Bare Stage When Thornton Wilder's *Our Town* was first produced, the use of the bare stage was greeted as a fairly new approach in theater. The use of two stepladders and a board connecting them suggested a house even to an audience not used to this kind of symbolic representation. And it added to the mood of a simple, small American town in ways an elaborate set could not.

But like so many experiments in theater, it was based on a very old tradition. The Elizabethan audience was perfectly prepared to use its imagination to visualize the rapid succession of scenes in Shakespearean plays. What Wilder did was simply to force the audience to use its "inner eye" in somewhat the same way as did writers of radio drama.

Picasso's extraordinary play, *Desire,* did equally well with a stage containing only a bench. In the off-Broadway production of this play, the director did not even use a curtain for a backdrop, preferring instead the brick wall of the theater itself.

The advantage of the bare stage is that it directs the whole at-

The Collection, showing emphasis on the modern apartment, with other areas dark.

The Collection, showing emphasis on the telephone booth, which is, in the play, some distance from either home.

The Collection, showing emphasis on the ornate apartment, with the other areas dark.

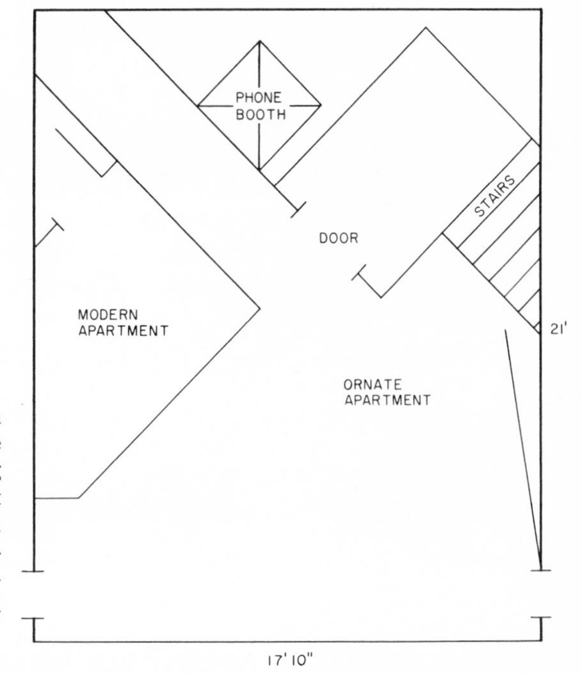

The Collection: a diagram of the stage, showing the technique of representing three entirely different scenes simply by shifts in lighting. Note how the unusual angles add both variety and depth even on a small stage.

tention of the audience to the actors themselves and to the lines spoken. This concentration of attention is particularly desirable in plays like Shakespeare's in which the language itself is often complex, filled with verbal nuances and, particularly in his comedies, a variety of puns. In the case of *Desire*, the language was important for an immediate and political reason: It was an anti-Nazi play made sufficiently complex so that the French audience of occupied Paris could catch the wit, laughing and applauding, while the German officials sat in bewildered and infuriated silence.

But the technique has been used sparingly in this century. There is so much that can be done with sets either realistically or symbolically that the bare stage is apt to be a limitation rather than an addition. It is a bit like writing free verse without the use of assonance.

The playwright who is considering the bare stage as a set should make sure that he is not doing it simply to be different. If he can analyze exactly how his play will be a fuller, richer performance by the lack of visual effects, then he is well justified in selecting this approach.

Costuming The playwright normally leaves the details of costuming to the director of a particular performance. But there are three different approaches which he should consider before he writes even the first line of dialogue: Are the costumes to be period, symbolically significant, or merely street clothes? These choices correspond roughly to the division of realism, expressionism, and bare staging already discussed.

The great majority of plays specify in the introduction that the costumes are of the period and are true to nationality and class. Certain differences, of course, can be suggested on the basis of personality. But the pattern remains: Most realistic plays employ realistic costumes.

Realistic costuming is also often used in highly expressionistic plays. Yank in *The Hairy Ape*, for example, normally wears just what one would expect a stoker on a coal-burning steamship to wear; Zero in *The Adding Machine* dresses as he would in a realistic play about accountants.

Symbolic or what might be called expressionistic costuming has been used only occasionally, but the effect is often striking. In

Desire, for example, the heroine wears pink tights with a black garter belt to suggest nudity. Hamlet, in the play *Hamlet of Stepney Green*, wears a silk blouse during the mad scene to suggest homosexuality. But one of the most original and successful uses of symbolic costuming was employed in the London production of *King Lear* already discussed.

Lear first appears in a flowing costume which, although it suggests no period and no particular country, is clearly regal. And it is decorated with a pattern which vividly resembles the distinctive peacock's tail complete with rainbow-colored eyelike spots. The symbolic association between the proud King Lear and the peacock is both startling and completely natural, but it is only a beginning. In the next scene the costume is so similar that the audience hardly notices that the center portion, the "eyes," of the design are no longer a part of the cloth itself; they are small holes. This is the point in the play when Lear's pride first begins to damage his position.

In the next scene, these holes have grown noticeably. And with each succeeding scene the costume seems to fall apart progressively as if some acid were working its way into the fabric. When Lear's ruin is absolute and he has at last been stripped of all pride, his costume has dissolved into great loops of dung-colored rags. At this point in the play, one remembers the Lear of Act I and has the distinct impression of having seen a man go through a lifetime. Rarely has costuming in any production created such an effect on the audience.

Street clothes are more commonly associated with readings rather than full productions. Like the bare stage, it is an easier approach and a less expensive one. One of the more famous productions, however, was Orson Welles' adaptation of Shakespeare's *Julius Caesar* in 1937. The modern dress in that case helped to draw a comparison between Caesar and Mussolini.

Lighting Lighting is the newest of all dramatic techniques. The Greeks depended on the sun and so did the Elizabethans. And from the time of the first enclosed theaters in the late sixteenth century until 1914, lighting consisted of a glare of footlights designed simply to illuminate actors.

In 1914 the first spotlights were hung on the balcony rail of

Wallack's Theater in New York. It is a sad fact that a good number of Broadway theaters have made no major improvements since then.

An increasing number of colleges and universities, however, have followed the lead of the Yale University theater by installing multistage light-control systems. Such equipment allows the operator to set up a combination of lights on one "bank" and then, on cue, let that combination take over automatically while he arranges the next scene on the other bank. In addition to ease of control, these lighting boards offer the widest range of color, intensity, and angle.

Returning to the playwright, there is no point in including extensive directions for lighting effects if the play is being written without any particular stage in mind. But the number of plays which are written for college competitions with the hope of production in a specific modern theater is growing every year. For this lucky group, lighting should be considered as important a visual effect as costume and most certainly should be included in the script.

The three factors which must be kept in mind are color, intensity, and angle. Little can be said about any one of these without taking the other two into account. Orange, for example, is a soft light and ideal for a gentle scene. Yet an orange light beamed from directly overhead gives the actor a demoniac look. Low intensity (that is, a dim stage) can lend itself to, say, a love scene if the angle is normal and the coloring on the warm side; but the same low intensity becomes eerie and grotesque if the light is flat-white and from above.

Undergraduates at Bowdoin College when working for the first time with an excellent light board were soon able to utilize a constantly shifting lighting arrangement to augment their own plays. The effect of blue hues shifting imperceptibly to red as an argument grows in intensity is extraordinarily similar to that of background music in cinema. Like music, it can be easily overdone. But like slant rhyme in poetry and stream of consciousness in fiction, it has become a part of the genre and adds immeasurably to it.

In addition to these effects, lighting also serves as a practical aid when the split set is being used. As pointed out earlier, several scenes can be suggested on the stage at the same time, as was done in *Death of a Salesman* and *The Collection*. This is a matter of set design. But lighting is also important here as a means of shifting the attention of the audience from one room to another or from an inside to an outside scene.

Occasionally it may be necessary to leave a character or even several characters in a darkened section of the stage. In the script it may seem rather artificial to have people "frozen" in positions of conversation while the play goes on elsewhere on the same stage. But audiences readily accept this convention and "forget" those left in dim light as readily as they have already "forgotten" those sitting next to them.

Like so many aspects of drama, lighting is not primarily a means of creating reality; it is one more convention which, if used with imagination and craftsmanship, can heighten the illusion which is so appropriately called *a play*.

The Playwright's Visual Imagination Most of the weaknesses in unsuccessful play scripts can be attributed to the fact that the playwright has read more plays than he has seen. Put more directly, he writes a play as if its primary purpose was to be read.

This lack of visual imagination can lead to both sins of commission and sins of omission. He can, for example, clutter his stage or require superhuman set changes for no good reason or ask for impossible tricks. It was an almost classic sin of commission on the part of my freshman who ended the final scene of his adaptation of *Winesburg, Ohio* with the stage direction: "Our hero takes one last look at the town and then hops on the rear of a moving freight train."

But the sins of omission are almost worse, for they do not stand out clearly. They cannot be laughed at. We finish the play with the vague feeling that it lacked "dramatic punch." The playwright may point out that he has had a man die of cancer and his sister pass into a catatonic fit, but such incidents are elements of plot and not necessarily samples of action. If the stage is not kept alive with meaningful things to see, the play may well be in danger.

There are, of course, plays which run this danger without ruin. But these are as rare as successful poems without assonance or novels without chapter divisions.

Drama has always appealed to the eye. Contemporary drama offers a wide range of possibilities both in the movement of actors, such as was discussed in the previous chapter, and in the use of the set, costumes, and lighting. If the playwright is to fulfill the potential of his art, he must master the ability to *see* each scene, each instant of his play, as he writes and reviews his own work.

26

REALISM AND EXPRESSIONISM

Realism in drama defined; aspects of *illusion* in realism; *expressionism* defined; the dangers of *false realism, fraudulent expressionism,* and *awkward blending* of the two techniques; two methods of *blending* realism and expressionism; *common objectives* in both approaches.

In the last chapter I used the terms *realistic* and *expressionistic* to describe differing approaches to set design and costuming. But the distinction between *realism* and *expressionism* deserves further examination, for it establishes the very premise on which the playwright bases every phase of his work from the original conception down to the final script.

In spite of their importance, these terms are frequently misunderstood. Realism in drama is not "real" nor is expressionism "unreal." They are both forms of dramatic illusion. But the techniques of establishing this illusion—the conventions used—are significantly different, and no playwright can afford to confuse the two.

Dramatic realism in its simplest sense means the technique of presenting the various aspects of the play, such as the set, the action, and the dialogue, so that they seem to reflect what we might see and hear in real life. Expressionism, on the other hand, is essentially the use of purposeful and overt distortion. Each of these approaches deserves careful study.

To be specific, the realistic set is one which appears to be taken directly from the physical world as we see it. As described in the previous chapter, it once surprised audiences with its ingenious fidelity to their environment; now it makes us feel "at home." When an audience applauds a realistic set, it is responding to an immediate sense of "being there." The visual details are familiar.

Further, realistic dialogue is that which appears to echo what we might expect to hear from a character of a particular type and background. We may be surprised at what a character says, but we are able to "justify" the statement on the same basis that we "make sense" of what our friends say in daily life.

This also applies to realistic action. We evaluate it just as we interpret actions in real life. When we say that a character's behavior lacks motivation, we imply that characters on the stage ought to echo the patterns of behavior which we are used to seeing in daily life. If one character slaps another, for example, we ask "Why?" The answer may not be given at that point in the play, but we assume that it will be given before the final curtain.

More basic than this, we insist that a realistic play not violate what are assumed to be the natural laws of the universe. Imagine a final act of *Death of a Salesman* in which Willy Loman departs in a chariot drawn by three dragons. Our taboo against a *deus ex machina*—a forced invention of any sort—is nothing more than a generally accepted convention.

I am using the word *realism* here as a purely descriptive term —not historical. It is in this sense that the distinction between the two poles, realism and expressionism, is so important to the practicing playwright. There are, however, two other uses of the term which should be mentioned here merely for the sake of clarity. The first refers to a school in fiction, and the second to a short-lived historical development in drama. The following diagram is designed to clarify this frequently misunderstood term and to show the relationship between the two traditional uses (numbers 1 and 2) and the definition which I am using in this text (number 3).

1. "Realism" as used in fiction is both an historical and descriptive term:

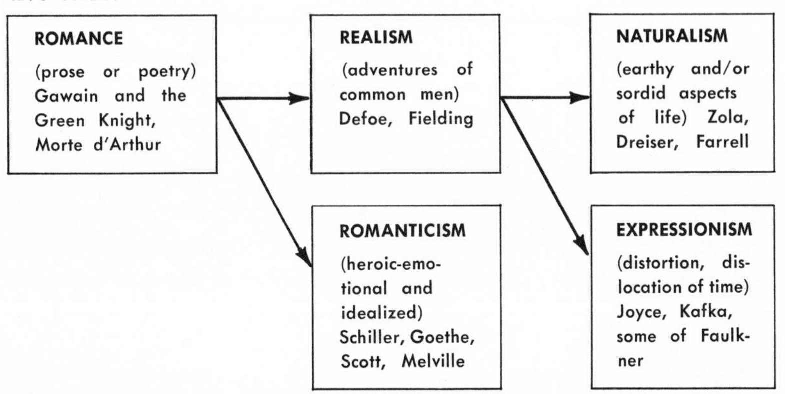

2. "Realism" as used in drama has also been used in both an historical and descriptive sense:

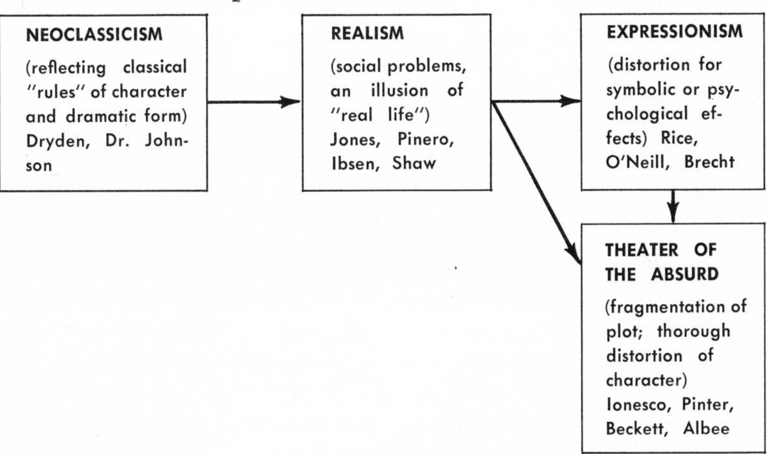

3. "Realism" as applied to drama in this text is a purely descriptive term which simply refers to characteristics which are the antithesis of expressionism:

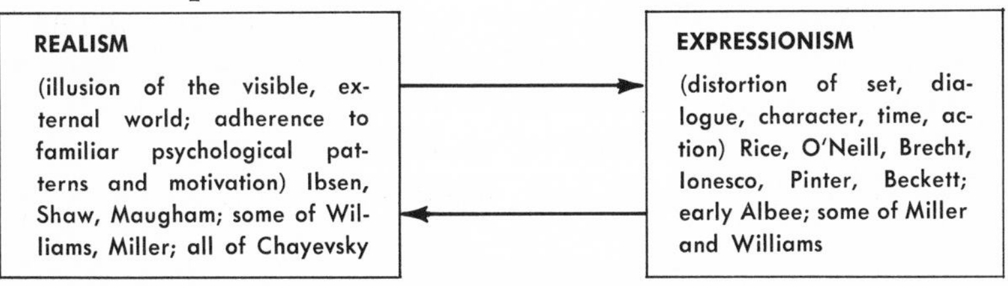

Concentrating on realism in this third sense, it is essential to stress the word "illusion." Regardless of whether we are dealing with the set, dialogue, or action, we must qualify the relationship between realistic drama and real life with such phrases as "appears to be" or "creates the illusion of." No matter how "real" a play may appear to be, it is still a set of conventions and an illusion.

The "realistic" living-room set referred to in the previous chapter contained only three walls. Such a room in real life would be grotesque; we accept it as "real" only because we have accepted the illusion as a valid representation of the familiar world. This is essentially the same psychological process by which we accept a highly representational (realistic) painting while at the same time knowing that it is merely a display of pigments on a flat surface.

Dialogue is discussed in more detail in Chapter 27, but it is worth noting here that it too is only an illusion of reality. Just as the volume and clarity of the actor's words is a clear departure from normal behavior in the home, so the speech patterns and the subject matter create only an illusion of real conversations. By way of specific example, notice our willingness to accept the "stage whisper" as if it were a real whisper in spite of the fact that it can be heard even by those at the rear of the second balcony. Or contrast the clarity of syntax in the speeches of such supposedly inarticulate characters as Willy Loman or Stanley Kowalski with the verbal confusion which is so evident in the transcripts of presidential press conferences. Or contrast the thematic unity in the dialogue during, say, the supper scene in Miller's *A View from the Bridge* with the chaos of themes and significance at even the most sophisticated dinner party you have ever talked your way through.

And even more than in the case of sets or dialogue, realistic action is only an illusion of what happens in the great jumble of activity we call life. As I have pointed out in Chapter 24, such action as exits and entrances, mobility on the stage, and even simple mannerisms and gestures must be carefully contrived to create a desired effect. They are "realistic" in that they *appear* to follow patterns of chance and normal motivation such as we are used to seeing in daily life.

Expressionism, on the other hand, employs a set of conventions which are purposeful and overt distortions of what we would expect to see or hear in real life. That is, for particular effects, certain aspects of the play are clear departures from the patterns we are used to, and these departures are recognized by the audience.

As noted earlier, we must accept realism as including certain distortions also; but they are covert. The key to expressionism is the fact that variations from the visible and audible world about us are made overt. We recognize the distortions as distortions *and cast about for a new system of logic.*

The clearest illustration of the various degrees and approaches to expressionism can be seen in set design. When O'Neill insisted that the price tags on the jewelry in a store window be made large enough to be read from the back of the theater, he was employing a distortion which could not be missed by the audience. The rest of the set was intended to be fairly realistic; but this one detail, reflecting the inner view of the character, was expressionistic. It is only a matter of degree which separates this scene from the one in Beckett's *End Game* where we see two characters living permanently in two ash cans. The logic in both cases is not based on a direct relationship with the visible world. O'Neill's price tags employ the logic of a metaphor. Beckett's play, like Kafka's novels, draws us into a wholly new world. His is the logic of a dream. Were *End Game* realistic in other respects, we would necessarily assume that the two ash can dwellers are insane. But given a new set of logical relationships, we take them to be parents dumped (metaphorically) like useless objects.

The same applies to dialogue. When Uncle Ben in *Death of a Salesman* actually comes on stage we are not being asked to believe in ghosts nor are we forced to consider Willy insane. These are the only alternatives if we insist that the play literally follow the logic of "real life." But it is also "real life" for sane people to think of themselves as talking with a figment of their imagination, and it is only mildly odd for us to allow this talk to become audible. When we see Uncle Ben actually standing there, we accept the premise that we are in Willy Loman's mind, viewing the scene as he does. Ben's portion of the dialogue is merely the dramatic version of the metaphor we use when we say "He argued with himself." Unconsciously we have begun with the simile, "He thought *as if* he were two people," and then translated the concept into a metaphor. Ben is this metaphor made visible and audible.

The same technique is extended and made the central device in Ionesco's *The Chairs*. Here the imaginary characters far outnumber the two visible characters on stage. Were this play realistic, we would have to take it as a psychological study of two utterly insane people. But the logic of the play insists that we take this symbolically; their castle in the middle of the sea is the sort of isolation many sane people feel their lives to be, and their "friends" are reflections of their needs and hopes and illusions.

These examples of expressionistic dialogue necessarily include expressionistic action. Willy Loman is not seen sleeping in a chair when Uncle Ben comes on stage because this is not a literal suggestion of a dream; he walks over to Uncle Ben and has his boys run out to meet him as well simply because it is not a dream. It is "real" in the sense that K.'s struggle to gain entrance into the castle is real, in the sense that the old couple's desire to please their "guests" in *The Chairs* is real.

From a writer's point of view, then, expressionism is not a literary period to be studied as an extinct phase of drama. It is one of two poles which present the playwright with a wide variety of techniques. On the one hand, we may rely primarily on the illusion of life as we perceive it, complete with certain expectations in motivation, character, and visual relationships. Or, on the other hand, we may employ some other system of logic, such as metaphors or purely symbolic relationships. Thus, realism and expressionism are as far apart as are a waking experience and a dream experience. In artistic terms, they are as removed from each other as the paintings of Hopper and Wyeth are from those of Picasso and Chagall.

Distinct as they are, it is a mistake to consider them mutually exclusive. The entrance of Uncle Ben in *Death of a Salesman* is an expressionistic device, yet whole scenes of that play are rendered as realistically as Ibsen's. The price tags and certain bits of action in *The Hairy Ape* are expressionistic, yet the opening scene in the boiler room of an ocean liner was commended for its high realism by oilers and stokers who saw the play. There are extreme cases of each approach: *End Game* is in its very essence expressionistic, whereas *Tea and Sympathy* is truly realistic—but a great many contemporary dramas make use of both techniques, and with those we must use the two terms as adjectives rather than as categorical nouns.

To this point I have been concerned with definition. Application is another matter. The first step in learning how to apply these or any other dramatic techniques is reading or seeing as many plays as possible. This is a truism, of course, but it is alarming how many students try to write drama on the basis of three Shakespearean tragedies, two Shavian comedies, and one televized version of Ibsen. No degrees of genius and no writing course, and certainly no text can even begin to substitute for a reasonable saturation in drama itself.

Assuming this background has been achieved, we can go on to three basic difficulties which are the most common causes of failure in this particular aspect of drama: false realism, fraudulent expressionism, and awkward blending of the two techniques.

False realism takes the form of stock characters, hackneyed dialogue, and conventional situations. It is rooted in a misunderstanding about the nature of realism. Take, for example, a play about a hard-driving businessman who has sacrificed love, loyalty, and ethics for material success. The first act shows him at work: an office scene in which he beats the old and honest board chairman out of fifty thousand shares, raises money through a shady character with underworld connections, and persuades an innocent but wealthy widow to support his scheme. For complexity, an honest but beautiful personal secretary is added whose function is to suggest "the right way" in hard-boiled terms. "Jim baby," she is made to say periodically, "you look great when you're riding high, but one of these days this whole thing is going to blow up right in your face."

The second act is a living-room set where Jim baby has to deal with his faithful, sad-faced wife and pampered son. We are given the impression that things are not going well on the home front. The climax is reached when we discover that this is their anniversary and he has, of course, forgotten all about it. With infinite charm Jim baby gets the diamond encrusted brooch he had intended to give the secretary and presents it to his wife. Unfortunately, the gift is inscribed with the secretary's name, and the act ends with tears (hers) and a vacant stare (his) suggesting some dim awakening of his conscience.

Act III is, of course, back at the office. Events have moved too fast and too far for Jim baby to back out. The underworld character closes in for the kill, the secretary calls the D. A. in a fit of conscience, the innocent widow turns out to be a federal agent, and the board chairman dies of a heart attack. Final scene: Jim is alone on the stage, tie undone, sitting in the director's chair at three in the morning, fingering his pearl-handled revolver. "Jim baby" he mutters to himself, smiling at the high irony of it all. The lights dim. "Bang!"

When scripts like this are presented in creative-writing courses, they are defended as "realistic." When they reach Broadway—which they do about once a season—they are advertised as "stark realism." But in what sense are they "real"?

We can't attack the basic situation as incredible because we know that real ambition can drive real people to suicide. But when we look at this play and examine the characters and this particular sequence of events, it is clear that we are not witnessing the illusion of reality; we are taking part in a ritual. Like the Western and the slick-fiction love story, this performance is true, not to the external world, but to the ritualized pattern of the form itself. It is far more narrow than religious ritual since it is confined to making a single and specific moral point, and it is far more rigid than ballet in that most subtleties and variations from the basic form are forbidden.

As soon as we see our hero placed in the business world and making ruthless decisions, we know what the outcome will be. And we know too what the moral point will be. We settle back in our seats, comfortable in the knowledge that this will not really disturb our sensitivities or our consciences.

There are as many formulas in drama as there are in fiction. But no amount of mechanical tinkering will make the formula drama true realism. In each case, it is fidelity to the pattern itself that dictates the action and the dialogue. True realism as defined at the beginning of this chapter involves the illusion of reality. Willy Loman in *Death of a Salesman* is "realistic" not because he echoes a formularized pattern of lower-middle-class-urban-American, and not even because he resembles actual people we have met, but because we have the illusion of dealing with a real person whom we have never met before. The play does contain elements which are also found in formula drama—there is an infidelity with shattering results, there is an ambitious-insensitive character, and there is a frustration-suicide final act. But they are imbedded in a situation which is convincing enough to include us as if this were an extension of our own lives.

Fraudulent expressionism has different origins, but the result is just as insulting to the audience as false realism. It usually springs, not from a respect for such playwrights as Strindberg, Ionesco, Albee, Beckett, and the like, but from a deep suspicion and dislike. The student, baffled and resentful of what he has not bothered to study carefully, mutters darkly, "Any idiot could write a play like that," and then sets out to prove it.

His first step is to find a bizarre setting—preferably down deep somewhere. He knows that cellars have been used by Beckett and Pinter (though he has never asked why), so he settles for a well-furnished mine shaft or a bomb shelter or a cave or the furnace room of an abandoned lunatic asylum or the cargo hold of a freighter which is moving through eternity without a crew.

Now that he has depth, he adds variety of character. He does this by selective aberrations: a hunchback, a harelip, a stutterer, and perhaps one whose eyes are constantly fixed upward, vaguely suggesting either Christ or the unpardonable sinner.

All that is left is the dialogue. There are various techniques of imitation in this area, but the most important involve discussing all serious subjects with hilarious wit and all inconsequential problems with intense profundity. No question can be answered directly, of course, and whenever possible characters should respond with emotions roughly opposite to what the audience might expect.

Picture, then, an opening scene in which our hunchback and our harelip are watering sunflowers, being careful not to step on their prone friend, a corpse.

> HUNCHBACK: "I never did like blue. Not even as a child."
> HARELIP: (to the corpse) "Where's my shoe?"
> HUNCHBACK: "But my mother insisted I was color-blind."
> HARELIP: "Hasn't *any*one seen my shoe?"
> HUNCHBACK: "So at the age of six she had me shipped off to the army. No one told her there was a war on."
> HARELIP: (beginning to cry) "Even a shoe*horn* would help."
> CORPSE: (significantly) "Why don't you two get married?"

This is one kind of drama which is more fun to write than to read. Worse, it is frustrating for anyone who attempts to take it seriously. No matter how complex a highly expressionistic play may be, we make the assumption that there is a symbolic language used which, with effort, can be mastered. As during our first month learning a foreign language, we take on faith the fact that there is order and an internal set of relationships which will eventually reward our effort. And this *is* the case in the most difficult plays from Strindberg to Ionesco. It is *not* the case in what I am referring to here as fraudulent expressionism.

Expressionism, then, is not Dadaism. It is not an abandonment of form, of meaning, or of intent. It offers to the playwright new forms, new methods of communicating meaning, and maintains essentially the same intent as realistic drama.

Blending the techniques of realism and expressionism presents one of the most complex problems in drama. When it is done awkwardly, we have the feeling that somehow two versions of the same play have been included in a single script—a kind of literary double exposure. And it is easy enough to tell the playwright that he must make up his mind, that he must use one convention or the other. But the advice is not fair, for there are too many successful plays which do combine the two conventions and do it very well.

This technique of blending the two is clearly seen in such plays as O'Neill's *The Hairy Ape,* Miller's *Death of a Salesman,* Eliot's *The Cocktail Party,* and Pinter's *The Caretaker.* But two different methods are involved: The first two plays link the distortions to the mind of a single character, whereas the second two simply slide in easy stages from an as-if-real situation to one which moves beyond into a symbolic logic.

As mentioned earlier in this chapter, *The Hairy Ape* begins with a highly realistic setting and situation. We are not made aware of any significant departure from this level of realism until the protagonist, Yank, sees the price tags in the jewelry store window and, later in that same scene, when he tries to strike a man of wealth and finds that he cannot even touch him. The invisible wall between Yank and men of means and power is symbolic as a general statement; but, more significant, it reflects Yank's personal view of the world. In essence, this is a technique of bringing point of view to the stage.

The same is true of Willy in *Death of a Salesman.* Every departure from what we call realism springs directly from the way Willy looks at the world or remembers past events. Every other character is seen externally through dialogue and action; this one character is seen internally through his own private interpretation of the world about him. The novelist does the same when he writes in the third person with the means of perception limited to a single character.

This first technique of blending realism and expressionism, then, depends on exploring the inner life of a single character. All physical action and dialogue of other characters not seen through the protagonist's own eyes are treated realistically. The audience makes the transition easily, drawing from the tradition of limited perception in fiction.

This is not so in the case of *The Cocktail Party* and *The Caretaker,* however. Like the other two plays, these open with a set and a situation which might easily suggest realism, but the situation slides away from realism in a much broader way. We begin to notice details which cannot be explained in realistic terms. Our first reaction may be "What's going on here?" In the case of *The Cocktail Party*, we are asked to accept the presence of spiritual "guardians" who look over the destiny of individuals like highly anthropomorphized gods. It is a minor distortion, and the play ends on a realistic level. Pinter pushes this same technique much further, sliding us into a world which is almost as detached from traditional relationships as Ionesco's *The Chairs*. Like Eliot, Pinter merely moves from the logic of real life to symbolic logic without suggesting that this might be the inner view of any one character.

The first of these two techniques is the easiest to work with. As mentioned above, it has it roots in fiction; it also echoes the soliloquy and certain aspects of the Greek chorus. As a result, it is familiar to us both as writers and members of an audience.

The second is more difficult. If the transitions from realism to expressionism are too abrupt or made too frequently, the devices become blatant and the play is apt to appear contrived. These transitions are even more basic than tonal shifts. They have to do with the fundamental assumptions from which the audience draws not only intellectual understanding but emotional acceptance of the play as something more than actors reading lines on the stage. It is for this reason that transformations are usually kept subtle and infrequent.

It is generally a waste of a writer's time to argue at length about whether realism or expressionism is a "better" approach. This is a matter of personal preference which is as unarguable as the relative merits of free and metered verse. The fact is that both methods do exist in twentieth-century drama. Although there are certain dangers inherent in each, the contemporary playwright is fortunate in having such a wide range of techniques from which to draw.

It is important to remember that no matter how different these two techniques may appear to be, they do share common goals. They are both concerned with the psychological trick of providing a new experience. They are both artistic methods of shattering previous conceptions or suggesting new relationships by creating an order out of chaos.

27

DRAMATIC DIALOGUE

The *multiple purposes* of dialogue in a play: revelation of *character,* a method of providing *peripheral information,* a technique of presenting *thematic elements,* a means of setting the *pace,* and a method of establishing *tone.*

The dialogue of a play resembles its counterpart in fiction in that it must serve several different functions at the same time. But the dramatist is necessarily more dependent on it not merely because he is deprived of certain fictional techniques, but because his very definition of drama is premised on the use of the spoken word. A story without dialogue is still fiction; a performance without the spoken word becomes either pantomime or dance. Further, it is difficult to conceive of a successful play with unsuccessful dialogue.

The playwright is for these reasons committed to the use of dialogue far more deeply than is either the poet or the story writer.

There are five different functions which the dialogue of a play generally serves. The first is the revelation of character. Second, it is a means of providing peripheral information—events which have occurred either previous to or outside of the action of the play. Next, it can develop thematic elements. Fourth, it is a means of controlling the pace. And finally, it is the primary method of establishing the tone of any one scene.

The experienced playwright can keep these concerns in mind without being fully aware of them in much the same way that any competent writer uses grammatical patterns quite unconsciously as he constructs a sentence. But regardless of experience, every playwright must make fully conscious use of them when attempting to diagnose a play which has gone wrong.

Revealing Character Of the five functions of dramatic dialogue, this one is probably the closest to fictional dialogue. The playwright would do well to review Chapter 6 on characterization and apply those points to the problem of creating a convincing character on the stage through appropriate dialogue.

First, remember that dialogue appears to be "convincing," not because it duplicates the speech patterns of the audience, but because, like the character it is developing, the dialogue is consistent and designed to reveal a complex set of attitudes.

By consistent I do not mean that it should maintain one level of emotion or even usage. On the contrary, it is impossible to understand a character on the stage unless he has shown a variety of responses to differing circumstances. If he is a placid character, for example, it helps if he is thrust into some situation which will drive him to rage or indignation; conversely, if he is generally hot-tempered, the audience will not really come to "know" him until it is able to see some circumstance under which he can be tender, cool-headed, or even passive.

The consistency comes when the audience is given a *pattern* of behavior by which to judge the character. Once this has been established, there is some measure of predictability. If, for example, a section of dialogue reflecting panic is planned for a crisis at the end of the play, some minor pre-echo would help to prepare the audience.

A good example of dialogue used to establish characterization is seen in the opening scene of Albee's *Who's Afraid of Virginia Woolf?* This portion of the play has been written off by some critics as pointlessly vulgar or mere "boob-appeal," but a second reading reveals the fact that every line contributes to an extraordinarily complex presentation of character. The reason these two characters are so fascinating is that although they each have the ability to be extremely ruthless, each also has areas of fearful vulnerability. The opening scene is comic on one level, and the audience laughs as readily as it would have had the comic lines been given for their own sake; but the comedy is also the means by which husband and wife defend themselves against each other. This opening "battle of the sexes" carefully defines the methods of attack and the points of vulnerability which are to become the very foundation of their characters.

After reading the play once—or seeing it once—the playwright should go back over this scene to analyze each line. There are four different types of information given through this bit of hilarious dialogue: those which expose the brutality of the wife, Martha; those which expose her pathetic childishness; those which reveal the strength in the husband, George; and those which dramatize his self-doubts, fear, and emotional impotency. One cannot predict from these lines whether one member of this anguished team will "win" or whether they will destroy each other or whether they will end in a draw. The last act of the play is a surprise to the most sophisticated theatergoer—perhaps *particularly* to him. But having seen the limits of each character through dialogue, the ending is credible.

These two characters are accepted as "real" not because they speak lines we have all heard but because what they say begins to take on a highly complex pattern as if we had listened to them over a period of years.

It is fairly easy to analyze this in the plays of others; it is far more difficult to achieve it in one's own play. The first step is coming to a full realization of the complexity of one's characters. The next step is to conceive of situations which will force one's characters to reveal the apparent contradictions which make them more than mere types. It is then that one faces the task of inventing dialogue which shines a light on first one and then another aspect of each character.

As with fiction, it is occasionally possible to base dialogue on conversations with a friend or relative. But it is extraordinary how rarely this serves as anything more than a jumping-off point. This is partly due to the fact that so many people in real life fail to reveal themselves through conversation at all. Even gin fails to lubricate the iron door behind which most individuals hide—and this is not necessarily bad. But if the playwright plans to offer something more rewarding than the superficial view given at polite gatherings, he must acquire material from some other source. For most, this source is the imagination.

I do not mean to suggest here that one should doggedly assign certain lines to certain aspects of character or specific attitudes. Imagination is liquid, not mechanical; a character well conceived should be allowed to write many of his own lines. What I do mean, however, is that the playwright must constantly ask himself: "What does this line suggest about this character?" and "Is she really *that* sweet?" and "Can't he relax for a minute?" These are the questions which keep characters from becoming flat.

Finally, when the script is ready for that agonizing period of revision, it is wise to review each line of dialogue to see whether it contributes to the total picture of a complex character. The writer of fiction can rely on thoughts and author's analysis; for the playwright, however, character is revealed through action and dialogue, and of these two it is dialogue which best lends itself to subtlety. He cannot afford to throw away a single line.

Providing Peripheral Information There are two types of peripheral information which must be presented by dialogue: significant events which occurred previous to the action of the play and any action which must for various reasons be kept off stage. Both are outside the audience's vision even though they may be dramatically important.

The first usually involves the opening of the play. This is a real danger point for the novice. It is extraordinary how frequently the opening scene is destroyed with lines like these:

MOTHER: You see, son, your father was a poor carpenter and left many debts.

SON: It's been hard on you, Mother, over these fifteen years.

MOTHER: Yes. At first I took in washing. Then I turned to sewing. Now I run my own little dress shop.

SON: And I got a paper route four years ago. Last year you gave me a bicycle. Then I could take on two routes.

Such openers are intended to introduce the audience to the characters, but too often they only introduce the characters to each other. The plain fact of the matter is that neither mother and son nor any other set of characters who have known each other for a long time are apt to sit down and review the facts of their lives.

Absurd as this little example is, it represents a problem which every dramatist has faced. And there is a wide variety of solutions. Often it involves secondary characters. Sophocles used servants in *Oedipus Rex* and so did Shakespeare in *Romeo and Juliet.* And the simple observer appears again in Thornton Wilder's *Our Town.* Less often, the main character enters alone and talks about himself, as do Shakespeare's Richard III and Beckett's Krapp. One of the most flexible techniques is to set one or more of the major characters against an outsider, such as Albee did in *Zoo Story, The American Dream,* and *Virginia Woolf.* This allows some discussion of material which close associates would not naturally review to each other, and it also avoids the somewhat artificial device of employing two outsiders.

No matter what the approach, however, one must be aware of the conventions on which the play is to be based. If it is the sort of work in which characters may address the audience directly (like *Our Town* or *Mother Courage*), one is operating under different rules than if the play is intended to employ the more traditional conventions. In the second case, background material must be slid in with some subtlety.

The other type of peripheral information is that which occurs off stage roughly at the same time as the action which is shown. This raises the question of what to include as action and what to present through narration. Generally speaking, there are three types of situations which are left to dialogue alone.

The first is the event which violates the taboos of the playwright's own society. The stage is in many ways freer from limitations than television, and this is a blessing which most playwrights value. But the Greeks, for all their freedom regarding sexual subjects, were strict in their refusal to have a death occur on the stage; and we, who are closer in this area to Rome than Greece, allow rather extensive bloodshed but place limits on sex. Contemporary audiences are quick to find *Lysistrata* "dirty," but the four murders which occur within five minutes in the last scene of *Hamlet* are generally considered good clean realism.

Morality and taste are private concerns and not the subject of this text, but the playwright must consider what effect a scene is going to have on his audience. If what he had hoped would be a point of high drama or delightful wit is shattered with a general reaction of embarrassment, the scene has failed by any standard. The solution in such cases is to leave the scene off stage and refer to it through dialogue.

The second type of action which is best handled through descriptive dialogue is that which is too complex to stage. Tennessee Williams is no coward, but he is dramatist enough to know that you can't have a pack of dogs tear the hero apart on the stage (*Orpheus Descending*) any more than you can have a pack of wild urchins devour a man (*Suddenly Last Summer*); and T. S. Eliot took the same approach when Celia was "crucified / Very near an ant-hill."

This is not always a matter of brutality. It is significant that in *My Fair Lady* it was decided to handle the all-important scene at the grand ball off stage, referring to it through dialogue. The imagination of the audience served better than all the extras could have even on the largest possible stage. This is, of course, essentially what Shakespeare did with his major battle scenes.

There is always a problem in these cases of how to keep the play moving when a character is assigned to relate something which has happened and everyone else on the stage is left standing there like a secondary audience. This is a matter of maintaining the pace of the drama which I will come to shortly.

The third situation which calls for narrating peripheral information is more general. It is a matter of unity. If the play seems to have too many scene shifts, or if its direction seems to wander aimlessly, the fault may be that too much is happening on stage. Writers who have moved from fiction to drama are apt to be most guilty of this. The fluidity of a novel does not lend itself to a play; the playwright must be highly selective. A scene in drama which serves no purpose but to fill in some minor part of the plot has no place on the stage. In many cases, such scenes can be summed up through references in the dialogue.

Presenting Thematic Elements This is generally the most dangerous use of dialogue. It frequently takes the form of a final monologue in which a character is given the task of analyzing what the playwright really wanted to say. Actors hate this role for the simple reason that they must step out of character and become social critics or even drama critics.

The need for such summaries was once formalized in the convention of the epilogue, and some contemporary playwrights have devised modified versions of this technique. The final scenes of *Death of a Salesman, Our Town,* and *Mother Courage* are all good examples.

More generally, however, contemporary drama leaves the summary to the audience. It is the total effect of the action and dialogue which makes the statement, not a chorus or an analytical spokesman.

If one wishes to follow this tradition, it is helpful to examine each reflective statement of each character. Although these lines may *reflect* the theme (or even the thesis) indirectly, they should not state it directly. It is generally agreed, for example, that *Mother Courage* has a strong thesis attacking war and man's inhumanity. But it is significant that there is considerable dispute as to whether Mother Courage herself represents those who take advantage of war for personal profit or whether she suggests the indomitable spirit of man which is able to endure such terrors with rough dignity. I personally feel that she is both and that this apparent contradiction is exactly the kind of paradox which makes Brecht's work so much richer than mere propaganda pieces. But regardless of what position one takes on this point, it is significant that even in a play which appears to be so highly thetic the protagonist has been given no line which states the thesis of the play directly. We judge the significance of theme and thesis through implications in action and dialogue.

Controlling Pace The pace of a play is all-important. Occasionally a play moves too rapidly. This is rare and the fault usually lies in the action, not the dialogue. Much more frequently, plays fail because of a pace which is too slow. We describe the play as "ponderous" or a scene as one which "sags." Here again, the solution may be found in adding action such as was described in Chapter 24. Frequently, however, the fault may lie in the dialogue.

In such cases, it is wise to examine the diction, the syntax, and the length of individual speeches. If all these appear satisfactory, one should review the degree to which dialogue has been blended with action and, finally, the amount of new information which is given through the dialogue.

Diction is often "heavy" in plays by writers who have a misguided admiration for Greek and Elizabethan drama. By "misguided" I mean a misunderstanding about the language used in those plays. Translations of classical drama vary tremendously, but many of them adopt a formal, Latinate style which a century ago was considered appropriate for "great" works. They miss the point that most Greek dramatists used a fairly simple style, echoing the speech of literate contemporaries and, particularly in the comedies, the dialects of illiterates as well.

The same is true of Shakespeare's dialogue. It appears formal and even elegant to us largely because so many words and phrases then in common use are no longer heard. Even the so-called great speeches are constructed mainly with simple, concrete nouns and active verbs.

Heavy diction, whether adopted for these reasons or others, consists of long words, Latinate roots, and excess modification. Certain types of characters are best shown through language like this, but they are rare. The best way of judging whether the diction of a particular character is natural and true to his nature is to read his lines aloud. A tape recorder is helpful. And the advice of actors is invaluable.

Heavy diction does reduce the pace of a speech and, in turn, the scene. The same is true of complex and involuted syntax. Such a style may be justified by the character himself, but even in those cases the playwright must remember that no matter how "real" it may sound, the scene is going to be slowed by it.

Large, unbroken blocks of speech are perhaps the major cause of tedium in dialogue. It is here that the Major Statements of Theme and Significance are apt to appear. But even when those

have been eliminated, the lines are apt to drag the scene down. What many playwrights forget is that when one character speaks at length, all the other characters on the stage are static. At worst, they have left the play altogether and joined the audience as listeners; at best, they are merely useless.

One way to solve this is to break up such speeches with action such as described in Chapter 24. Another method is to add replies from other characters. This may take the form of a discussion or even an argument. In either case, the other characters are used, and the result is an increase in the pace of the scene.

For all this, there are some plays which ignore most of this advice by giving extraordinarily lengthy speeches and yet still maintain a fairly rapid pace. O'Neill's *Long Day's Journey Into Night* is one example. It should be remembered that this play was written at the end of a long career in drama; as such it serves as a rather dangerous model for the novice. But some explanation should be given concerning why plays like this maintain enough pace to be lauded by a good number of critics.

Part of the explanation is due to the poetic quality of the language itself. Shakespeare was able to roll out long speeches which hold the attention of at least the trained portion of the audience through exactly the same qualities which capture those at a good poetry reading. Some critics, but not all, feel that O'Neill achieved this.

More to the point, however, is the amount and degree of information which is presented through such lines. An audience will be bored with a thirty-line speech if it fails to reveal much about character or the dramatic question; the same audience will be fascinated with a hundred-line monologue if there are a series of revelations about the speaker or the situation.

Pace, then, is not merely a matter of diction, syntax, and length of speeches; it also depends on content. In Chapter 23 I suggested that the play as a whole must have some sort of dramatic question to keep the audience alert and committed to the play; the same is true of long speeches. To test the dramatic voltage of a single speech—particularly a long one—the playwright must determine just how many new insights are offered through this dialogue. I do not include vague and general statements about Life and

Beauty and Death as insights; I am referring to those all-important discoveries about the inner nature of the speaker and the real significance of the situation.

Determining Tone Tone is created both through action and through dialogue. But of the two, dialogue is a more basic factor. The action of *Arsenic and Old Lace* is essentially serious, but the tone is kept delightfully light through the dialogue. Within limits, it is not so much what happens that determines tone but the attitude of those to whom it happens as revealed by what they say.

Traditionally, light tone and serious tone were given separate scenes, the former often coming in the form of "comic relief." This is still followed by many playwrights. The comic relief is used mainly to keep the audience from emotional exhaustion and occasionally to echo the major theme. An easy way of handling this is to add a comic or a "light" minor character (an echo of Shakespeare's clowns) whose function is to provide relief through either witty or cynical dialogue.

One of the most significant trends in this half of our own century, however, is the linking of light and serious tones in the same scene. One can trace this development in fiction from Nathanial West through Joseph Heller. The same pattern can be seen in drama by studying Brecht's *Threepenny Opera,* Ionesco's *The Chairs,* and Albee's *Zoo Story* and *Who's Afraid of Virginia Woolf?* It was Ionesco who coined the phrase "tragic farce," and although some of these works are closer to farcical tragedies, the term should be accepted as meaningful and significant.

This technique cannot be learned from any text. It is a stylistic paradox which appears outrageous at first viewing and is only later adopted as an acquired taste. I point it out here only to indicate that in the manipulation of tone through dialogue extraordinary effects are possible. The grave scene in *Hamlet* comes close to tragic farce, but it is only in our own century that the technique has been applied to entire plays.

Regardless of what approach one takes, it is important to remember that dialogue is the primary means of determining tone—not only light versus serious, but calm versus tense, sentimental versus bitter or ironical, and the like. The playwright who wishes

to maintain control over the tone of his work must necessarily be master of his dialogue.

These, then, are the five primary functions of dialogue in a play. As a basic rule, no line should serve only one function and many should reflect all five. Obviously one cannot check each line in a script against this list. But if one uses it frequently to analyze individual scenes, the principles will eventually be internalized. This is the point at which one is able to use dialogue with true facility.

28

SELF-CRITICISM—DRAMA

The *three steps* necessary to evaluate one's own play: an uninterrupted *silent reading*, a *spoken reading* to judge playing time and fidelity of dialogue to character, and a *group reading* to imitate the effect of a full production; a *checklist* of questions to ask about one's own work.

There are three basic steps in analyzing one's own play. One should use all of them before even considering the possibility of producing the work on the stage.

The first is reading the play silently. One has, of course, been doing this through the course of writing. What I am referring to here is a complete, uninterrupted reading from beginning to end. This is not always easy to do—students are apt to have roommates, parents have children, and everyone has Very Important Things to do when the alternative is reading a work which one has wrestled with for months.

Yet such a reading is essential. Most plays are not only more intricately structured than stories but longer as well. Because of this, the playwright tends to think in terms of scenes, and his creative energies are focused singly on first one and then the next. The uninterrupted, silent reading is necessary to unify one's view of the play.

This silent reading has an advantage over a spoken reading because it is faster. But to be effective, it should be conducted literally without a single interruption. This means not taking notes or even making the simplest mechanical correction. Those can be done later. This is not a proofreading nor is it a critical reading. In many cases, it is the playwright's first introduction to the totality of his creation. Think of it as the foot soldier's first aerial view of territory which he once fought for day by day and town by town.

The second of these three steps is reading the play out loud. Ideally, this too should be uninterrupted; but it is not as important as it was for the silent reading because the intent is different.

One mechanical purpose is timing. The total playing time can be estimated fairly accurately if one allows for those few scenes in which silent action takes place. This information will be needed if the play is to be entered in a contest. More important, it is a way of judging the nature of the work itself. If it turns out to be a long one-act play, it may be worth expanding into a full-length work. If, on the other hand, it is a three-act play which runs only eighty minutes, one should consider either expanding the work or cutting it back to one act.

The difference between a so-called one-act play and a full-length play is about as vague as the distinction between a short story and a novel. A one-act play can be divided into several scenes which may resemble acts, and a full-length play can replace the traditional three acts with a number of scenes which structurally resemble the one-act play. Greater length allows for greater complexity in plotting, but it does not demand it. For these reasons, plays are classified by playing time. The so-called one-act play usually runs from ten to sixty minutes; the full-length play, from two to four hours. In between there is an awkward length which, like the novella, is discriminated against for purely commercial reasons. Playing time is both a practical bit of information and a way of defining the work.

It is also helpful to have a record of how long each scene takes. If a scene is tedious, it is important to know whether it is disproportionately long or merely seems that way.

In addition to these mechanical concerns, the spoken reading is one of the most effective ways to judge the quality of the dialogue.

Most of the concerns discussed in the last chapter and reviewed at the end of this one are best analyzed through a spoken rather than a silent reading.

After corrections and revisions, one is ready to take the final step in self-criticism: the informal group reading. The readers should be quite familiar with the script, but there is no need to memorize the lines. If possible, the reading should be taped for further study. Naturally, some of the parts will appear better or worse depending on the talent of the reader, but no matter how informal the performance may be, it provides the playwright with his first real conception of what the play might be like in full production.

It is pleasant to have a small audience of friends for such a reading, but it is not at all essential. The real value comes from translating the written script into something close to what it is intended to become: action and dialogue on the stage. If possible, allow time after the reading for a discussion of the characters, the theme, the pace—in fact, any of the concerns discussed in this text. Those who have participated in a reading are apt to have insights into the work which the playwright had never considered.

After each one of these steps, the playwright should review and revise his script. The following checklist is similar to the ones which concluded the other two sections of this text. It should serve to stimulate effective revision after each reading of the play.

1. Is this play in some way poorly suited for production on the stage? (See Chapter 21.)
   a. Does a lack of compression suggest that it might be more successful as a story or a novel?
   b. Are the scene shifts such that it would be better as a film?
   c. Have individual characters or entire scenes been borrowed from television conventions?
2. Is the play primarily one of theme or thesis? (See Chapter 22.)
   a. If this is a play of themes, are there several related concerns which give the play richness and depth?
   b. Does the thematic approach slide into a didactic thesis at the end of the play?
   c. If the play is essentially thetic, is there some measure of irony or wit to keep it from being more assertive than literary?

   d. And are there enough qualifications to keep the play from the level of propaganda?
3. Is there a dramatic question and if so is it compelling? (See Chapter 23.)
   a. Is there a dramatic question posed early in the play?
   b. Does it continue to hold interest either by itself or in conjunction with other questions?
   c. Does it echo the thematic elements of the play, or is it merely employed as an end in itself?
   d. If the dramatic question is weak, could the work be made more effective in the form of fiction, poetry, or a dramatic dialogue intended mainly for reading?
4. Is action on the stage employed effectively? (See Chapter 24.)
   a. Are exits and entrances used to establish a meaningful pattern of secondary scenes?
   b. Do characters move about on the stage, or are they mere posts from which dialogue pours forth?
   c. Are characters provided with business to keep them visually alive?
   d. If there is no physical contact between characters, does this represent a dramatic weakness?
   e. If physical contact *is* used, is it well motivated? Is it a means rather than an end?
   f. If there is very little action in this play, is it possible that the story form would serve as a better vehicle?
5. Has enough attention been given to the set and costuming? (See Chapter 25.)
   a. If the set is realistic, is there some imaginative use of detail?
   b. Is there or might there be a visual focal point in this set?
   c. If the set is expressionistic, is there a symbolic unity to the details?
   d. Does it merely add further obscurity to an already clouded play?
   e. If the two approaches are combined, has this combination been made meaningful or is it merely careless?
   f. If the bare stage has been used, is there some reasonable justification for it?
   g. Would it be more effective to select some other type of set than the one in this draft?

   h. Would the play be improved by shifting the type of costuming either from realistic to expressionistic or the reverse?
   i. Is there any point in the play which might be dramatized by the artistic use of lighting?
   j. In general, has the play reflected a visual imagination on the part of the playwright?
6. Has the play made full use of either the realistic or the expressionistic tradition? (See Chapter 26.)
   a. If realistic, does the play fall into the category of "false realism" by borrowing stock situations, characters, and dialogue?
   b. If expressionistic, does the play represent only the private and inner world of the playwright?
   c. In either case, will the audience be drawn into the events as if he were sharing either an as-if-real experience or an as-if-real dream?
7. Does the dialogue generally serve more than one function? (See Chapter 27.)
   a. Do the lines reflect the character of the speaker sufficiently so that in most cases we could tell who was speaking without being told?
   b. Do the lines continue to expand our view of the speaker so that we know him far better as the play develops?
   c. Is dialogue used to provide peripheral information?
   d. If not, is there any scene which might be more economically handled through reference by dialogue?
   e. Or has some crucial scene been left off stage?
   f. Do characters tell each other information which they already know merely to help the audience?
   g. Are thematic elements introduced through dialogue in an obvious or "preachy" way? Are there final monologues which force an actor to abandon his role to become a one-man "chorus"?
   h. Could the pace be increased by simplifying diction and syntax or reducing the length of speeches?
   i. Is the dialogue blended with action?
   j. Does the dialogue continue to present new information about characters and the plot?
   k. Is the tone maintained successfully through the dialogue?

l. Would the play be more successful if the tone were shifted through revisions in dialogue?

8. Have your critical readings of this play been honest attempts to analyze deficiencies and weaknesses? Or have you mesmerized yourself into the role of an enthusiastic audience?
   a. Have you allowed as much time for revisions as you did for the original writing?
   b. Have the revisions been based at least in part on a professional view of what the play actually has become?

PART FOUR

Appendices

A

SUBMISSION OF MATERIAL FOR PUBLICATION

Unfounded *myths* about publishing; the *tests* of whether one is ready to submit material; *mechanical considerations* of the manuscript itself; *what to submit; where* to submit; the *vanity presses;* the use of *personal contact;* the dangers of *double submissions;* the value of *agents; placing a play;* and the reasonable approach to publication.

The number of novice writers who submit material long before there is any chance of publication is almost as large as the number of those who refuse to submit even after they should enter the public market. This absurd situation exists because so few writers analyze their work or the problem of marketing with any degree of rationality.

The field is cluttered with unfounded myths. One hears, for example, that nothing is published without "pull," that neither fiction nor drama can succeed without sex, that poetry must be unintelligible, that agents are generally dishonest, and that Madison Avenue has a death grip on every phase of publication. Equally fanciful is the claim that if a piece of writing is "good" it will eventually be published without the slightest effort on the part of the writer.

In addition, there are a number of personal delusions which occur so frequently that they are almost archetypal. This country is full of pathetic individuals who have lost a trunk, suitcase, or even a crate of manuscripts which, if it were found, would astound the literary world. Meanwhile, they populate writers' conferences. And then there are those who have written a brilliant work which was "stolen" and published under another title with "only minor revisions."

There are two essential facts to remember: First, publication is no more fair than life itself; there will always be good works which are not accepted as well as thoroughly rotten material which is. Second, if talent, practice, and a practical system of submission are combined, one can alter the odds in one's favor.

The test of whether one is ready to submit material is twofold. First, one should have written in that particular genre for some time. So-called "first novels" are usually preceded by considerable practice in short stories and quite frequently from one to four unpublished novels. This may be partly due to the timidity of publishers, but in many cases it is a great blessing.

In addition, one should be perfectly familiar with the publications to which one is going to submit. This is particularly true for poets. Those who live in large cities should buy little magazines from bookstores, and others should order them by mail. A good list of titles and prices is given in *Trace,* the address of which is given later in this appendix. The purpose of studying literary magazines is not imitation but familiarity with the standards and tastes of each publication.

If one has passed these two tests of creative maturity, one is ready for a long, sometimes agonizing program of submitting material.

Mechanical Considerations The manuscript must be typed with a dark ribbon on a good grade of standard typewriter paper (16- or 20-lb. weight with at least 25% rag content). The type should be pica (not elite or the new varieties). The margins at left and at the top should be 1½ inches, the bottom one inch, and the right roughly one inch without excessive hyphenation. All material except name and address should be double spaced. The title should be placed about one-third of the way down the first page together with the writer's name, address, and brief explanatory material as shown here:

A WINTER'S NIGHT

Joseph P. Author
50 Bellweather Place
Chicago 10, Ill.

A short story
Approx. 4,500 words

The story begins two double spaces below this. Only in the case of novels or plays should the title be placed on a separate sheet. For poems, substitute the number of lines for the number of words. For plays, give the total playing time in the same place.

The pages should be numbered in Arabic numerals which together with the last name of the author should be placed in the *upper right* corner of every page after the first: Author 2, Author 3, and so on.

Do not place the manuscript in a folder or binder, and do not staple it. A simple paper clip will do. Novels should be sent loose in a box. Covering letters are not at all necessary, but if you do include one, make it brief and factual. Never defend your own work.

If all this seems rather restrictive, remember that originality belongs in the art form itself, not in the manuscript.

For mailing, the envelope should be large enough so that the manuscript need not be folded. This applies to single poems as well. If one buys 9½" × 12½" envelopes for sending, one can include a self-addressed, stamped 9" × 12" envelope for its return. If this is too complicated, merely fold the second 9½" × 12½" envelope so that it can be placed inside the first with the manuscript. In either case, be sure that your address and proper postage is on it. Failure to do this not only infuriates the editor but increases your chances of never seeing it again.

Poems may be sent first class. A fairly recent ruling by the Post Office Department permits heavier manuscripts to be sent at "special 4th class: manuscript" * very much cheaper (novels used to cost about $3.00 each way by mandatory first-class rates).

---

* Certain post offices are confused on this point. Have them look up Section 135.13 and 135.214f of the Postal Manual. The fact that these sections *do* include unpublished manuscripts was verified by Roy L. Sheridan, Director of Mail Classification Branch, Post Office Department, Washington, D.C., on February 27, 1964.

Allow about four weeks for poetry and short stories and an agonizing three months for novels. Resist that temptation to enquire about work sent until at least twice the expected time has passed.

If you know no one on the staff, merely send the manuscript to the fiction or poetry editor at the address given in the magazine. But if you have met or have had correspondence with an editor or even a junior reader, send it to him.

Keeping records is extremely important. It is impossible to remember what went out when and to which magazine. In addition, it is invaluable to have a record not only of which editors had a kind word or two but of which magazines sent specifically worded rejection slips. The lowest level of rejection slip is merely a printed statement saying that they appreciated receiving your work and were unable to use it. In addition most magazines have one or two special slips with wording like "this was of particular interest to us" or "we hope to see more of your work." Take these seriously. Next on the scale is the penned comment on the bottom of the slip like "good dialogue" or "try us again." These are infuriatingly brief, but they are worth recording. Be careful, however, not to inundate a magazine with weekly submissions. An editor who has commented on one poem is not going to be impressed with a flood of inferior material. Treat him as a potential ally who deserves only your best work.

The highest point on this scale is the *letter* of rejection. Even if brief, this is close to acceptance. If they suggest specific revisions which seem wise, revise and resubmit. If not, send your next really good piece. These are two situations in which a short covering letter is definitely required.

What to Submit This decision must rest ultimately with the author. Although the advice of other serious writers is often helpful, beware of being influenced by friends who do not know what you are doing. For example, if a classmate or neighbor never reads contemporary poetry, he is the world's worst critic. The same applies to fiction or drama. Every writer has many friends who know nothing whatever about literature—just as lawyers or doctors associate with those who have never been introduced to even the terminology of law or medicine. It is pleasant enough when such friends enjoy something you have written, but one should not either send material out prematurely or file manuscripts away on the basis of such judgment.

Poets should select a group of four to six poems. Writers of fiction should limit each submission to one story. Once the choice is made, keep sending the work out repeatedly. A single editorial rejection means absolutely nothing. A manuscript is not "dead" until it has been turned down by at least ten magazines. The best approach is to send the work out on the very day it is returned—otherwise you are apt to lose courage. As a practical matter, just as many manuscripts are accepted after six or eight rejections as after only one. This is largely due to the fact that so many nonliterary factors go into selecting a work for publication, such as the number and kind of manuscripts on hand, the balance of a particular issue, and the personal preferences of the first reader.

There is no easy rule concerning what should be sent out; but once the decision is made, stand by it until you have cumulative proof that the work is unpublishable.

Where to Submit The writer should have his own file of magazines which seem to be interested in his own kind of writing. Addresses can be found in *Trace* (Villiers Publications, Hollywood, California). Single copies are available, as well as subscriptions for the four copies published each year. This is a quarterly of fiction, poetry, and comment, but its major and unique contribution is the listing called "The Chronicle, An Evolving and Biased Directory." Ask for the International Directory Number; other issues simply add to this basic list. The information they give about the magazines is sadly minimal, but it is at least enough to judge whether one should order single copies. Briefer listings are also found in the back of *New World Writing* and in the excellent annual anthology edited by Martha Foley and David Burnett, *The Best American Short Stories*. *Writer's Yearbook* has a good listing, and such publications as *Writer's Digest* and *The Writer* are sometimes helpful.

Never submit material to a magazine on the basis of these listings alone. Always review at least one issue of several magazines and make your marketing decisions on the basis of these.

Novels can be handled in the same way, but one can gain a familiarity with which houses handle what kind of material by reading the book sections of any large newspaper. Generally speaking, book publishers are more catholic in their literary standards than are magazines. For this reason, most writers simply work their way through the list of thirteen to fourteen major publishers without much regard to order. This takes about three long years—time enough to complete the next novel.

Circulating a novel raises four points which in various degrees apply to placing other types of writing as well. First, don't be seduced by the so-called vanity presses unless absolutely desperate. The vanity press is one which charges the author a percentage either for publication costs or for revisions. Some of them are perfectly honest, but it is rare indeed that a vanity press with its minimal system of distribution can do much with a novel which has been rejected by the major publishers. Collections of poetry are sometimes handled in this way and distributed by the poet himself. This is legitimate and honorable—though the poet should make sure he understands the contract even if (or perhaps *particularly* if) the editor is a friend. Novelists, however, should remember that good publishers are searching for good manuscripts. If a new novel is rejected by thirteen major publishing houses, it is time to shelve it.

Second, never be too proud to make use of a personal contact at a publishing house or magazine. It will not, generally, get a bad manuscript published, but it may bypass that first reader who has a great many manuscripts to review. In the case of rejections, the writer is apt to receive a lengthier comment if the reader has some personal interest. I can testify to the fact that such personal contact is not a prerequisite for having stories or novels accepted; but it is neither unethical nor a waste of time to make use of any interested reader or publisher.

Third, never submit copies of the same work to different publishers at the same time. This applies to stories and poetry as well. And with novels, one should not even have two *different* works in circulation at the same time. The publisher assumes that if he accepts a novel, he is investing in an author. Standard contracts insist on a first refusal not only of later works but of book-length manuscripts already written. This is true only of novels, and it is perfectly ethical to have any number of stories or poems out at the same time as a novel.

This is frustrating and, to my mind, unfair to the writer who has two novels which he would like to circulate. But it is one of the facts of the publishing world. It is simply not worth trying to violate what editors so nicely call "publishers' ethics."

Finally, there is the world of agents to consider. Reputable agents charge a flat ten per cent of all material sold through them and make no other charges whatever, regardless of how much postage or time they may spend. In return they expect to see *all* your work. If an author is unpublished, it is sometimes difficult to find an agent who will be willing to handle his work. But it is not impossible. Once an agent has decided to handle a particular client, he is often willing to maintain faith through a decade of absolutely profitless submission.

There are also agents who charge for reading each manuscript. Some of them may be of help to those in specialized fields like juveniles or mysteries, but any writer whose interest is at least partially literary will have little to learn from them. More serious, some of these agents have a way of flattering incompetent writers into paying one fee after another for such services as "editorial analysis" and "professional revision" which end up finally with an expensive offer from a vanity press. The only way a writer can be sure that he is dealing with a reputable agent is to have an agreement in writing which makes no financial demands but the flat ten per cent for work sold.

There is not much point in seeking an agent if one plans to submit primarily to little magazines. Placing material in such publications is an honor well worth struggling for, but they pay very little and most agents cannot afford to work for love alone.

There is, however, an argument for submitting to agents if one has a reasonable body of fiction (five or six potentially publishable stories) which might be considered by quality magazines and the slicks. Manuscripts submitted to magazines through agencies usually receive more careful scrutiny by a mature reader with more authority.

There is an even stronger argument for working with an agent if one has written a novel. Not only does one reap the benefits mentioned above, but in the event of acceptance, one receives invaluable legal advice regarding the contract. Although magazines do not offer contracts (one merely accepts the rate offered) publishers do. And *all contracts are negotiable.* Those without an agent should hire a lawyer, and it is not easy to find one who is familiar with this rather specialized field. These contracts contain three or four pages of very fine print covering, not only a graduated scale of royalties, but highly complex agreements concerning serial rights, film rights, translation rights, and the like. Since you should turn to an agent at this point to protect your rights, you might as well have him handle the submissions from the start.

But this should not deter a writer who is unable to find an agent who will handle his work. Many first novels and stories have been accepted directly from an author.

All this has only partial relevance to the problem of marketing a play. There are several directions the playwright can take—none of them as neat and simple as the methods of submitting fiction and poetry.

First, the playwright can try working through an agent. Most large agencies have drama departments, and some small agencies specialize in this field. Second, he can try every drama contest in the country—and there are many. Announcements of contests are usually found on bulletin boards in colleges and universities. Third, those who are fortunate enough to be on campuses with a good stage and an active drama group can try to have their work produced locally. This may not be Broadway, but the satisfaction is deep and lasting. It is also professionally valuable. Fourth, it is worth submitting to those publishers who specialize in plays; though here it is much more important to know exactly what their editorial policy is than it is in the case of novels. Most of these concerns have a particular type of play which they consider acceptable for publication. Fifth, one-act plays can sometimes be placed in magazines like *New World Writing.* It is worth writing a letter of inquiry first. Finally, one can try to find a producer directly. There is probably no other branch of the arts which is more committed to personal contact than drama. To put it more brutally, "pull" is extraordinarily valuable. If one knows a producer, director, actor, or even a stagehand, write him. This situation is not merely a matter of commercial corruption. The fact is that although book publishers come to know potential writers through little magazines (which they read with professional care), producers have little contact with the young playwright whose work has not yet appeared on the stage. This situation will continue until there are more little magazines willing to specialize in original plays and more low-budget stage companies in the smaller cities. Meanwhile, the playwright must struggle with this particularly difficult task of presenting his material.

The writer who is serious about his art must be realistic when considering publication. It is naive to assume that the word *marketing* is crass and beneath him. Publishers have no way of discovering a writer who does not make his work available. Yet, on the other hand, a mania to publish at all cost can easily become a poison to the creative process. It leads first to imitative and conventionalized work, and finally to the most negative type of self-delusions designed to protect one's ego. To avoid these most unrewarding routes, one must begin with an honest evaluation of one's own work and follow through with a planned, long-range program of submissions. There are, of course, writers who achieve wide recognition very suddenly; but this is rare and not always a blessing. Ideally, creative work is a way of life, and the effort to publish is an important but not a central portion of that life.

B

GLOSSARY-INDEX

This combined listing may be used either as a glossary of terms or as an index listing the primary references within the text itself. In some cases, a quick review of the definition may save thumbing through the text.

Definitions are limited to the senses used in the text. Numbers refer to pages and italics are used for relatively fuller treatment. Italicized words indicate cross-references either in the same or in closely related form. Thus *metered* refers to an entry headed *meter* and *rhyming* to *rhyme*.

Alliteration, 117, *143*, 148. The repetition of consonants in *verse*, particularly those at the beginnings of words.

Ambiguity, *184*. That which suggests two or more different meanings. Ambiguity which is not resolved is frequently considered a liability because it tends to shatter the *internal logic* of a work. But ambiguities can be effective when the two alternative meanings join to make a broader or more profound suggestion or when the two alternatives are harmonious.

Anapestic feet, *131*, *132*. See *meter*.

Archaic language, *172*. Words which are primarily associated with an earlier period and are no longer in general use.

Assertive writing, *4*, 9, 213. See *descriptive writing*.

Assonance, 117, *143*. The repetition of similar vowel sounds in *verse* regardless of their position in the word.

Automatic writing, *14*, 95. See *stream of consciousness*.

Blank verse, 132. Unrhymed iambic pentameter (see also *verse* and *meter*).

Business, 237. Generally, any unit of action in a play; more specifically, an activity which does not involve relocation of a character —tying a necktie, combing one's hair, and the like.

Caesura, 136. A pause or complete break in the *rhythm* of a *line* of *verse* frequently occurring in the middle of that line.

Catalyst, 66. A literary element which causes or speeds up some change in the work, as in chemistry a catalytic agent causes another substance to change without itself being altered. The literary sense (first suggested by T. S. Eliot) can be applied to such elements as *conflict, setting,* or some sequence of action when they are used to stimulate character development or to dramatize a *theme.*

Chronology, 33, 34. The arrangement of events in the order of their occurrence. This corresponds to Forster's use of *story* (see also *plot and story*).

Cinquain, 133. See *stanza.*

Cliché, *167ff.* A metaphor or simile which has become so familiar from overuse that the vehicle (see *metaphor*) no longer contributes any meaning whatever to the tenor. It provides neither the vividness of a good metaphor nor the strength of a single, unmodified word. "Good as gold" and "crystal clear" are clichés in this specific sense. The word is also used to describe overused but nonmetaphorical expressions such as "tried and true" and "each and every."

Commercial writing, *5,* 13. Prose—both fiction and nonfiction—which is *simple* and conforms to certain rigid *conventions* usually for the sake of publication and profit. Fictional forms include "pulps" (confessionals such as *True Romance*) and "slicks" (McCalls, Redbook, and the like). Slick magazines have, however, published *sophisticated* work from time to time.

Conflict, *65ff.* A clash of forces which in *sophisticated literary* works may serve as a *catalyst* and in *simple* works is generally an end in itself. The most common types of conflict pit man against nature, against society, against another man, and against some aspect of himself.

Consonance, 117, *143.* A similarity of consonantal sounds in verse. This is distinguished from *alliteration* if the latter is restricted (as it is in this text) to initial sounds.

Convention, *13.* Any pattern or device in literature which is repeated in a number of different works by many different writers. It is a broad term which includes basic devices like *plot, dialogue, meter,* and the divisions of acts and *scenes;* it also refers to general patterns like man against nature in *fiction,* young-girl-and-spring in poetry, and the recognition scene in *drama.* It excludes that which is unique in a work.

Couplet, 132. See *stanza.*

Creative writing, *5ff.* Any form of *sophisticated literary writing.* This term is generally used to describe college courses in the writing of fiction, poetry, and drama, or any combination of these. It excludes courses in assertive writing and thesis writing.

Curiosity, 76, *77.* A form of *tension* in which withheld information is played against the desire to find out.

Dactylic feet, *131,* 132. See *meter.*

Descriptive writing, *4,* 9, 218. Any verbal system in which meaning is ultimately linked with the real world and so can be judged as generally valid or invalid. This is the opposite of *literary writing* which contains its own system of *internal logic* and cannot be judged as valid or invalid. *Descriptive writing* is synonymous with assertive writing and includes such forms as the essay, thesis, editorial, article, and text.

Dialogue, *87ff., 269ff.* Any phrase or passage which appears to quote a character's words directly regardless of whether such material was uttered aloud or merely thought. That which is stated is called external dialogue; that which remains unspoken is internal dialogue, one form of which is *stream of consciousness.* The term "monologue" is limited to solitary speeches, spoken or silent. "Soliloquy" usually refers to monologues in *drama.*

Dimeter, 132. See *line.*

Double rhyme, 145. See *rhyme.*

Drama, 207ff., *211.* That form of literary writing intended primarily for presentation by performers speaking and acting on a stage. Drama is further characterized, generally speaking, by the fact that it is a continuous art, by its frequent use of conflict, and by its dependence on visual and auditory communication.

Dramatic, 211. In addition to being an adjective for drama, this term usually implies a rapid *pace,* the use of *conflict,* the presence of a *dramatic question,* and some measure of *curiosity* or *suspense.*

Dramatic question, 222ff. The emotional element in a play which holds the attention of an audience before the *theme* or *thesis* becomes clear and which usually continues through to the resolution. The dramatic question (or series of questions) is usually a *simple,* emotional appeal based either on *curiosity* or *suspense.* When the dramatic question dominates the play, the result is usually *melodrama.* Dramatic questions are also found in *fiction* and narrative poetry.

End-stopped line, *134.* A technique in *verse* of completing the grammatical construction (usually with a comma or a period) and a unit of meaning at the end of a *line.* This is contrasted with *run-on lines* in which meaning and construction continue into the next line usually for the sake of muting the rhythm.

Epiphany, 27. The moment of awakening or discovery by a fictional character, the reader, or both. The literary use of this term was first suggested by James Joyce. It is associated almost exclusively with the short story.

Feet, *131,* 132. See *meter.*

Feminine rhyme, 145. See *rhyme.*

Fiction, *4ff.* That form of *literary writing* which tells a story in *prose.* It may be very *simple* like most *commercial writing* or it may be *sophisticated.* In either case it establishes its own special world which is guided primarily by the rules of *internal logic.* Fiction is also classified by length and breadth: The short story is usually less than 40 manuscript pages and explores the lives of only one or two characters; the novel is usually more than 200 manuscript pages and frequently develops more than two characters and explores a wider variety of themes. The novella is a short novel.

Figurative language, 152, *158.* See *image.*

Flashback, *34ff.* A break in the chronology of a narrative made when the *plot* turns back to events which occurred earlier. The term is not used for a simple reference to past events; the shift must involve the creation of an entire scene.

Formula, *14ff.* Popular *conventions* which characterize *simple fiction* and *drama.* These conventions are usually patterns of *plot* combined with *stock characters.* Sample: The Sincere-brunette who competes with the Scheming-blond for the attentions of the Rising-young-executive who at first is "blind to the truth" but who finally "sees the light."

Frame story, 36. (1) A story within a longer narrative; (2) any narrative which begins and ends with the same scene, making the body of the work a kind of extended *flashback.* Chaucer's *The Canterbury Tales* is an excellent example of the first type, and Conrad's "Youth" illustrates the second.

Free verse, *189ff.* *Verse* which is written without *meter* or *rhyme* scheme; which in varying degrees derives rhythmical patterns from *line* length, syntactical elements, and repetition (see *prose rhythm*); and which creates sound patterns from the use of such devices as *assonance* and *alliteration.*

Genre, *vii.* Any of several types of *literary writing.* In common usage, genre refers to *fiction, poetry,* or *drama.*

Gimmick, 19. An unusual twist of *plot,* characterization, or occasionally *setting.* A colloquial term, it usually suggests that which is only tricky or contrived.

Hackneyed language, 169. A broad term which includes *clichés* as well as nonmetaphorical phrases and single words which have been weakened by overuse. Such language is closely associated with *sentimentality* and with *stock characters.*

Heptameter, 132. See *line.*

Hero, 49. See *protagonist.*

Hexameter, 132. See *line.*

Hyperbole, 160. A figure of speech (see also *image*) employing extreme exaggeration, usually in the form of a simile or *metaphor.*

Iambic feet, *131,* 132. See *meter.*

Image and **figurative language,** 124, 125, *152ff.* An image is any significant piece of sense data in a poem. It may be used in a literal statement, in a figure of speech, or as a *symbol.* Figurative language (same as figure of speech) is an image used suggestively by means of such devices as *irony,* personification, *metaphor, pun,* or *hyperbole.*

Interior monologue, 87, 93. See *dialogue.*

Internal logic, *54.* A system of consistencies within a *literary* narrative which determines what is possible, impossible, likely, or unlikely for that particular piece. This is an inductive system which makes use of every detail in a work—action, *dialogue,* descriptive material, *style,* and the like. It is the internal logic of a work which makes characters, actions, and events "credible" to a reader or a viewer even when they are contrary to what he might expect in real life.

Irony, *80ff.,* 176ff. A form of *tension* in which the literal statement or actual event differs significantly from the intended meaning, a special meaning known only by the audience, or the generally expected outcome. The first of these three forms is verbal irony in which the author or speaker knowingly expresses himself in terms which are literally the opposite of his meaning (like the man who says, "Great day for sailing" as he watches his house being washed out to sea). The second is dramatic irony in which the speaker unknowingly makes a statement which has a second meaning for the audience or for the reader (like the man who innocently says, "Great day for sailing" when the audience or reader knows that his son has been drowned. The third is cosmic irony which is usually thought of as a reversal of normal expectation (like the Olympic swimmer who drowns in his bathtub).

Line, 115, *132,* 190. A unit of verse which when printed normally appears in a single row the length of which is determined by the poet alone. The inclusion of the line as a part of the art form rather than merely a printer's concern is one of the fundamental distinctions between *verse* and *prose.* In *metered verse,* lines usually contain the same number of feet (see *meter*); in *sprung rhythm* and *alliterative verse,* lines are linked by having the same number of stressed syllables; and in *free verse,* the length of lines is more of a visual concern (see *typography*). The following represent eight types of lines used in metered verse: (1) monometer (one foot), (2) dimeter (two feet), (3) trimeter (three feet), (4) tetrameter (four feet), (5) pentameter (five feet), (6) hexameter (six feet), (7) heptameter (seven feet), (8) octometer (eight feet).

Literary writing, *4.* Any verbal system in which meaning is ultimately self-contained because it has created its own system of logic (see *internal logic*) which may or may not resemble that with which we interpret aspects of the real world. In essence, literary writing creates its own universe, as opposed to *descriptive writing* which is designed to explain or comment on some aspect of the real world. Literary writing, a synonym for *literature,* is a nonevaluative term and includes both *simple* and *sophisticated* samples of *fiction, poetry,* and *drama.*

Means of perception, 39ff. The agent through whose eyes a piece of fiction appears to be presented. It is synonymous with point of view. When the first person is used, the means of perception is necessarily the narrator; with the third person, the means of perception is that character whose thoughts are presented directly to the reader. Short fiction usually contains only one such character.

Melodrama, 19, 230. Any sample of *simple writing* (usually *drama*) which is dominated by suspense. *Sophisticated* forms of writing also use *suspense;* the distinguishing characteristic of melodrama is its simplicity—its failure to do anything *but* play hopes against fears. Melodrama usually employs *stock characters* and exaggeration as well.

Metamorphosis, *27.* Radical transformation of an experience or of an existing draft of a story or play in order to create fresh *literary* work. It is usually employed (consciously or unconsciously) for one of three reasons: to clarify existing patterns, to break up patterns which appear contrived, or to help the author work with greater objectivity and control.

Metaphor and **simile,** *158ff*. A simile is a figure of speech (see *image*) in which one item is compared with another which is different in all but a few significant respects. Thus, "He fought like a lion" suggests courage but not the use of claws and teeth. The item being described is called the tenor (the true subject) and the one utilized is the vehicle. (Terms originally suggested by I. A. Richards.) A metaphor implies rather than states this same sort of comparison and so becomes a statement which is literally untrue, but when successful, figuratively stronger than the simile. "He was a lion in battle" is not taken literally because the reader recognizes it as a literary *convention*. In both cases, the base or starting point is the tenor. The reverse of this—using the vehicle as base and merely implying the tenor—is a *symbol* ("It was the lion, not the lamb that ruled England in those years").

Meter, 130ff., *132*. A system of stressed and unstressed syllables which creates rhythm in certain types of *verse*. The conventionalized units of stressed and unstressed syllables are known as "feet." The following five feet are the most common:

iamb	(iambic)	ex*cept*
trochee	(trochaic)	*Mi*das
anapest	(anapestic)	disap*point*
dactyl	(dactylic)	*hap*pily
spondee	(spondaic)	heartbreak

Monologue, 87, 88. See *dialogue*.
Monometer, 132. See *line*.
Mood, 10. See *tone*.

Octave, 133. See *stanza*.
Octometer, 132. See *line*.
Off rhyme, 145, 148, 193. See *rhyme*.
Onomatopoeia, 117, *143*. A word which either sounds like the object or action it describes or appears to echo it in some way like "slap" and "buzz."
Open-ended plot, 36. See *plot* and *story*.
Overtone, 10, 120. The unstated suggestion implied by a word, phrase, passage, or any other unit in a *literary* work. This term includes everything from the connotative aspects of a word or phrase to the *symbolic* significance of a character, *setting*, or sequence of actions.

Pace, *275ff*. The rate at which new events occur in a *literary* narrative, such events including action, discoveries about character, insights into *theme* or thesis, and the like.
Paradox, 76, *83*, 180. The form of tension found in a statement which on one level is logically absurd, yet on another makes a reasonable assertion. For example, "As a pacifist, he fought a bloody battle against war."
Pathetic fallacy, 63. The literary use of nature as an echo of human

emotions, actions, or characteristics. This term, John Ruskin's, is used particularly in those cases which strike the modern ear as contrived or artificial.

Pentameter, 132. See *line*.

Person, *42ff*. See *means of perception*.

Plot and **story,** *31ff.*, *33*, 36. Plot is a narrative of events which, for the sake of explaining causality, may be presented in a nonchronological order. Plot may, for example, use the *flashback* or the *frame* or any other sequence. "Story," as defined by E. M. Forster, is a "narrative of events arranged in their time sequence." "Story" in this sense is the day-by-day or hour-by-hour sequence of events which the writer may either use directly or refashion into some more elaborate plot. For the conventional use of *"story,"* see *fiction*. Formal plots are characterized by one or more rises in dramatic action, some measure of suspense, a climax, and usually a resolution. In contrast, open-ended plots are generally less dramatic and are concluded without a clear resolution.

Poetic, 116ff. In addition to being an adjective for poetry, this term when applied to fiction or drama usually implies a concern for *rhythm, sound devices, figurative language, symbol,* and compression of meaning.

Poetic diction, *165ff*. The theory, held by some and rejected vehemently by others, that certain words are appropriate for poetry and others are not.

Poetry, *115ff*. See *verse*.

Point of view, *39ff*. See *means of perception*.

Pornography, 18, 20. The quality in *simple writing* which is dominated by sexual words, phrases, or scenes. *Sophisticated* forms of writing can also present sexual material in abundance; the distinguishing characteristic of pornography is its simplicity—its failure to do anything *but* stimulate the reader sexually.

Propaganda, 9, 18, 275. The quality in *simple writing* which is dominated by a strong message or *thesis. Sophisticated* forms of writing can also present political, social, or religious theses; the distinguishing characteristic of propaganda is its simplicity—its failure to do anything *but* argue a case.

Prose, 115. That form of writing which is consecutive, the length of the line having nothing to do with communication or the art. This is, of course, in contrast with *verse*.

Prose rhythm, 138. A type of *rhythm* used in both *prose* and *verse* (particularly *free verse*) and created by balancing or repeating syntactical elements or by repeating key words and phrases or by a combination of these. Striking examples may be found in the prose of the Bible, the fiction of Thomas Wolfe, and the poetry of Whitman and Allen Ginsberg.

Protagonist, 49. The main character in a piece of *fiction,* play, or narrative poem. The term is broader than "hero" which suggests greatness. Protagonists who are perpetual victims are sometimes referred to as "anti-heroes."

Pulp writing, 5, 13. See *commercial writing.*

Pun, 181. A figure of speech (see *image*) in which two different but significantly related meanings are attached to a single word. Most sophisticated uses of the pun are a form of *metaphor* with the tenor and the vehicle combined in a single word as in Dylan Thomas's use of "some grave truth."

Quatrain, 133. See *stanza.*

Quintet, 133. See *stanza.*

Realism and **expressionism,** 53, *257ff.* Realism is the literary illusion that the various aspects of a play or piece of *fiction* reflect what we might see and hear in real life. Expressionism is here used to mean the purposeful and overt distortion of such aspects. Note that both forms are illusions. For those traditional uses of these terms which are not used in this text, see diagrams on page 259.

Rhyme, 117, *145ff.*, 193. A device found exclusively in *verse* and consisting of two or more words linked by an identity in sound which begins with an accented vowel and continues to the end of each word. The letter preceding the accented vowel in each word must be unlike in sound. This definition applies to "true rhyme." "Slant rhyme" or "off rhyme" is defined in the same way but with the word "identity" replaced by "similarity." "Double rhyme" (also called "feminine rhyme") refers to those rhymes in which the matching sounds occur in the last two syllables of each word.

Rhythm, 116, *130ff.* A systematic variation in the flow of sound. This is achieved by such devices as *meter, prose rhythm, sprung rhythm,* and *visual rhythm.*

Run-on line, 134. See *end-stopped line.*

Satire, 76, *83, 178.* A form of *tension* in which an exaggerated view of characters, places, or institutions is played against the "reasonable" view for the purpose of ridicule. At least some small measure of exaggeration (if only through a biased selection of details) and ridicule or criticism must be present.

Scanning, 131ff. The analysis of *meter* in a sample of *verse,* identifying the various feet (see *meter*) and the type of *line* used. Also called scansion.

Scene, 232, 281. In *drama,* this word is used in two different ways: as a formal subdivision of an act marked in the script and shown to the audience by lowering the curtain or dimming the lights; and, second, as a subtle subdivision of the *plot* marked only by the exit or the entrance of a character. In *fiction,* the scene is a unit of action marked either by a shift in the number of characters or, more often, a shift in time or place.

Sentimentality, *17,* 19. A form of *simple writing* which is dominated by an appeal to the emotions of pity and love. *Sophisticated* forms of writing can also arouse these emotions; the distinguishing characteristic of sentimentality is its simplicity—its failure to do anything *but* appeal to these emotions. Popular subject matter includes that which is small (children, puppies, kittens), that which is old (Mom, Dad, Grandma, Ireland), and that which is reputed to be pure (young lovers, country living, girls with freckles). In most cases, *hackneyed language* is used.

Septet, 133. See *stanza.*

Sestet and **sextet,** 133. See *stanza.*

Set, *243ff.* That portion of a dramatic performance which the audience sees, excluding the actors themselves.

Setting, *99ff.* Strictly, the geographic area in which a plot takes place; but more generally, the time of day, the season, and the social environment as well. In most cases, geographic, temporal, and social setting are emphasized unequally.

Shock, *84ff.*, 220. A form of tension in which the incredible is made credible. This apparently *paradoxical* technique is achieved by means of *internal logic* sustained throughout the length of a work.

Short story, *4ff.* See *fiction.*

Simile, 158ff. See *metaphor.*

Simple writing, 5, 119. The distinguishing quality in any unit of writing which is limited to only a few literary effects or is overwhelmingly dominated by one. This term includes the adventure story and the horror story (*melodrama*), many love stories and most greeting-card verse (*sentimentality*), most patriotic verse and politically dominated fiction and drama (*propaganda*), and that which is single-mindedly sexual (*pornography*). The antonym is *sophisticated writing.*

Slant rhyme, 145, 148, 193. See *rhyme.*

Slick writing, 5, 13. See *commercial writing.*

Sophisticated writing, 5, 119. Any work which combines many different literary effects within a single system having *internal logic.* It is the opposite of *simple writing.* It is a relative term roughly analogous to the biological distinction between the *sophistication* of a bird and the *simplicity* of a jellyfish. This literary use of the word should not be confused with its popular use.

Sound clusters, *144,* 150. Subtle similarities in the *sounds* of verbal groups in a particular *literary* work. Quite often a group of words with *e* and *i* sounds are played against a second group with *o* and *u* sounds, possibly without a single clear sample of assonance.

Spondaic feet, *131,* 132. See *meter.*

Sprung rhythm, 137. A technique of rhythm in verse which is based on the number of stressed syllables in each line, disregarding those which are unstressed. It is primarily associated with the work of Gerard Manley Hopkins.

Stanza, *117,* 132. A division within a poem consisting of a certain number of lines. In *free verse* the stanzas vary in length and are distinguished visually by typography. In *metered verse* the stanzas are usually of the same length, and where rhyme is used, of the same rhyme scheme. These are the more common types: (1) verse (single line), (2) couplet (two lines), (3) tercet or triplet, (4) quatrain, (5) quintet or cinquain, (6) sestet or sextet, (7) septet, (8) octave.

Stock characters, 7, *263.* Characters in *fiction* or *drama* which are *simple* and which also conform to one of a number of types which have appeared over such a long period and in so many different works that they are familiar to readers and audiences. The good-cowboy, the bad-cowboy, the rising-young-executive, and his long-suffering-wife are all examples.

Story, 4ff., 31ff., *33,* 36. See *plot and story* and *fiction* for two separate uses of this word.

Stream-of-consciousness writing, 14, 50, *94ff.* A literary device (now a *convention*) which creates the illusion of consecutive and apparently random thoughts of a character in *fiction.* Note that in using this device, the author must be in complete control if he is to maintain the *internal logic* of his character's personality. This is in sharp contrast to automatic writing in which the practitioner writes rapidly and without conscious direction for long periods of time with the hope of achieving some sort of psychological insight concerning himself.

Style, 10, 115ff., 120, 165ff., 275ff. The manner in which a work is written; the total effect of all the author's decisions, both conscious and unconscious, about technique, such as the type of words used (simple, complex) and their juxtaposition; the type of phrases (long and involved or terse); the type of sentences (simple, complex, compounded, fragmented); the absence or presence of *poetic* techniques (*sound devices, rhythmical* patterns, figurative language, *symbols,* and the like); and *tone* (serious, witty, satiric).

Substitution, *134.* The technique in *metered verse* of replacing a foot (see *meter*) which has become the standard in a particular poem with some other type of foot. A common form of substitution is the use of a trochee for emphasis in a poem which is generally iambic.

Suspense, 76, *78.* A form of *tension* in which hope for a particular outcome is played against the fear that it will not turn out that way. Unlike *curiosity,* suspense is limited to what will or might happen.

Symbol, *162ff.* Any verbal detail, such as an object, action, or state, which has a range of meaning beyond and usually larger than itself. Public symbols are those which have become a part of the general consciousness—the flag, the cross, Madison Avenue, and the like. Private symbols are made public slowly either through single works or in a series, such as Dylan Thomas's use of the color green to suggest youth and vitality. In most cases, the reader is first introduced to the vehicle (see *metaphor*) and then slowly perceives the tenor or true concern. This is in contrast with similes and *metaphors* where the writer works directly with his tenor and pauses briefly to suggest a provocative vehicle.

Synecdoche, *160.* A figure of speech (see *Image*) and a form of *metaphor* in which a portion of something (the vehicle) represents the whole (the tenor) as in "a city of 30,000 souls" and "the young man asked for his daughter's hand in marriage."

Syntactical rhythm, 138. See *prose rhythm.*

Tenor, 159. See *metaphor.*

Tension, *76ff., 175ff.* A type of conflict in which the clash of forces is between *literary* elements. Specifically, tension can take the form of *curiosity, suspense, irony, paradox, satire,* and *shock.* In addition, tension can be established between two thematic elements (see *theme*) and two or more *tones* and from certain types of *ambiguity.*

Tercet, 133. See *stanza.*

Tetrameter, 132. See *line.*

Theater of the absurd, 259. A somewhat loosely defined dramatic "school," including such contemporary playwrights as Ionesco, Beckett, Pinter, and Albee (before *Virginia Woolf*) and consisting of three characteristics: (1) a development of *expressionistic* techniques and a corresponding rejection of *realistic* devices, (2) a tendency to reject the formal structure or organization of traditional drama, (3) a partial acceptance (except by Albee) of the existential suggestion that life is "absurd" in the sense that man's system of values is beyond proof.

Theme and **thesis,** *213ff.* Theme is that portion of a *literary work* which can be summarized as an abstract suggestion or a group of suggestions. It is the central intellectual concern of a work. Thesis, on the other hand, is a stated or implied proposition of policy within a *literary work.* Whereas theme explores, thesis proposes.

Tone, *10,* 186. The emotional quality of a literary work itself as well as the author's attitude toward it. Some critics prefer to separate the two aspects of this definition, but most writers think of them as two forms of the same quality. Tone, then, is described with adjectives like exciting, sad, gay, eerie, and depressing as well as with terms like satiric, sardonic, ironic, and dramatic.

Trimeter, 132. See *line.*

Triplet, 133. See *stanza.*

Trochaic feet, *131,* 132. See *meter.*

Typography, *194ff.* The technique in *verse* (particularly free verse) of arranging words, phrases, and lines on the printed page mainly for rhythm. These effects take the form of vertical spacing (leaving space between two lines) and horizontal spacing (indentation).

Vehicle, 159. See *metaphor.*

Verse, *115ff.,* 132. That form of *literary writing* which is exclusively characterized by including the length of the *line* as an aspect of the art, and more generally characterized by a concern for rhythmical devices, sound devices, the stanza, the compression of meaning, and the intricacies of individual reflection. *Verse* is occasionally used as a synonym for a *line,* a *stanza,* or a refrain. More frequently it is used as a synonym for *poetry,* though some prefer to reserve that term for verse which is truly *sophisticated.*

Viewpoint, *39ff.* See *point of view.*

Visual rhythm, *190ff.,* 194. A technique of *rhythm* in *verse* based on the arrangement of printed words and lines on the page. This is associated particularly with *free verse.*